WAR AMONGST THE CLOUDS

WAR AMONGST THE CLOUDS

MY FLYING EXPERIENCES IN WORLD WAR I
AND THE FOLLOW-ON YEARS

**AIR VICE-MARSHAL HUGH GRANVILLE WHITE
AND GROUP CAPTAIN CHRIS GRANVILLE WHITE**

GRUB STREET • LONDON

Published by
Grub Street
4 Rainham Close
London SW11 6SS

Copyright © Grub Street 2019
Copyright text © Chris Granville White 2019

A CIP record for this title is available from the British Library

ISBN-13: 978-1-911621-43-0

Cover design and maps by Richard White
Typeset by Caroline Teng

Printed and bound by Finidr, Czech Republic

Dedicated to Joy.
Loyal and supportive wife and devoted mother
who moved house some twenty-five times during Hugh's RAF career.

And their elder son John
who served over thirty years in the RAF and died before his time.

CONTENTS

FOREWORD

The war of 1914-18 was an historic watershed in being the first where aircraft were involved on both sides. The Royal Flying Corps and its successor the Royal Air Force crammed four generations of aircraft development into four years – such is the imperative of war. The dramatic achievements of those 'in the field' outpaced the administrative organisation which failed to match the courage and imagination of those who flew or maintained the aircraft. Initially there was little, if any, exchange of views between training schools until the great innovator Smith-Barry standardised flying training. Even operational squadrons flying the same aircraft type had no control system for the exchange of ideas or tactics. The issued flying clothing did not protect against frostbite, and both air and ground crews struggled with equipment which would cause a public outcry today with the instant communication to the fighting man. However, the pressures of conflict worked fast, and a proper training organisation ultimately evolved to include such details as instructional posters, for example 'Watch for the Hun in the Sun' to bring home the lessons learnt the hard way.

Hugh White was my mother's brother. His experience was both typical of many, and yet unique. Barely eighteen when he joined his first squadron in France with just over thirty hours flying, he survived against the odds – flying exacting operations, air combat, escorts, bombing, reconnaissance, photography and ground strafing – all essential for the support of those fighting in the carnage of the trenches. Fewer than five per cent of aircrew served as long as he did on an operational squadron. Although buoyed by the assured confidence of youth, (i.e. 'it will never happen to me') it was his undoubted skill as a pilot which he built up by flying anything and everything, that contributed to his longevity. Hugh White developed technical application and intricate knowledge of his aircraft, which served him well at a time when unreliability was the norm. Anyone trained by him during his spell as a flying instructor was fortunate, as he deliberately induced aircraft to spin (a hitherto fatal manoeuvre) and perfected the recovery technique. This contributed to the standardisation of flying instructors at Smith-Barry's School of Special Flying.

In his second tour in France in a pure fighter squadron, Hugh White was in his element, and showed fearless skill in six victories. The last when his own aircraft was severely damaged in collision with his victim, which he nevertheless followed in a dive and destroyed – an act mirrored by a similar event in the Battle of Britain, resulting in an immediate award to the pilot.

In 2004, the memorial to the British Air Services in the Great War was unveiled at St Omer, which figures strongly in Hugh White's experiences. I was privileged to be asked to speak and give the welcome and introduction to the ceremony. I took great pride in being able to say that my father, his two brothers and my mother's brother all fought in the skies under which we were standing. They were all members of a very special generation which laid the foundations for air power that we know today and, with their colleagues, will never be forgotten.

Hugh White went from strength to strength in a full and successful career in the Royal Air Force – but that is another story for the 'follow-on years' later in this book.

Air Marshal Sir Frederick Sowrey, KCB, CBE, AFC

PREFACE AND ACKNOWLEDGEMENTS

Hugh White was born on 1st March 1898 and grew up in rural Kent, where his father was a successful and well-known hop farmer, during the peaceful Edwardian years of the early 1900s. His life could easily have been cut short in his teenage years as a Royal Flying Corps pilot on the Western Front during the First World War. But he survived that dreadful conflict where so many young lives were lost and he flew on through the vibrant 1920s, spending nearly five years in India; and into the 1930s when once again the dark shadow of war hung over Europe.

By the time of the Second World War he was back from three years in peaceful Singapore and serving in senior roles within RAF Technical Training Command and as commandant of the School of Technical Training at Halton.

In the immediate post-war years, he was back in occupied Germany as he had been a quarter of a century earlier after the previous conflict. His final years in the RAF during the early 1950s saw him as the air officer commanding of successive groups within Maintenance Command.

The story of his long and varied military career, with its considerable amount of survivor's luck during the early years, needs to be told. This is the story beginning with his own account of flying in the First World War which he wrote several decades afterwards. He was then aged eighty, but it reads as if written by the young man he was at the time of those momentous events.

Family photo at the Poplars, Maidstone c.1912. Beatrice and Herbert White with their children Beresford, Hugh (centre), Margarita (Rita).

Haymaking at the Poplars 1907. Hugh, Beresford and Rita having fun.

11

My grateful thanks to family, friends and colleagues who have helped and encouraged me in writing the Follow-on Years; and to those whom I have contacted for specific information, or whose books I have referred to.

In particular, I would like to thank:

› My cousin Air Marshal Sir Freddie Sowrey for his inspiring foreword to this book.
› Air Marshal Sir Dusty Miller for being such a diligent and constructive proofreader.
› Air Commodore Graham Pitchfork for his invaluable advice on publishing.
› Group Captain 'Min' Larkin for sharing freely with me his encyclopaedic knowledge and understanding of the RAF Aircraft Apprentice scheme and RAF Halton.
› Dr Steve Bond for expert advice on many detailed aspects of historic aircraft.
› The Royal Air Force Historical Society and Defence Studies (RAF) for access to their report of the seminar on 'The Royal Air Force in Germany 1945-1993' held at the Joint Services Command and Staff College, Bracknell on 9th December 1998.
› Dr Joyce Hargrave-Wright for allowing me to draw from her first-hand experience as a young airwoman working in the Air Traffic Control Co-ordination Centre at Bad Eilsen during the 1948-1949 Berlin Airlift. It was a delight to meet Joyce on 30th June 2018 at her home in Cornwall on the day after her ninety-first birthday.
› Herr Manfred Tegge of Bremen for permission to include information from his comprehensive article on his website, relikte.com about the move of the Focke-Wulf technical and design team from Bremen to Bad Eilsen in 1941.
› Keith Skinner and the Bad Eilsen Reunion for providing much interesting background information from his time working in Headquarters BAFO at Bad Eilsen.
› Malcolm Barrass for his brilliant 'rafweb' website 'Air of Authority – A History of RAF Organisation' which he has created and continues to develop to provide a wealth of accurate historical information. This has been of immense interest and value to me.
› Wing Commander Ian M Philpott's outstandingly informative *Royal Air Force – An Encyclopedia of the Inter-War Years Volumes 1 & 2.*
› The Texas A&M University Press for permission to use background information about planning for a possible airlift to Vienna in 1948 from *To*

Save a City': The Berlin Airlift, 1948-1949 by Roger G Miller.
› The Cudmore family and George Hogg for background information on the
  German 'Windfall Yachts' which were sailed from the Baltic to England by
  British servicemen after the Second World War.
› Scott Hamilton the webmaster of The Aerodrome forum (webmaster@
  theaerodrome.com) in connection with the RFC/RAF flying of Lieutenant
  Billinge RFC as a pilot after he had been my father's first observer/gunner
  during 1916.

And very importantly, our younger son Richard who created the book cover and
formulated the six India maps to illustrate the flying activities of 28 Squadron
between 1924 to 1928; and the maps of post-Second World War occupied Germany
and occupied Austria. Richard also spent many hours 'cleaning' and enhancing
electronically photographs taken by his grandfather Hugh.

Group Captain Chris Granville White, CBE
(Hugh's younger son)

NB: The author's proceeds are being donated to the RAF Benevolent Fund.

Hugh with 'Peter' by his S.E.5a of 64 Squadron, Froidmont, France in January 1919.

PART 1
FLYING EXPERIENCES IN WORLD WAR I

CHAPTER 1

IN THE BEGINNING

My interest in flying originated in 1909 when I was at Glengorse Preparatory School, Eastbourne. Our recreation periods were usually spent on the downs, at or around the school's playing fields below Bullock Down. This was an ideal area for flying our model aeroplanes, which were by then becoming available in the larger toy shops. My particular model, a birthday present, was a well-constructed wooden frame model covered with red silk. A tractor biplane powered by rubber strands of square cross-section. Although it never flew very well, it managed to cover quite a good distance before crashing (which never did it much harm). On one occasion we were surprised to find a full-size real man-lifting glider at the top of Bullock Down inland of Beachy Head. It was a biplane of heavy wood construction, with a skid undercarriage supplemented by the pilot's legs as he would either have to hang or lie in the centre of the framework. We never saw it flown and it disappeared after a few weeks.

The glider on Bullock Down.

It was about this time (24th July 1909) that Louis Blériot flew across the English Channel for the first time, thus winning the Lord Northcliffe prize of £1,000 for being the first to achieve this feat. On 11th August of that year, my mother and I made an ascent in a captive balloon to about 1,000 ft at the Maidstone Athletic Ground.

During the next few years, my interest in aviation was non-existent for the simple reason that it was intended that I should follow a naval career which entailed entering the Royal Naval Cadet College, Osborne, at the age of twelve-and-a-half years old. Unfortunately, when attending an interview by their Lords of the Admiralty (about a dozen bearded horrors) and a complete medical examination (which included being stripped naked, climbing a rope, and later an eyesight test) the medics pronounced me to be colour blind. By the time another test could be arranged, which proved beyond doubt that my eyesight was 100 per cent perfect in all respects, the total quota for entry at Osborne had been selected and therefore I could not be included.

The only alternative in those days was to join HMS *Conway*. This was a vintage wooden battleship like HMS *Victory*, anchored in the River Mersey off Rock Ferry. The total number of cadets was about 200, made up of a majority being trained for careers in the Merchant Marine Service and a lesser number of much younger cadets, better known as 'squeakers' or Osborne cadets, whose educational curriculum was similar to that taught at the Royal Naval College. It was a tough and unhappy two years of my life and rather a wasted effort as I failed in French when taking the final examinations at Osborne, which debarred me from going on to the Royal Naval College at Dartmouth.

Left: HMS *Conway* – the naval training ship school.
Below: The staff and cadets on board HMS *Conway* in May 1911. Hugh is in the front row, second from the left with the dog.

As a naval career now seemed to be out of the question, it was decided that I should join my brother Beresford at Eastbourne College. Beresford was then in the army class and later passed into the Royal Military Academy, Woolwich, and commissioned in the Royal Artillery. I, on the other hand, failed to obtain the higher marking at the Civil Service Commission examination that was required for the RMA Woolwich (I had flu at the time of the examination). However, the marks were sufficient for the RMC Sandhurst, which was confined to the training of cavalry and infantry officers. So, in August 1915 I went there instead.

It was, however, whilst at Eastbourne College that my interest in flying was revived. On 30th January 1914 I cycled out to the Eastbourne airfield (near the gasworks) to see Gustav Hamel giving a flying exhibition of the quite novel art of 'looping the loop'. Also at the OTC camps near Laffan's Plain and Farnborough in 1913 and 1914, we used to see Colonel Samuel Cody in his 'Flying Cathedral' and others flying round at low altitude on calm evenings.

During my nine months as a cadet at RMC Sandhurst (21st August 1915 – 7th April 1916), I spent several Saturday afternoons watching some elementary flying at close hand at Farnborough. On one occasion I was taken up for a short trip which made me late for our turn at riding school (I had already earned my spurs) and was then put on a charge and awarded fourteen days restrictions. This was not so good, as amongst other things it meant attending 'putty parade' for an hour each evening in full kit with pack, rifle and entrenching tools and being drilled for an hour by a succession of cadet NCOs.

By the time we were interviewed about our preference for particular regiments, my interest in flying was sufficiently great to ask, in addition to being commissioned in one or other of the Kentish regiments, whether I could also be attached to the Royal Flying Corps, for training as a pilot. And so, I was later notified that I would be commissioned second lieutenant in the Buffs, East Kent Regiment attached to the Royal Flying Corps, from 7th April 1916, and was to report to No. 5 Reserve Squadron RFC at Castle Bromwich, near Birmingham, on that date.

Hugh, Rita and Beresford all in uniform at the Poplars during 1915 when Hugh was at Sandhurst.

CHAPTER 2
LEARNING TO FLY

After reporting my arrival at Castle Bromwich, I was sent to the officers' mess to wait, with two other new arrivals also from Sandhurst, for the tender to take us to our billets in a large private house several miles away. We were collected the next morning and after being issued with flying clothes, consisting of a leather flying cap, leather coat, sealskin gauntlets and calf-length flying boots we and other pupil pilots gathered in our hangar or on the grass outside waiting to be taught to fly.

Hugh with his issued flying clothing at the Poplars.

An additional item of flying clothing issued on temporary loan to ab initio pupils was a large crash helmet, mostly of cork, which, apart from affording some protection in the event of a crash was also useful when flying for indicating whether a turn was side slipping inwards or outwards. It also had its uses as a football substitute for any sort of game which would help pass the time while waiting to be taken into the air.

In my case it was a fortnight before receiving any flying instruction, and then only for ten minutes at 8.29 a.m. on 21st April 1916 and a further thirteen minutes at 6.13 p.m. in the evening of the same day. The type of aeroplane was a Maurice Farman Longhorn, a pusher-type biplane powered by a 70 hp Renault engine with a maximum speed of 59 mph at sea level. My instructor was Lt Turner, better known as 'Wind-up Turner'. The form of instruction consisted of resting my fingertips lightly on the spectacle-type joystick and my feet even more lightly on two pedals which moved up and down as the instructor worked his rudder bar. On landing after the second flight, which was a very hurried affair, Lt Turner remarked that he had felt faint! I never saw him again.

During the next three-and-a-half weeks I had no less than six different instructors on nine separate occasions, each flight lasting between five and twenty minutes. On one flight, my third, with Capt Greenwood, we flew for thirty-nine minutes. This was the best of the lot as he allowed me to control the aeroplane most of the time.

So, on 14th May, three weeks after my first flight and a total of two hours and forty-eight minutes so-called instruction, I was told I could go solo. Having therefore offered up a short prayer or two I jammed the throttle full open and proceeded to juggle with death as best I could. After the rudder pedals, I had to get used to the rudder bar in the rear pilot's cockpit, a position I had not previously occupied. However, apart from side slipping on turns, I managed to do two successful landings in the space of ten minutes.

After another four solo flights (averaging fifteen to twenty minutes) I was taken in hand by a seventh instructor, Capt Albrect, who converted me to the Maurice Farman Shorthorn.

Meanwhile, and still flying solo on Longhorns, I managed to pass the tests for an aviator's certificate on 19th May. This consisted of performing a specified number of figures of eight and of fetching up on landing within the airfield marking circle in the centre of the landing area. This certificate was issued by the Fédération Aéronautique Internationale, British Empire, and familiarly

Top: Maurice Farman Longhorn at Castle Bromwich. April 1916.

Middle: Maurice Farman Shorthorn at Castle Bromwich. May 1916.

Bottom: Hugh's aviator's certificate (exterior).

referred to as our 'fly paper'. It contained a photograph of the holder and a request in six different languages as follows: 'The civil, naval and military authorities including the police are respectively requested to aid and assist the holder of this certificate.' The number of my aviator's certificate was 2984.

Hugh's aviator's certificate (interior).

On 27th May I was transferred to 34 Squadron, also stationed at Castle Bromwich but equipped with the B.E.2c. This was a tractor biplane with a 90 hp RAF engine. Its maximum speed was 72 mph at 6,500 ft with a service ceiling of 10,000 ft.

Here I had a further six different instructors covering some three hours flying time, followed by three days of concentrated solo flying up to six flights a day at higher altitudes from 4,000 to 6,000 ft.

An interesting point is that most of my flying up to now had been carried out between six and nine o'clock, either in the morning or the evening, my pilot's logbook doesn't say. The point is that if the wind sock was indicating more than about thirty degrees from the vertical all the Maurice Farman aircraft were wheeled back into the hangars, hence the expression 'wind up'. It seems that there was less wind early and late than during the rest of the day.

The most frightening experience I met with up to this time was on taking off in a southerly direction towards the local cemetery on a hill. It was evident that the engine wasn't giving sufficient power to climb over it. I therefore swung right, hopped over a railway bridge on the railway line bordering the aerodrome and found myself flying at only a few feet above the railway line towards Birmingham which was six miles distant. With telephone wires and other such hazards on either side I couldn't take my eyes off the way ahead. I groped for the throttle and found that I could move it forwards and to my relief obtained full power and was able to climb out of my predicament just as Birmingham hove into sight. The only explanation I could think of for this happening was that having pushed the throttle lever forward for take-off, the sleeve cuff on my raincoat must have caught on it and pulled it back part of the way.

On 13th June I was on the move again, this time to 33 Squadron at Tadcaster, near York, which was also equipped with the B.E.2c. Although only with this squadron for ten days, I managed to put in fifteen hours solo flying time and covered all the requirements for the award of my pilot's wings (No. 1509), on 22nd June. These included a minimum of two cross-country and return flights to Doncaster. On the journey there was

B.E.2c at Castle Bromwich. May 1916.

only one map available between two of us in separate aircraft, so it was decided that I should have it on the first leg of the journey and the other aircraft would formate on me, whilst on the return journey the other pilot should do the navigating.

Shortly after taking off from Doncaster on the return trip, the other aircraft disappeared into thick cloud and I never saw him again. I was completely lost and with no means of finding my way home except that I knew that York was somewhere up north. So steering a northerly course for half an hour or so and seemingly getting nowhere fast, I decided to land in a suitable field adjoining a road on which a man was driving a cart, in the hope of finding out where I was.

Apart from learning the approximate distance to York, this farm labourer was little help in providing information about the proximity of any main road or railway that might lead me in the right direction. I therefore took off again and continued flying in a northerly direction until I caught sight of a town in the growing darkness (by this time it was after 10 p.m.). I decided to land once again in another suitable field on the outskirts of the town, and here I found out that the town was

York itself. As Tadcaster was only ten miles away I hoped to be able to pick it out before it was completely dark. As luck would have it they had lit some oil drums in a line preparatory to doing some night landings, so I was able to pick it up quite easily and land without difficulty.

The next day I was sent for by Capt Birch, the squadron commander, and had some explaining to do. I had also been seen looping the loop on the previous day, an unheard of thing, and was told off severely for endangering the lives of other pilots who might have to fly the same aeroplane after me. (I had in fact done fifteen loops in the three days since my first one.) He added that I was to be posted to an F.E. squadron equipped with aircraft which couldn't be looped. How wrong he was, for though we never did so for pleasure, we certainly did all but on many occasions in combat.

I was then posted to No. 9 Reserve Squadron at Norwich on 27th June. I was only with them for three days – or should it be two days – because I left on the second day returning on 30th June to collect my kit. I had sewed my wings on in the train on the way to Norwich, and then received further posting instructions. On my first day with 9 Squadron, I was taken up as a passenger in an F.E.2B by Capt Moore for a twenty-five-minute flight. This aircraft was a 'pusher' biplane with a 120 or 160 hp Beardmore engine and a maximum speed of 73-81 mph at 6,500 ft, and a ceiling of 9,000 ft (120 hp) or 11,000 ft (260 hp) and an endurance of three-and-a-half hours. After this slight introduction to a new strange type of aircraft at 6 p.m., I made two further flights solo that evening, finishing up at 9 p.m.

The following day (28th June 1916) at about 4 p.m. I was told to pack a bag and report back at the Boulton and Paul Aircraft Co hangar to take one of their newly manufactured F.E.2Bs to Farnborough airfield. I took off that evening at 6.30 p.m. and ran into a heavy rainstorm that appeared to have no ending at any height, so I turned back and set down again at Norwich until it had passed over. After taking off again, I once more ran into bad weather, so I decided to land at Thetford airfield and continue the journey the next day. Later in the officers' mess I met several other pilots who were making for Farnborough with ex-factory F.E.s who had also run into bad weather. We agreed to go in company next day.

The next morning, we took off one after the other and formed a loose formation with the senior and most experienced pilot leading. With only twenty-five hours solo, I was about the least experienced and so placed my trust in the one leading – until I was shocked to see him go down and circle round a railway station trying to read the platform name boards. Thereafter, we broke formation and it was a case of every man for himself. After a while I managed to locate my position on the map and decided to make for Hendon and refuel to be on the safe side. This worked out quite well and I was off again in half an hour and found my way to Farnborough without difficulty.

On reporting my arrival there, I was told to get some lunch at the officers' mess and to be back by 2 p.m. to fly the same aircraft to No. 1 Aircraft Depot, St Omer in France. So later, having collected the necessary maps, an air gunner and two Lewis guns and ammunition, we took off at 4.30 p.m. and arrived safely at St Omer two hours later. Another pilot leaving Farnborough later overflew the trenches, landed at Lille and was taken prisoner.

CHAPTER 3

ON ACTIVE SERVICE

On my return to Norwich I was told to report to the Air Board office, Strand, London, for posting to the British Expeditionary Force (BEF), France. Having done this and been told the time and date for departure from Charing Cross station, I just had time to return home to The Poplars, Maidstone, to collect my valise, spend the night at home and catch an early train to London. My valise contained my flying clothing, sleeping bag and a sort of a cricket bag containing camp bed, canvas bath and camp table etc. The troop train for either Dover or Folkestone left Charing Cross at about noon, and it was a kindly thought of my elder brother, Beresford, to travel down from the Royal Field Artillery at Ipswich to see me off. He gave me a large box of cigarettes and some other items, which, having already served a long stretch in France, he thought might come in useful to a newcomer. It was the last time I should see him as he was killed in France the following April.

Hugh's elder brother Beresford as a second lieutenant in the Royal Artillery. Beresford died after being kicked by a horse during a unit move in France on 13th April 1917 (See Appendix F).

On arrival at Calais I prided myself on being one of the first off the boat, only to be nabbed by an officer organising disembarkation procedure and was detailed to march a large number of soldiers coming off the ship to a rest camp several miles away. Thus I learnt my lesson early and was never caught again.

When I eventually returned to the dockside to collect my camp kit, I reported to the railway transport officer's (RTO) office and was given a railway warrant to proceed to St Omer. I was told that once there I should ask the local RTO to contact 20 Squadron for transport to collect me. In due course I arrived at my destination, which was Clairmarais aerodrome on the east side of Clairmarais forest, and in typical French farmland country. The airfield was surrounded by hedges and there was a pond in the centre surrounded by wild bushes. There was a line of Bessonneau hangars on higher ground, and across a road from them was the domestic campsite consisting of wooden huts used as messes and Armstrong Whitworth canvas-covered wooden frame sleeping units, each holding two officers. These were extremely hot in summer and bitterly cold in winter. In winter, the limited daily supply of fuel for the stove was often exhausted early in the day.

Left: Hugh with Scamp in front of the officers' mess at Clair-marais.

Right: Lt Billinge, Hugh's F.E.2D observer/gunner outside their hut during the early weeks on 20 Squadron.

In the long, severe winter of 1916-1917, it was not unusual to find a sheet of ice on the bedding where one had been breathing. Also, some items of clothing, for example flying boots and gloves, were found to be frozen stiff on getting up in the morning. I shared one of these huts with my observer, Lt Billinge.[1]

So, here I was on 4th July 1916 at the age of eighteen years and three months, with a total of thirty-three hours solo flying experience on four different types

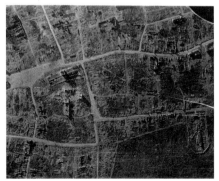

Destruction of a town in the Ypres-to-Armentières war area by repeated shell fire. (20 Squadron photo)

of aircraft, about to do battle with the enemy in the air. This airspace was along and above and beyond a series of trenches facing each other with barbed wire entanglements between them. The surrounding countryside for miles on either side was bare of vegetation and pitted with overlapping shell holes and the ruins of towns and villages.

Every now and again one side or the other would concentrate troops and guns and launch an attack aimed at smashing through the opposing line of trenches, and the net result was to produce a salient or bulge extending for a mile or so in the line of trenches. As seen from above, these changes were hardly noticeable, yet the cost of achieving them would be quite appalling and run into tens or hundreds of thousands of casualties on either side. These trenches or 'the Front' or 'lines' ran from Nieuport near Ostend in the north, all the way to near Basle on the Swiss border. Throughout the twenty months I was with 20 Squadron, we operated on a thirty-mile section of the front from Lizerne just north of the Ypres salient, where Belgian and British lines met, to Béthune La Bassée in the south and to a depth over the lines of up to seventy-five miles.

Above: 'A' Flight 20 Squadron October 1916. Back row: Lt Dennis, Lt Wooley, Lt Spicer, Lt Gibbons. Centre row: Lt Wainwright, Lt Gordon-Davis, Capt Reid, Lt H G White. Front row: Lt Gower and Lt Lewis.

Major Malcomb was the CO of 20 Squadron at Clarmarais when Hugh arrived in July 1916. In the background is a F.E.2D.

The squadron CO was Major Malcomb and the flight to which I was allotted was commanded by Capt G R N Reid who later because AVM Sir Ranald Reid.

The squadron had only recently been re-equipped with F.E.2D aircraft, a greatly improved version of the Beardmore (160 hp) powered F.E.2B. It was powered by a 250 hp Rolls-Royce aero engine 'Eagle' which was later increased progressively to 300 hp and enabled us to reach 18,000 ft, and a speed of 85 mph at our normal operational height of 10,000–14,000 ft. The aircraft was a pusher biplane and its armament consisted of two movable Lewis machine guns and one fixed Lewis machine gun operated by the pilot. The rear Lewis gun, which was attached to a telescopic mounting, could be used either by the pilot or his observer, but it meant standing up to do this and leaving the aeroplane to fly itself for a while. The alternative bomb load was either eight 20-lb bombs or two 112-lb bombs.

The pilot operated the bomb sight and the bomb release gear. The leading aircraft also carried a vertical-fixed camera and a handheld oblique camera. Only one safety strap was fitted, and only for the pilot, but this was seldom used. The reason being that in the event of a crash, we all preferred to be thrown out rather than crushed beneath a hot engine. At times in a dogfight, the observer would be in danger of leaving the aircraft except for his grip on a machine-gun handle, whilst the pilot would seek safety by holding on to the circular top of his joystick.

The aircraft was not fitted with windscreens, oxygen or parachutes, and these deficiencies, coupled with inefficient and inadequate flying clothing made it pure torture flying for three hours on end at 14,000 ft in severe winter weather. Casualties due to frostbitten hands and feet were so numerous that urgent action was taken to improve clothing, but this did not produce results until the winter of 1916-1917 was nearly over. Meanwhile, we bought ourselves fur coats at 110 francs at St Omer, and also well-designed fur-lined flying caps, goggles and chin pieces which covered the face completely, from Andree in Piccadilly (near Fortnums). But that side of it was to come later.

The Royal Navy had first call on the output of RR Eagle engines and they would only release sufficient to equip a single squadron of F.E.2Ds for the RFC. Thus 20 Squadron was the only one equipped with F.E.2Ds for the better part of a year. As a result of its good all-round performance at this stage of the war, the F.E.2D's role became a general-purpose one, and was always the one to be chosen for any special mission or task on the First Army Front. Its normal duties included line

F.E.2D with three-gun armament, bomb sight and bomb racks. There was no windscreen for the pilot. The distinctive large radiator immediately behind the pilot denotes this as a F.E.2D (not an earlier F.E.2B). Hugh can be seen in the pilot's seat behind the observer/gunner position in the nose with the reconnaissance camera. Photo taken at Yatesbury in July 1917.

and offensive patrols, bombing of enemy airfields, railway sidings and marshalling yards, ammunition dumps etc., general visual and photographic reconnaissance, escorting and protecting aircraft of other squadrons engaged on distant bombing objectives or on artillery co-operation duties. One of the more unpleasant duties when battles were raging, was dawn reconnaissance of important railway points behind enemy lines to detect the tail-end of any overnight troop reinforcements. This entailed taking off in the dark an hour or so before dawn to reach possible rail disembarkation areas just as dawn was breaking, and at a very low altitude so we could see clearly what, if anything, had been happening under cover of darkness. We also carried a full load of anti-personnel 20-lb bombs to drop at our discretion on fleeting opportunity targets we might happen to come across.

Another unpleasant task was taking panoramic photographs covering certain lines or areas under construction well to the rear, for example defensive trenches such as the Hindenburg Line. This required flying straight and level which was exactly what the anti-aircraft gunners needed to score a hit or cause serious damage to our aircraft. We were also constantly harried by enemy aircraft which sometimes turned up in large numbers. We would then form a circle, one behind the other so that we could guard each other's tail, and provide covering fire for those of us who were being attacked at any one time. During a pause in the fighting we would continue taking photographs until all plates were used up and we were free to fight our way home.

My flying ability on F.E.2s was not all that it might have been during the first few weeks, and my logbook tells me that I was taking two or three attempts to land before touching down within the airfield boundaries. I was also side-slipping on turns, so must have scared the life out of my observer and anyone else who happened to be watching. My first few days were spent on practice reconnais-sance in the St Omer-Dunkirk area, followed by line patrols between Ypres and Armentières, or the southern one down to La Bassée; also machine-gun practice at the pond on the aerodrome.

It was only a week after I joined the squadron that the CO, Major Malcomb, and his observer Lt Chancellor crashed on taking off from St Omer airfield and were both killed. I and other officers who were not on duty at the time attended their funeral at St Omer cemetery. Afterwards, with an hour or so to spend before the tender returned to pick us up, my observer Billinge and I repaired to the Hotel de Ville where, knowing little about a suitable French drink for three o'clock in the afternoon, I fell in with Billinge's suggestion of a green Chartreuse, of which he had slight acquaintance. As it seemed quite a harmless drink, we had three each before it was time to go. Upon standing up we found that our legs weren't working properly. Nevertheless, we eventually made it to where the tender was waiting for us and were lifted up and laid on the floor in the back to sleep it off. That was 'drink lesson number one'.

The new commanding officer, Major Mansfield arrived within a few days and remained the whole time I was with the squadron.

When operating in formation, the only means of communication between aircraft was by arm or hand gesture or by firing a red or white Verey light. The red light indicating enemy aircraft (EA) in sight, and the white one that we could break formation and proceed home individually in our own time. The latter generally happened on crossing the lines on completing a mission. Apart from the leader, who had photographic plates to be developed and reconnaissance reports to deliver, the rest of the formation would either bang about for a while if we had sufficient petrol left, and watch any artillery or other activity going on in or near the trenches. Also, if we had any ammunition left we would expend it by firing it into the enemy trenches.

On one such occasion early on, I went back over the lines and attacked an enemy observation balloon. Although its crew jumped out by parachute, and it was hauled down, it failed to catch fire as we didn't have tracer bullets until a little later. An hour or two after landing, enquiries were made as to who had fired at an enemy balloon. When I admitted it was me, I was ordered to report to 11th Wing HQ, where, instead of getting a commendation I was ticked off and told I was awarded a 'black mark' for not

No. 20 Squadron F.E.2D at Clairmarais. From left to right: Major Mansfield (CO), Lieutenant H G White (obscured beyond Mansfield), Colonel Murphy, Captain Child.

making myself acquainted with orders relating to German balloons. These stated that we were to 'tame' them by ignoring them for a period, and then carry out a major attack by surprise. My excuse was that I had only been with the squadron a few days and had seen no such orders. Also, that I thought we were supposed to hit the enemy whenever we could.

My first encounter with enemy aircraft was on 10th July, six days after my arrival in France. When on line patrol at 10,000 ft. I came on a German Morane, and whilst chasing it back from the lines I was attacked by a Fokker aircraft. After a brief engagement, he dived away eastwards at a higher speed than I could achieve, so I returned to carry out my duties of preventing any EAs from approaching or crossing the lines between Ypres and Armentières. This task was also to protect any of our aircraft operating down low, while directing artillery fire on to specific targets such as enemy batteries. On this flight a piece of anti-aircraft shell went through my flying coat without touching me.

Shortly after this, on 20th July, I was part of a formation that took off at 5.20 a.m. to carry out a forward patrol. The leader was Capt Teele, who had been transferred from a F.E.2B squadron in another sector of the front, and only arrived a day or two earlier. As usual, we rendezvoused at 10,000 ft and set off over the lines, although the lines themselves and the land to the east were totally obscured by what appeared to be low cloud. After flying for about an hour and a quarter, the leader fired a white Verey light meaning that we could break formation and proceed home separately. It also indicated that he was lost, and so were the rest of us.

There was no alternative but to fly a westerly course to be reasonably certain of crossing the lines, and in the hope of finding a break in the cloud and possibly locating our position on the map. We all followed slightly different courses and soon lost sight of each other. Except, that is, for the leader (Capt Teele) who tacked on to me of all people, despite my signals to indicate that it would be better to change positions so I could follow him. He wouldn't go in front and stayed with me until my main two fuel pressure tanks were empty. It was then necessary for me to turn on to the gravity tank which would last only fifteen minutes. We had then been in the air for three hours, and not having found a break in the clouds I thought it was high time I went below.

I entered the cloud at about 1,000 ft. After descending until my altimeter indicated 100 ft, and with zero visibility I levelled off, and as I did so bounced off the ground. It was only then that I realised that the cloud was pea-soup fog, so I decided to climb above it again and then descend under power at a gentle angle and hope for the best. Capt Teele had followed me into the fog and crashed in a quarry, killing both himself and his observer. When near the ground on my second attempt, a church spire and some poplar trees flashed by, and I hopped over a hedge and landed in what turned out to be a wheat field.

The first thing to be done was to find out where we were, and which side of the lines we were on. Leaving my air gunner Corporal Ward to look after the aircraft, I set off in dense fog across the countryside, leaving flying clothes on fences and hedges here and there so I could find my way back to the aircraft and destroy it if on the German side of the lines. I eventually came to a road which brought me to a village called Haut Maisnil, where I came upon a group of farm labourers apparently waiting to set off to work once the fog cleared. As I couldn't make myself understood, they escorted me, complete with harvesting tools, to the mayor's house. After some discussion, he got it into his head that I was a German aviator, and more or less placed me under arrest – which solved the problem as to which side of the lines I was on. By this time the fog was starting to lift, and as the mayor insisted on checking the nationality markings on the aircraft before accepting my word that I was a British officer, we set off en masse to retrace my route to the aircraft – which we found, after some difficulty locating my pieces of flying clothing. Thereafter, they couldn't have been more helpful, and the mayor let me use his telephone to get through to my squadron to say where I was, and that I wanted petrol and help to get airborne again. It was then that I heard that except for one other aircraft (Sgt McCudden's) all the others in the formation had crashed and were either dead or seriously injured.

We waited all day beside the aircraft, and it was not until late in the evening that the tender arrived with squadron personnel and petrol. There was some doubt whether I should succeed in taking off from a field of standing wheat, but I decided to have a go without the air gunner, and managed to get airborne at 9 p.m. I made for Hedin, which was the landing field for General HQ for the RFC in France, and put down there for the night. I was met by General Brooke-Popham (deputy adjutant and quartermaster-general of the RFC in France) who took me to the officers' mess and arranged for some food to be provided. Whilst waiting we talked over a couple of whiskies. But having been up since 4.15 a.m., and with no food all day (not even breakfast), the effect of the whiskies put me out completely and the mess steward, failing to rouse me, left me where I was to sleep it off overnight.

Next morning, I was preparing to set off for Clairmarais, when word came that an enemy aircraft was coming in our direction and that I was to go up after it. General Brooke-Popham would act as my air gunner. As I was starting the engine with the general on board, another message came to say that the EA had turned back, so there was no hope of catching it. I therefore flew solo back to Clairmarais.

There then followed the almost daily grind of bombing and reconnaissance missions over a wide front and deep into enemy-held territory, interspersed with line and offensive patrols. Fights with enemy aircraft were frequent, and although many were sent down out of control, we rarely had an opportunity to watch them down to the ground as we had to continue with the job we were doing. Also, they generally took place above 10,000 ft and well beyond the enemy lines, so the results could not be confirmed by any army observation points or balloons. In fact, we seldom bothered to report air combats other than to say that we were attacked by so many EA of a particular type and fought them off.

About this time, we were suffering from a spate of trouble with our fuel pressure systems. The petrol in the two main tanks had to be under pressure to reach the

engine carburettors, and for this were
dependent on a 'windmill' pump which
sometimes broke off during a dive at
high speed. When this happened, the
only option was to use a hand pump fitted on the left side of the cockpit. A further complication was a pressure-release
valve on the instrument panel, which
blew off when the pressure exceeded a
certain amount. This also used to fail
on occasions, and was liable to freeze
up in the air during the winter months.
Another problem was that the system
only allowed for running on one tank at
a time, and if the pilot hadn't previously
pressurised the other main tank when
the first one ran dry, the engine would
stop. It would then take some time to
build up sufficient pressure to re-start

Bombing of Courtrai railway siding on 2nd
August 1916 photographed from 13,000 ft.

it. Meanwhile, if flying in formation, it probably meant dropping several thousand
feet in height when this happened. This could result in never catching up with
the formation again and being a sitting target for any EAs in the vicinity or on the
way back to the lines. We lost a number of aircraft for this reason.

This problem happened to me early on (before I was fully conversant with the
highly complicated system and its many taps), and as I was unable to get things
going again, I turned on to the gravity tank as a last resort – but this didn't work
either. By this time, I was so low that I started to look around for a suitable landing
area and having found a likely spot came in to land. As I touched down the engine
suddenly came to life, and I was able to take off again with bullets flying all around
me. I crossed the trenches at 300 ft, and just made it to the nearest aerodrome,
Abeele. I discovered later that the fifteen-minute gravity tank would not start
up on a glide because of suction on its overflow pipe, but as soon as the air flow
causing this was reduced, i.e. when landing, it would start to function again. After
this experience, I studied the pressure system in detail, and learned also how to
take the pressure-release valve to pieces and reassemble it again when in the air.

By the beginning of October, squadron casualties had built up to such an extent
that I was required to lead some of the bombing and reconnaissance missions.
Around the same time, a 'one-off' R.E.7 three-seater biplane with a Rolls-Royce

engine was delivered to the squadron for test under active service conditions. It was fitted with a number of innovations, including Constantinesco interrupter gear for firing through the propeller, a telescopic bomb sight, and a new type of bomb of 500 lbs.

As I was the only one who had flown a tractor-type aircraft, I was detailed to carry out the trials in addition to my normal duties on F.E.s. These entailed carrying out lone bomb raids on selected targets up to twenty miles over the lines. I was supposed to collect any squadron aircraft doing north or south section patrols on my way over, to act as my escort, but as often as not they pretended not to see

R.E.7 – Reconnaissance Experimental No. 7 Aircraft No. 2299 which Hugh flew for the trial with 20 Squadron. (Courtesy of RAF Museum)

me and I had to carry on alone. After dropping a number of these 500-lb bombs, none of which exploded, I decided to wind off the safety vanes on both the front and rear detonators (which were only supposed to unwind after the bomb was released from the aircraft). As chance would have it, on this flight the engine cut out shortly after take-off and I had to force land straight ahead in a sodden ploughed field. The bomb was well and truly buried in the ground by the time we stopped, and if it had functioned as it should have done, we would have been blown sky high. My two observers scuttled out and ran for it as soon as we stopped, and gingerly I removed myself too walking back to the aerodrome, hoping that the armourers would be sent out to defuse the bomb. Not a bit of it! I was ordered to do this, and to supervise the collection and return of the R.E.7 to the aerodrome. After offering up a prayer (which I was doing quite a lot since taking up flying) I set to and managed to refix the safety vanes. I then climbed into the cockpit and released the bomb, so that we could manhandle the aeroplane away from it. And so to breakfast, and the start of another day! Only one of these new 500-lb bombs ever exploded over a period of four months of trials.

As the days began to draw in and the weather produced further hazards, opportunities occurred to spend an occasional evening in St Omer. Not that there was much to do there after the few shops were closed, but it made a pleasant change from playing Vingt-et-Un or poker in our small flight messes or sleeping huts. First we would go to the field cashier's office and draw the limit of about £7 in French Francs, and then start spending it on a few necessities. After that, it was on to a very good ladies' silk 'undies' shop to buy a present or two to take home when our next three-monthly leave came round. There was also a very good fur shop which could produce long warm fur coats which made do as flying coats in winter. We would then go on to the Hotel de Ville for a few drinks followed by dinner, and perhaps afterwards to a better class of brothel, known as No 4. Here, as long as we bought some champagne, we could sit and talk to the girls attired only in transparent gowns, make-up and perfume. Some might absent themselves upstairs for a while and re-appear in time for our return to camp.

My observer, Billinge, and I were particularly lucky in being invited every Sunday evening to dinner at the mayor of Clairmarais' farmhouse, which adjoined our aerodrome. The *curé* was always there and also occasionally our army doctor. The family consisted of the mayor's wife and innumerable daughters, aged about eighteen downwards, and as we had difficulty in remembering their names referred to them as Mark 1, 2, etc. The food was always excellent and plentiful and so was the wine and, later, the liqueurs. After dinner, one of the girls would play the piano, and we would stand around it and try to sing French songs. They were indeed happy occasions, and especially Christmas Day 1916.

New Year 1917 started well for me, as I was given fourteen days' leave, starting on 1st January. I had been in France for six months by then, which was about the limit anyone in the RFC had survived. I had seen the squadron aircrew through completely, once at least. On the way home the Channel crossing was terrible. Most of the passengers, all military, were being sick, lying about on the decks and being hurled from side to side as the boat rolled. One man was lost overboard early on, and the captain ordered everyone on the upper deck to go below. A colonel and I who were occupying a snug position behind the funnel pretended we had not heard the order and remained where we were, undetected until we arrived in harbour. I have never seen such a shambles as it was between decks when we eventually went down to disembark.

On my return from leave in mid January, I found the squadron packing up, and in the process of moving to Boisdinghem, a new aerodrome eight miles or so back from St Omer, some twenty minutes flight from Clairmarais. My first job was to fly three aircraft, including my R.E.7 over there, returning each time in a motorcycle side-car driven by a RFC dispatch rider.

The hutted accommodation at Boisdinghem was a great improvement to that at Clairmarais, and much warmer, which was just as well with the worst of the winter yet to come. Also, the large squadron mess was conducive to a better unit spirit than existed with the separate flight messes.

We had barely settled in at our new airfield when it began to snow, and we soon learned what it was like living and operating under 'arctic' conditions. It turned out to be the worst winter of the war and was really terrible. Difficulty in starting aero engines made it impossible to stipulate who, and how many, would take part in the day's operational requirements, nor at what time they would start. The only solution was to begin starting up engines at dawn, and when a sufficient number were running to make the operation worthwhile we would allocate positions in the formation and then take off. If the tasks for the day were photographic or general reconnaissance (e.g. noting trains, directions of travel, number of trucks or carriages, movements of troops, etc.) we would take off when only a few aircraft had started up. But if bombing raids had been planned, it was necessary to have the maximum number of aircraft available. This might take an hour or more, and the first to start up (mine was usually one of these) were kept running while others having difficulty had their water drained out for fear of freezing up, and then refilled with hot water which was always in short supply. Then, once the last one was started up, we had to top up the petrol tanks of the earlier starters which all took time.

When we eventually took off we experienced the agony of flying at 85 mph through the air, starting at sub-zero temperature on the ground, and getting progressively colder as we gained height without any protection (not even a windscreen) apart from our wholly inadequate flying clothing. We became more and more chilled as we gained our operational height, and by that time we had lost all feeling in our hands and feet. Also without oxygen, coupled with the never-ceasing anti-aircraft fire from the ground – it was pure undiluted hell.

On our return from these missions, we either had to be helped out of our aircraft, or just left to thaw out which was the most painful, and inclined to induce tears. My fitter and rigger, like a couple of nannies, used to climb up and massage my arms and legs whilst making sympathetic noises. They would eventually help me out of the aircraft. They always took a close interest in what I had been doing in the air, and on several occasions I came across them threading a long thin cord through bullet holes entering and leaving the wings and aligning them to see how near they came to the pilot's position. Sometimes, they were so engrossed they didn't see me approach, and I'd hear them say things like, "that was a near one, Bill, just missed me nose!" When it first happened and they caught sight of me they hurriedly put the cord away in case it might upset me, but I told them to carry on because after all they had missed me which was all I cared about.

There was a continual drain of aircrew at this time due to frostbitten hands or feet. One or two observers had removed their gloves to clear a jammed gun, and in the process their hands had swollen so they couldn't put their gloves on again. The Lewis guns too were inclined to freeze up unless a few rounds were fired now and again.

I was now leading all the main operations, because of my longer experience than anyone else in the squadron. I had also acted as flight commander ever since the departure of Captain Reid, back in October the previous year.

On 1st February, we were told that the R.E.7 trials were to cease, and the aircraft was to be returned to No. 1 Aircraft Depot at St Omer. As I took off for its final flight with the squadron, the radiator burst when a few hundred feet up. I came down to land again, but with steam and hot water blowing in my face, combined with the snow on the ground, I badly misjudged things and dived into the ground crashing the aircraft. I hit the top of the heart-shaped joystick across my eyes and nose, tearing the skin badly, and after walking back and being patched up temporarily, I was taken into No. 1 Field Hospital in St Omer. After sewing up the cuts, they expressed concern about my eyes, the whites of which were all red, so they bandaged them up and kept me in hospital. After a few days, the bandages were undone and a couple of doctors examined and discussed my eyes and the prospect of my being able to see again, as if I wasn't there. This was most alarming, as my sight had become somewhat blurred. However, my eyes were re-bandaged and would be examined again in about a week. This made it difficult to pass the time, and I wanted to find out what had happened to my last observer, Lt Golding, who was shot in the forearm in a scrap we had over Roulers [French pronunciation of Roeselare] at 12,000 ft a couple of days earlier. He was in an upstairs ward which

I had visited before, so having got someone to lead me to the bottom of the stairs, I set off by myself. I couldn't have timed it worse, for as I was told afterwards, the matron appeared at the top of the stairs and stood waiting to gobble me up, but not before I reached the top. Suddenly, all hell seemed to break loose, and sisters were called to bundle me back to bed. However, everything turned out well in the end, and I was back flying again after three weeks and able to see normally, though it was a long time before the redness wore off.

One incident occurred in connection with the R.E.7 which is worth mentioning before I leave it altogether. It was when General Trenchard visited the squadron at Clairmarais. We pilots had been warned that the first thing after his arrival he would be inspecting all the aircraft in the squadron, and we were to take up position in front of our particular one. They were all under cover in the Bessonneau hangars at the time. My F.E. aircraft was at the end of one hangar, and the R.E.7 was the next one he would come to in the adjacent hangar. After asking me a number of questions in front of the F.E. he turned away and I dashed out of the back of the hangar into the next one. I was just in time to get in front of my R.E.7 before he arrived. After saluting him he said, "I seem to know your face, where have I seen you before?" As I hesitated a bit, he said, "Speak up, boy, where was it?" I replied, "The last machine, Sir." "Well," he said, "You've been very quick."

I told him about this many years later after he had retired, when my wife Joy and I were having lunch at his house one day, and he roared with laughter. He had a notoriously bad memory for names and faces.

From March onwards, we were beginning to meet with increased opposition when carrying out our operations over the lines, not only were we being attacked or harried by larger numbers of Fokker fighters (fourteen or twenty at a time), but a new type of fighter, the Albatros, was also beginning to appear in increasing numbers. Anti-aircraft fire was also heavier and more accurate. In what was to be known as 'Bloody April', our casualties and those in other squadrons on our sector of the lines, were severe.

A typical example of conditions at this time taken from my logbook on 18th March 1917 was a photographic reconnaissance of such importance that three Nieuport fighters were provided to give us additional protection after crossing the lines. The lines of trenches we had to photograph ran from Lille to Wervicq and Menin, known as the Hindenburg Line, which was under construction at the time. We were attacked on and off for the whole hour-and-a-half it took us to do this job, and we lost two aircraft; one Nieuport shot down and one F.E. which had to make a forced-landing in enemy territory – against one Fokker shot down.

This defensive fighting whilst carrying out a task gave us no satisfaction, nor any spectacular results, as the enemy could turn away as soon as he heard the opening shots directed at him, whereas we had to stick to what we were doing and open fire each time they tried to close in.

On 1st March, which was my nineteenth birthday, I see in my logbook that on my second mission of the day I led a reconnaissance over the Lille area and had to fight off fourteen enemy aircraft, almost twice our number of eight. Whilst otherwise engaged, a lot of bullets were fired at me from an unsuspected direction, but apart from a number of holes in the wings, no structural damage was discovered.

A few months earlier, the British government, under pressure from many parents, laid down that no service personnel aged nineteen or under were to be sent to any operational zone, and those already there were to be returned to the UK. There were four of us on the squadron under nineteen at that time, and all aircrew, and we went together to the CO to ask if we could be made an exception, but without result except for me. We had again reached a stage where due to the number of the casualties, one other pilot and I were the only two left with sufficient experience to be capable of leading offensive and reconnaissance operations. So, authority was obtained for an exception to be made in my case.

With so many new aircrew arriving, I started them off by doing line patrols only, and accompanying them for part of the time in a second aircraft. On one such occasion, we were attacked by two German Albatros fighters, and a dogfight ensued. After a while, everything started to go wrong. First, the other F.E. was shot down, although he managed to land safely on our side of the lines. Then our front Lewis gun jammed, and my air gunner (a private who had never been in the air before), was lying helpless and being sick on the floor of his cockpit. Meanwhile, the two Albatros were attacking from opposite directions, fore and aft, passing over the top then turning and repeating the performance. Each time they attacked I shut off the engine and stalled the aircraft, which foxed the one coming from behind, as he overshot me each time just as he was going to open fire. In the case of the one attacking from the front, I stood up and used the rear Lewis gun on telescopic mounting to return his fire and continue firing as he passed overhead. The second time this happened, it was obvious that one of them was in difficulties, and the other one left him and made off for home. I therefore caught up with the damaged one and flying close alongside made signs that he was to fly west over our side of the lines, or else! I stayed with him until it was clear that he could not return to his side of the lines and watched him crash-land near Neuve-Église.

On the way back, my engine was giving trouble and I had to put down at Clairmarais aerodrome, which was still unoccupied. My air gunner had by this time partially recovered, and implored me not to say what had happened, otherwise they would return him to the trenches in the infantry. I agreed, so long as he cleaned the mess up in his cockpit. The upshot was that he was awarded the Military Medal, and I the windmill-type air-speed indicator from the Albatros (which is now in the RAF Museum at Hendon).

The pilot of the Albatros was Ltn Josef Flintz of Jasta 18. I looked in and saw him in Baillieul Hospital next day and gave him a hundred cigarettes. Amongst other things a bullet had shattered the top portion of his joystick and damaged his hand, which was his sole wound. He was a well-built man of 6 ft, and he expressed his resentment at having been shot down by one so young. I had difficulty in explaining the meaning of a piece of lead hanging on a string over his head with a notice saying 'to be swung daily'. German humour did not descend to that short of thing.

On 7th April 1917 I was promoted to the rank of acting captain, which merely confirmed my status as a flight commander, which I had been in practice for some six months. As spring advanced to summer, our operations were increased, and included the bombing of enemy aerodromes. The inevitable Luftwaffe reaction to this, coupled with added numbers of enemy squadrons moved up to our section of the front to support military offensives which were raging all along our part of the line, meant greatly increased enemy air opposition over their side of the lines.

Our squadron continued to suffer severe losses, and on several occasions I only just made it back to our lines to land at Abeele aerodrome with a dead or failing engine because of bullet holes in the water cooling system or oil tank or both. The engines would continue to run for half an hour with either system out of action, and about a quarter of an hour with both affected.

On 16th April 1917, 20 Squadron moved from Boisdinghem aerodrome to Sainte-Marie-Cappel (near Cassell) which was much closer to the lines. I took off soon after 8.30 a.m. for a twenty-five-minute flight to our new airfield. Nos. 20 and 45 Squadrons were based there when the photograph was taken by 20 Squadron during June 1917 (see overleaf).

About this time I got a message saying that General Trenchard wanted to speak to me on the 'phone. He told me that enough F.E.2Ds were now available to re-equip 25 Squadron at Auchel, which up to then had been flying F.E.2Bs. It seems that one F.E.2D was delivered and shot down the first time they used it, and therefore got a bad name. Therefore the squadron was asking to be allowed to carry on with their old-type aircraft.

I was told to go down there and ask the CO to produce his best pilots to take me

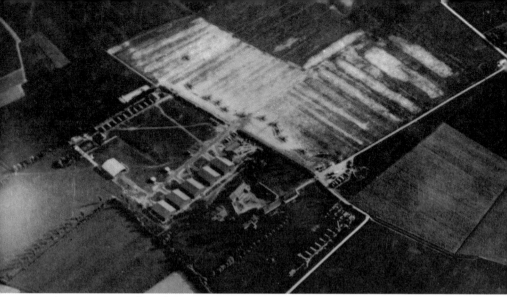

Sainte-Marie-Cappel aerodrome, June 1917.

on in mock combat. I took them on one at a time, and after giving them the choice of position at the start, I quickly turned the tables on them to such an extent that they were wholly convinced of the considerable advantages of the F.E.2D over the inferior F.E.2B They now agreed to accept the F.E.2D, and the CO informed the General Headquarters RFC accordingly.

By May I had been in the squadron for ten months, the next senior only one month, and the remainder only a matter of weeks and days. I was therefore told I had no chance of returning to the UK until some of the others had gained sufficient experience to fill my job of leading the main operational missions.

My chances of survival after such a long spell, and yet more to come were just about nil, but I tried to think about other things – which was not all that easy, bearing in mind that we had no parachutes and therefore no means of escape if we caught on fire, or broke up in the air. Also, after avoiding the many bullets that came my way during combat, and being fired at by AA gunners for an hour or so almost every day for months on end, it now seemed just a matter of time before my name was added to the long list of 20 Squadron casualties. There were seventy-five names listed at the back of my logbook (see Appendix H), not counting the frostbite victims, and others I forgot to include. I certainly noticed my nerves were beginning to get rather tightly strung towards the end, when we were crossing the lines and waiting for the first AA shells to arrive, which were often the most accurate. After that, I would vary height, direction and speed slightly every thirty seconds or so, to mislead and confuse the AA gunners, and this would restore my nerves to their normal equanimity.

So, into June 1917, when I was surprised at being handed a type-written sheet of paper which read:

No. A.528.

Capt H. G. White.

You will proceed to England this day, 3rd June 1917, and will report forthwith on arrival to Air Board Office, Strand, London W.C. for further orders.

In the field.
3rd June 1917.

This, coming so soon after being told I'd have to stay for a while yet, made me wonder. I later heard that following the death of my brother Beresford in France, my father had contacted Lord Londonderry (whom he knew quite well, and was the Air Minister at the time) and said he felt that I had been on active service in France too long at one stretch and would he look into it. This explains my sudden and unexpected return to the UK, after eleven months with the BEF in France.

Meanwhile the terrible destructive effects of artillery and bombing through 1917 and into 1918 are shown in the series of 20 Squadron reconnaissance photos below.

YPRES-COMINES CANAL
LOCK Nº 4

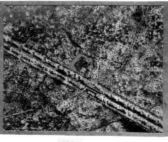

Ypres Comines Canal lock No. 4 1917 and 1918. (No. 20 Squadron photo)

1917

1918

BAT WOOD. 28.P.S.C.

1917

1918

MONT KEMMEL 28 N 20d

1917

1918

Left: Bat Wood 1917 and 1918. (No. 20 Squadron photo)
Right: Mont Kemmel 1917 and 1918. (No. 20 Squadron photo)

X ROADS at 28.T.32.b.

1917

HOLLEBEKE CHATEAU

1917

1918

1918

Left: Bombing around crossroads in 1917 and 1918. (No. 20 Squadron photo)
Right: Hollebeke Chateau 1917 and 1918 (No. 20 Squadron photo).

Royal Navy block ships were sunk in the entrance to Zeebrugge harbour to prevent its use by enemy submarines 22-23 April 1918. (No. 20 Squadron photo)

CHAPTER 4

INSTRUCTING FLYING TRAINING

On my return to England, I was granted ten days' leave, after which I joined 59 Training Squadron at Yatesbury, Wiltshire as a flying instructor and flight commander. It was then that I realised that I didn't know the first thing about the art of flying, and was therefore not likely to make a very good instructor.

Hugh as an acting captain.

But help was at hand. My CO Major Davey and a Major Smith-Barry at Gosport, had got together trying to work out the basic principles to be followed when instructing pupils to fly. Not only had they covered the normal requirements of take-off, climbing, turns, gliding and landing, but they were now turning to the other side of the picture of how not to fly. In other words, they considered that pupils needed to be taught both how to fly and how not to fly at one and the same time. Most of the accidents occurring with the types of aircraft used for training at this stage of the war were due to stalling, either on take-off or when coming into land, or when producing conditions in a turn that would result in a spinning nose dive. All too many of the crashes resulting from these causes were fatal.

Major Davey, therefore, required his instructors not only to teach the basic principles of good flying which he and Smith-Barry had so far evolved, but also called 'stall-control', which meant making pupils fly at the borderline of a stall so they would get the feel of the danger area where loss of control commences. This could only be done when flying straight, because if done on a turn it would probably develop into a spinning nose dive, which up to then no-one had discovered how to get out of, before hitting the ground.

Captains Hugh White, Wren, Leask and Major H B Davey (CO) at Yatesbury in 1917 with R.E.8 aircraft.

Hugh beside a D.H.1A at Yatesbury during 1917. At Yatesbury Hugh also flew the F.E.2B, F.E.2D, B.E.2c, B.E.2d, B.E.2e, B.E.12, R.E.8, Avro and Bristol Fighter.

It so happened, that on my first familiarisation flight in a D.H.1A (with which my flight was equipped) I got into several spins, and from which I recovered after a turn or two. Major Davey, who was watching my performance, was most interested, and after I had landed he questioned me closely on how I had induced a spin, and more importantly how I had recovered from it. Since I was unable to explain this, he decided to come up with me and see if I could do a repeat performance.

After committing to all the things one shouldn't do flying (if hoping to live to a ripe old age) we managed to get into a spin, and then I followed my usual practice when in a dogfight. Sometimes strange things happened, and if the aeroplane would fail to answer the controls, I just left the controls alone and the aeroplane would right itself. This seemed to do the trick all right in a spin, whereas by following the normal procedure of pulling the stick back to bring the nose up, it merely locked one in the spin more tightly. We therefore concluded that pending further research and experiment, the best way of getting out of a spin was to centralise the controls and hope for the best.

During the following weeks when flying solo doing engine and rigging tests, I also persevered with this spinning problem, and more particularly, how to induce it in the simplest manner. In the course of my experiments, which often included an 'Immelmann turn' (i.e. a loop, with a roll off the top), I also accidentally invented the 'flick roll' – which although spectacular when performed on a Bristol Fighter, nevertheless played havoc with the aircraft rigging, and therefore came to be frowned on when flying biplanes. However, a make-shift method of inducing a spin was evolved which consisted of stalling the aircraft, pulling the stick right back and applying full rudder.

Thereafter, what had previously become a feared panic-stricken vertical spin into the ground, with invariably fatal results, could now be demonstrated or included in the early instruction of pupils as a controlled manoeuvre.

Unfortunately, up to now there was no system for disseminating vital information concerning flying practice and procedure. The senior formation of the RFC consisted largely of army officers having no experience or interest in aviation, who seemed to act in an administrative capacity only.

Thus, although flying instruction in our squadron was widened to include aerobatics such as loops, spins and Immelmann turns, we had not one single accident involving injury throughout the time I was with the unit. On the other hand, there was seldom a day without at least one fatal accident with the other squadrons operating on the other side of Yatesbury aerodrome.

A few of the many crashes which Hugh photographed at Yatesbury during 1917. Clockwise from top: F.E.2B on fire, B.E.2e, Sopwith Camel on its nose and another B.E.2e.

This policy of turning out pupils who wouldn't crash through faulty flying, and could at least live to join an operational squadron on one of the fighting fronts, impacted adversely on the number of pilots turned out each month. The powers that be laid down a definitive number of pilots to be turned out each month, without regard for weather or quality of training. However, although we worked long hours, from 6 a.m. to as late as 9.40 p.m. seven days a week in the summer months, we seldom reached the target. The result was that Major Davey was sent for almost every month for the customary ticking-off and to explain, in extenuation, that all his pilots were fully trained up to operational standards and that unlike other training units, we had not suffered any casualties in the process. He also refused to alter his training methods in any respect, or to lower his standards.

Major Davey continued his consultations with Major Smith-Barry at Gosport, who was something of a law unto himself and equally interested in improving the standard of flying training, and it was due to their combined efforts that a School of Special Flying was set up at Gosport at the end of 1917. This was for the sole object of training flying instructors under Smith-Barry, who at the same time was promoted to lieutenant colonel. The effect of the efforts of this school on the standards of training was marked and widespread. It was not long, therefore, before Smith-Barry's capabilities were recognised, and resulted in his promotion to major general and being posted to Northern Command with its HQ at York.

The first thing he did after taking over was to concentrate all the flying training units on one airfield close to his HQ, and to introduce various innovations which failed to meet the approval of higher authority. In particular, I gather, paperwork was greatly reduced by the simple process of not answering official correspondence. When it got to such a stage that somebody was sent to investigate why no replies were sent to important letters, he was reported as saying, "Well, I expect those were put into the BB file". When asked what the BB stood for he replied, "The bloody balls file, or wastepaper basket".

After a few weeks he apparently realised that he wouldn't be allowed to have his own way, and sent off a signal to the Air Board, London, saying 'Major General Smith-Barry left HQ York by air for Gosport'. A few hours later another to the effect that 'Lt Col Smith-Barry arrived at Gosport to resume command of the School of Flying' – where I believe he remained for the rest of the war!

In July 1917 we ceased training F.E.2D pilots, and turned over to training R.E.8 and Bristol Fighter pilots. My A Flight, which covered full ab initio training, changed from the D.H.1A to B.E.2e and B.E.2d. From then on we made a further change in our method of instruction, but which only applied to our squadron, and to my flight in particular. Whereas the instructors had previously occupied the pilot's seat and the pupil the observer's seat, we now reversed the positions so that the pupil would become accustomed to flying the aircraft from the pilot's position from the outset, instead of suddenly changing over at the time of going solo for the first time. The only disadvantage of this was that the dual-control system was such that the pilot's cockpit controls were more powerful than those in the observer's cockpit. This slight danger was discounted, on the grounds that a pupil was unlikely to think he knew better than his instructor in the case of an emergency. There was also a speaking tube for communication between the instructor and his pupil, but this was not very efficient.

On only one occasion the unexpected happened, when a ham-fisted pupil put us into a spin and completely lost his head. He wouldn't act on my earphone instructions, or let go of the controls, and as attempts to overpower him were unsuccessful it seemed that a crash was inevitable. However, at the last moment, he did let go, and I was able to recover with a few feet to spare behind the Yatesbury White Horse Hill.

Rita with a colleague in her Crossley staff car in 1918.

Apart from a week's leave at the end of July, there were very few days when we weren't instructing in the summer of 1917 from 6 a.m. to 9 p.m. or later. It was a pleasant relief when the days started to draw in and deteriorating weather conditions allowed us sufficient time to visit, and possibly spend a night in Bath or Bristol. My sister Rita happened to be stationed at Netheravon as a driver in the Women's Legion, and she invited me over to dances organised by the station, and held in Devizes.

On 1st November 1917, the squadron moved to an airfield near Beaulieu in Hampshire, and was re-numbered 38 (T) Squadron. We only remained there for a few days before being moved once again to Rendcomb, near Cirencester in Gloucestershire on 12th November.

Rendcomb was an enjoyable station, and there was plenty of social life in the neighbourhood around Christmas. I got to know a lot of the local people, including the Marquis of Bath who invited me to dinner, and also to take part in a pheasant shoot.

Shortly after arriving at Rendcomb, I was invited to a private dance at a nearby house, and there met, among others, a charming girl by the name of Lettice Wykeham-Musgrave, and she seemed to rule my social life throughout the short three-month period I remained with the squadron. Her parents lived in a large manor house, Barnsley Manor, about five miles from Cirencester. Her brother, who had been torpedoed in the Battle of Jutland, was at home on sick leave at the time.[2] I was repeatedly invited over for meals or parties, where we played all the favourite parlour games, also with her father to shoot wood pigeons coming in to roost in the surrounding woods at dusk. Transport to and from being rather difficult, I often used to fly over and land in a field near the house during the lunch break, or when weather conditions put a stop to instructional flying. I was also bidden on one occasion by Lettice to attend, by air, a meet of the local hunt at their house. I often replied to her frequent letters by dropping them in a message bag in front of the house. One day, the message bag caught in the branch of a high tree and she had to get her father to shoot it down for her.

I was invited out to lunch at various times by several other people who said there were suitable fields to choose from for landing near their respective homes. One invitation by two unmarried sisters turned out to be a little unfortunate. The date for us to visit was left open, and they said that we were welcome to take pot luck. On the day we turned up, they said they had already had an early lunch but there was a cold partridge apiece that we could have. A day or two later, I was to learn that our hosts had not had an early lunch at all, and they had given us what was intended for themselves. God bless them!

On 19th February I was ordered to report to the Air Board, London, for posting overseas for the second time. Before leaving, I took advantage of an S.E.5 aircraft which had been left overnight in my hangar. Having taken a fancy to it, I put in sufficient time to qualify on this new type of fighter, which was then two hours.

Next day, when interviewed at the Air Board, they looked up my records and said that I would be joining a Bristol Fighter squadron in France. I said that I was also a qualified S.E.5 pilot, and would much prefer to join an S.E.5 squadron instead. I pleaded in vain, and was given a chit to take to another section of the Air Board in Duke Street. As it was nearly 1 p.m. I decided to go to the RFC Club in Bruton Street first for a spot of lunch. Whilst having a drink in the bar, I opened the envelope containing the chit I should have to hand over that afternoon. All it said was 'Herewith Capt H G White, a Bristol Fighter Commander'. I found it not too difficult to delete the words Bristol Fighter and to insert S.E.5 in its place, and thus did I tempt fate which is not a very wise thing to do in the midst of war. However, it probably made the difference between death and survival, and I have often wondered about this.

Anyway, my subterfuge was undetected when I reported to the Duke Street office in the afternoon, and I was duly posted to 29 (Fighter) Squadron. I was, however, to regret my action a few days later, on learning the type of aircraft with which the unit was equipped.

CHAPTER 5

SECOND PERIOD OF ACTIVE SERVICE

I crossed over to France by sea on 26th February 1918 on the commencement of my second period of active service. On arrival at Calais I took the precaution of waiting until there was no longer any danger of being picked on to march some of the troops to the rest camp (several miles outside the town), before I left the ship and reported to the RTO to get a railway warrant and find out where 29 Squadron was located and how to get there.

I learnt that it was at an airfield called La Lovie, four miles north of Poperinghe and five miles from the front line of trenches. I went some of the way by train, and from the point where the railway terminated I found an airman with a Crossley tender who had been sent to collect me and my camp kit. On the way to the aerodrome, I asked the driver what type of aircraft the squadron had, and to my horror he replied Nieuport Scouts. It was then that I bitterly regretted hoodwinking the Air Board into posting me to an S.E.5 squadron instead of one equipped with Bristol Fighters.

At this stage of the war, the Nieuport Scout was long out of date, and completely outclassed and out-gunned by the latest type of German Albatros and Fokker fighters now opposing them. They were powered by the 110 hp Le Rhône rotary engine, and its only armament consisted of a Lewis gun mounted on the upper plane firing over the top of the propeller.

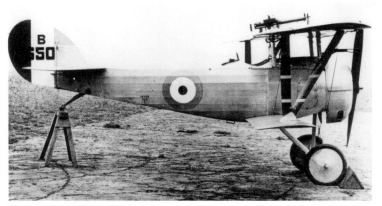

Nieuport Scout B3650 of 29 Squadron during 1918. After Hugh's first ten-minute flight in a Nieuport Scout on 28th February 1918 he commented in his logbook: 'First time in one. Quite nice.'

I had not previously flown an aeroplane powered by a rotary engine, and so had to get my flight sergeant to show me how to start and run it up. The trouble with this type of engine was that it was controlled by two levers, one which regulated the quantity of petrol supplied, and the other the air needed to correct the petrol/air mixture. It was a complicated business, and required a lot of juggling of the two levers to obtain full power, and also had to be continually adjusted in the air, as too much or too little air entering the air intake (depending on whether one was climbing or diving) would result in a loss of power or even complete cut-out. Anyway, I got the flight sergeant to file marks on the throttle/air quadrants when the engine was producing full power on the ground. Then I took over, ran the engine up and thereafter controlled it (in the usual way when taxying with a rotary engine) by alternately pressing and releasing the 'blip' press button on top of the joystick.

After getting airborne, I was also to discover some other unexpected happenings due to the centrifugal effects of a rotary engine, and which I found most disconcerting. Thus, when doing a quick turn to the right, the nose of the aircraft would rise steeply, whereas when doing a quick turn to the left the nose would dip steeply. Also, it almost flicked round, turning in one direction due to engine torque, but showed unwillingness to turn in the opposite direction. However, after a few more practice flights, I felt sufficiently confident to take part in the normal squadron operations.

One such operation was a two-aircraft line patrol, the second I did on that particular day. Before take-off, I told the other pilot that I should be doing a 'cast' well over enemy territory, to get the feel for Archie (AA fire) once again, and also to see if there were any enemy aircraft about. I told him that he need not come over with me and that I would rejoin him on the patrol line later.

Shortly after breaking away, and only a few miles over the line, and flying just beneath a 9/10 cloud layer at 8,000 ft, a formation of eight enemy Fokker aircraft suddenly came diving through a gap in the clouds which I was just passing under. They couldn't have been more surprised than I was to find a lone Nieuport Scout in the middle of their formation, and flying in the same direction. There seemed to be nothing I could do about it once they closed in tight around me, and their leader (who was close alongside my aircraft) pointed in the direction I was to go. But after a while, they opened out into a fairly loose formation, and I took my chance without thinking and did a flick climbing turn until I reached the cloud layer. There, after a lot of cat and mouse business in and out of the clouds, I eventually managed to shake them off. I managed to complete the line patrol by myself, as the other line patrol pilot had returned to report that he had last seen me amongst eight enemy aircraft and assumed that I had been shot down. Just imagine their surprise when I returned unscathed from the 'dead' at the end of my patrol period!

Due to the imminence of the squadron being re-equipped with S.E.5 aircraft, and the all-round inferiority of the Nieuport Scout at this stage of the war, the squadron's operations throughout March and April 1918 were confined to line and offensive patrols and bomber escort duties. As I was the only pilot who had flown an S.E.5, I had the additional job of returning the Nieuports to the depots at St Omer and Marquise, from where I collected the replacement S.E.5s.[3]

The S.E.5 was the Hurricane of World War One. Powered by a 200/240 hp Hispano engine, it had a speed of 132 mph at 6,000 ft, and a ceiling of 20,000 ft. Armament consisted of one Vickers gun firing forward through the propeller, and one Lewis gun on the top of the centre section.

Whilst the re-equipping was going on, the squadron was moved from La Lovie to Téteghem (behind the quieter Belgian-held trenches) on 11th April, and from there to St Omer on 22nd April. From mid-May, by which time the squadron had been fully re-equipped with the S.E.5, and all pilots familiar with them, we reverted to carrying out the normal duties of a fighter squadron, i.e. offensive patrols over enemy territory.

It was an anxious time on our sector of the military front. The German offensive had pushed our front back to a serious extent in the Bailleul-Hazebrouck area, and whereas British troops previously held this part of the line, certain areas were now allotted to French and Portuguese troops. At the height of the offensive the Portu-

No. 29 Squadron pilots at La Lovie, April 1918. From left to right: back row – Lt H A Whittaker and Lt Reid; centre row – Lt Largesse, Lt Humphries, Lt C G Ross, Lt Reid, Lt Prior, Lt Tims, Lt Beavan and Lt Durrant; front row – Capt J B Coombe, Capt J S Rusby, Lt Macloulin and Lt Venter.

guese troops abandoned their position and left a gap of three to four miles, which the enemy could have advanced through if they had realised the situation in time.

As it was, a British Cycle Corps was thrown in to hold the ground until the French and British reinforcements could be brought up. During this period, even cavalry regiments appeared on the scene for a while. We also took part with other squadrons in machine-gunning any German troops seen approaching the gap from the other side. Feelings ran so strongly against the Portuguese, who, incidentally pinched the Cycle Corps' bicycles to speed their flight from the enemy, that an army order was issued forbidding the habit of referring to the Portuguese as 'Pork and Cheese', and in future they were to be known as 'our gallant Allies, the Portuguese'!

There was plenty of enemy air activity at this time, as well as military activity on the ground, and it was a joy to be flying a fast, well-armed and strong fighter aircraft after the flimsy ill-armed and slow Nieuport. We started to make ourselves felt almost daily from early May onward, as shown by the following examples.

› On 8th May my flight engaged twelve Fokker Triplanes over Bailleul, and I shot down one. The following day I got two out of seven Pfalz.
› On 15th May we drove down several observation balloons and caused the observers to jump out.
› On 17th May we met eleven enemy aircraft over Armentières at 15,500 ft, and I shot down one in flames.
› On 18th May we intended doing another balloon strafe, but there were none up, so instead we found and engaged seven enemy aircraft over Merville, one of which I shot down in flames.

On 19th May we set out on another observation balloon strafe, and started in on a line of them at 6,000 ft, taking one a-piece so as to damage the greatest number of them before they could winch them down, at speed. All the seven balloon occupants were parachuting down, when I spotted nine German fighters coming down towards us from high up. I fired a red Verey light as a warning and recall signal, and went up to meet the enemy aircraft, which turned out to be Pfalz D.IIIs. My flight members were a bit slow in catching up with me and I was alone for a while after engaging the EA at about 10,000 ft. I fired a hundred rounds at the first one I came to at close range, and it zoomed up and hit my right top plane, smashing some of the wing structure and the propeller. The force of the collision was such that my triplex goggles were starred and became opaque when my head had hit the windscreen. When I pushed them up I found that I could see again. The other aircraft was immediately below me in a vertical dive, and I was following it. I fired a further burst, which caused his wings to break away. I then turned for home with the engine shut down, as it was shaking itself to bits with the damaged propeller. I found that it was just possible to control my aircraft at 130 mph, otherwise it would go into a spin.

I was attacked twice on the way back, from close behind. Fortunately, the first one's gun jammed after firing a few shots, and when another took its place I threw a Lewis ammunition drum over the back, and this damaged his propeller and caused him to turn away. By this time the rest of my flight had driven off the remaining aircraft and I was just able to reach our side of the line. I did a cartwheel crash amongst our third-line trenches, finishing trapped upside-down in what was left of the fuselage.[4]

It seemed a long time before I heard an English voice asking, "Where's the body?" and some sort of reply in French. I shouted, "the body's still in here, and for God's sake get it out". Thereupon, they lifted up the tail-end enough for me to drop down and crawl out practically unharmed, to find that my helpers were a Padre and two French Poilus. I was invited to take shelter from possible shelling in a British regiment's dug-out nearby, where I was kindly given a whisky, with which I experienced some difficulty in downing without shaking it out of the tumbler.

Hugh's flying logbook for May 1918.

As I was due for a week's leave on the following day, the squadron MO arranged for me to attend a RAF Medical Board in London, as I had been suffering excruciating head and facial pains when descending from high altitudes on the completion of operational missions.[5] It had reached a point where I could only descend in painful slow stages of a few hundred feet at a time, and it would take me up to twenty minutes on occasions to get down from 14,000 – 16,000 ft. The outcome was that the Medical Board recommended a full month's leave.

A further Medical Board a month later failed to pass me for high-altitude flying, seemingly due to tonsillitis. I was therefore posted on 3rd July as a flying instructor to 9 Training Depot Squadron, Shawbury, near Shrewsbury.[6] I was only there for ten days before being promoted to acting major on 12th July 1918, and posted to No. 30 TDS

Hugh with his sister Rita at the Poplars while on leave May-June 1918.

at Northolt on 17th July, to be officer i/c Flying Training. The station commander was also a major, named Wynne-Eyton.

I was still at Northolt when hostilities ended on Armistice Day, 11th November 1918. I finally left when posted on 6th January 1919 to command 64 (F) Squadron at Froidmont, France [in north-east France towards the Belgian border] at the ripe old age of twenty years. The previous CO had been killed on Armistice Day when taking part in a mock battle on the airfield between pilots mounted on MT vehicles and armed with Verey Light pistols. He had been hit in the head from close range.

Left: Hugh as an acting major while at Northolt. July 1918.

Right: Hugh (sitting on the grass second from left) with his pilots at Northolt in 1918. At No. 30 TDS Northolt, Hugh flew the S.E.5 (including two of the small number of two-seat S.E.5 produced), Sopwith Pup and Avro 504K.

CHAPTER 6

POST-WAR SQUADRON COMMANDER IN FRANCE AND OCCUPIED GERMANY

No. 64 Squadron was equipped with S.E.5 aircraft, and we also had two of the latest German Fokker fighters to try our hands at. One of these was crashed soon after I took over by my wing commander, one 'Crasher' Smith, who thought he'd like to try it, and duly lived up to his name.

Above: Captain Foster in the Fokker D.V11 which Hugh flew on 18 January 1919. He commented in his logbook: 'Not a bad machine, very light. 2 landings.'
Right: The Fokker D.VII later that day.

My time in command of 64 Squadron was very short-lived, when only a month after arriving I was instructed to reduce it to cadre on 8th February 1919. I was then to proceed to Bickendorf aerodrome on the north-west edge of Cologne in Germany, to take over command of my old squadron (No. 29). This was still equipped with S.E.5s, and one of nine squadrons on this airfield. There were ample hangars to keep all the squadron aircraft under cover, and an ex-Zeppelin hangar to house all the MT vehicles. The other rank personnel were accommodated where the German Zeppelin personnel had been, whilst the officers were billeted on German civilians in the better residential part of Cologne. Each squadron had its own officers' mess which was a complete house.[7]

Our working hours were only 9 a.m. to 12.30 p.m., but for seven days a week, up to the time when the peace treaties were signed and air activity could be relaxed. Ample sporting facilities were available; including golf, tennis, cricket, football, swimming and trout fishing. There was an excellent officers' club where meals were available, and tickets could be obtained for the asking for theatres and the Opera House.

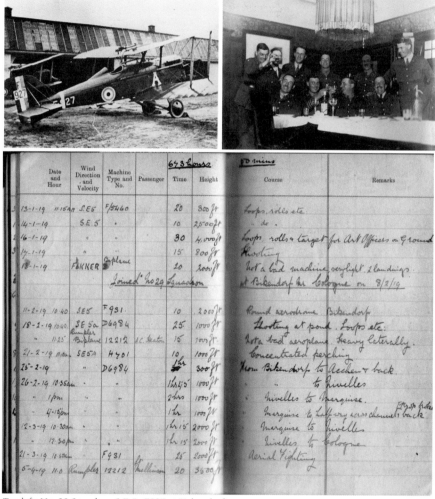

Top left: No. 29 Squadron S.E.5a F927 at Bickendorf.

Top right: A cheery evening at Bickendorf with the Army Service Corps. Hugh with the rank rings visible on his sleeve as acting squadron leader.

Bottom: Logbook pages with flights in a German Fokker D.VII & Rumpler biplane. At Bickendorf there was a German two-seat Rumpler biplane (serial no. 12212) which Hugh flew on four occasions with various passengers between February and April 1919, including two flights over Cologne with their Padre Popham.

During my time in command of 29 Squadron, my adjutant came across a cita-tion for the recommendation of an award for a certain Capt H G White, that was submitted when I was previously with 29 Squadron, and which he thought I'd be interested to see. [A copy of this non-award is enclosed as a matter of interest at Appendix A.] Also, more than half a century later I came across a copy of an early official Royal Air Force War Communiqué 1918 in the Eastbourne Library which contained a mention of my name. [see Appendix B.]

When the first RAF permanent commission list was issued in the summer of 1919, little attention seemed to have been paid to our records of service, or even our current appointments. Thus, although I was commanding a squadron at the time, and had considerably longer service than my three flight commanders, they were all granted a permanent commission in their acting ranks of flight lieutenant, whereas I was amongst the flying officers. Furthermore, those coming over from the RNAS on the formation of the RAF did so one rank higher than the strict naval equivalent. Complete uproar resulted, and the first list was cancelled and replaced by a second one. However, this was much the same, especially as far as the RNAS ranks were concerned, because of overwhelming naval political pressure and to disinterest of the army high-ups.

When I questioned the absurdity of my position, General Sir John Salmond said I was to continue to command 29 Squadron with the acting rank of squadron leader, and promised to take my case to the Air Ministry. He was, however, re-lieved of his command at about this time, and I heard nothing more until I took up the matter again in 1920 and was then told that my age had debarred me from holding a higher substantive rank. Thus when I appeared on the promotion list on 1st January 1921, I was now at the bottom instead of near the top of the flight lieutenant list.

I continued to command 29 Squadron until 13th August 1919, when the run-down of the British Army of Occupation of the Rhine was well under-way, and my squadron then listed for reduction to a cadre on that date.

I returned to Britain on 15th August 1919 as a rather despondent flying officer, having had to relinquish my two acting ranks of flight lieutenant and squadron leader. Also, the home that I had loved was now about to break up, because my father had died a few months previously in February, and my brother Beresford had been killed on active service with the Royal Artillery in 1917. [See Appendix F.]

So ends my experiences in the First World War.

The centre section of a 29 Squadron group photo at Bickendorf in May 1919. Hugh presented the full-length original photograph to 29 Squadron during the sixty-fifth anniversary at RAF Coningsby on 7th November 1980.

Verse from RFC song sung to air of 'The Lost Chord'.

We meet 'neath the sounding rafters
The walls all around us are bare;
They echo the peals of laughter;
It seems that the dead are there.
So stand by your glasses steady,
This world is a world of lies.
Here's a toast to the dead already;
Hurrah for the next man who dies.

PART 2
THE FOLLOW-ON YEARS 1920–1983

Hugh enjoying a litre of German beer in the Stadtwald beer garden in Cologne, April 1919.

CHAPTER 7

REFLECTIONS

Surviving the First World War

Somehow it doesn't seem right to leave the twenty-one-year-old Hugh White as a 'rather despondent flying officer' in 1919 (reduced by two ranks from his acting rank of squadron leader) after his time as a front-line squadron commander, as this would leave the reader wondering what happened later in his life. So this follow-on narrative provides a comprehensive account of my father's life after the dramatic events of the Great War.

I wasn't born until more than twenty years after Hugh's account finishes in 1919, so I have had to rely on his flying logbooks, his meticulous photo albums and his collection of official correspondence and newspaper cuttings, for much of the early information about which he rarely spoke.

The life expectancy of a pilot during the First World War was precarious and often short-lived, with many pilots and observers lasting just a few weeks or only days. Indeed, I recall my father saying that when he left 20 Squadron after nearly a year on the front line, none of the other pilots at that time had been on the squadron for even a full month.

Now, thirty-six years after his death in 1983 at the age of eighty-five, there are many things which I wish I had discussed with him. But for the most part he was a man of few words who shared relatively little of his thoughts. Looking back, I wish I had taken the time to probe below the surface, because when I look through his flying logbooks (reading them with my own knowledge as a RAF pilot flying in similar tactical roles in a later era) I can sometimes read between the lines to detect the changes in the type of flying in which he was involved as newer aircraft entered service. For the most part the logbooks just give a factual list of flights, with the occasional cryptic comment. But I am not fooled by the odd tongue-in-cheek comment such as when he records the name of his crew for his first flights in a B.E. 2e; in a Bristol Fighter; in a R.E.8; and sometimes when collecting or delivering a two-seat aircraft on his own, when he recorded his crew as 'Lt Sandbags' or 'Lt Ballast' – as I too have flown (in my case air testing a glider) with sandbags as ballast strapped to the other seat to keep the centre of gravity within limits, when it might not have been appropriate to put another person at risk.

His brief comments (often just asides) about each aircraft type which he flies for the first time are illuminating and interesting. During the First World War the operational biplane he flew initially with 20 Squadron was the F.E.2D two-seat scout and reconnaissance aircraft. Later, with 29 Squadron, he flew the single-seat Nieuport Scout and S.E.5a fighter aircraft; or 'fighting scouts' as they were sometimes termed. The primary task of the scout/fighter aircraft was to impose local air superiority over areas of enemy territory to enable the reconnaissance aircraft to take photographs of enemy positions and identify any changes or significant movements of troops or equipment. They were also used to spot for the artillery.

Later, during the 1920s and early 1930s he mostly flew two-seat army co-operation biplanes. With some of these aircraft there was not an opportunity for a dual flight before flying solo if they were configured for pilot and observer/gunner and only had flying controls fitted in the pilot's cockpit. In some instances, a new pilot might be given a short flight as passenger in the observer's cockpit to gain an indication of the aircraft's flying characteristics or techniques required by the pilot. In Hugh's case, after his initial flying training in 1916, almost all of the thirty or so different types or variants he flew after this were flown without any dual introduction.

Sometimes when flying a new aircraft type Hugh simply recorded 'First time in one, quite nice' or 'learning to fly' or 'getting used to machine'. Comments on further familiarisation flights as he got used to a new type were sometimes noted as 'getting used to the bus'. He also recorded minor damage after a few tricky landings, and on a back page of one logbook under 'Crashes' he listed 'R.E.7 (three-seater Rolls-Royce engine) on fire 1/2/17' and 'S.E.5a Collision with Hun 19/5/18'. In some ways the detail is remarkable, with lists in the back pages of the logbooks of the aircraft types flown, and names of the seventy-five aircrew wounded, missing or killed during nearly a year with 20 Squadron (see Appendix H). Did he compile this human list wondering whether his turn might come one day, or did he have the optimism of youth that he would survive? The grim reality, as he noted in Chapter 3 towards the end of his time on 20 Squadron, was that it seemed 'just a matter of time before my name was added to the long list of 20 Squadron casualties'.

Somehow, in that conflict, I doubt that there would have been much justification to feel confident about survival: especially when aircrew weren't allowed to have parachutes in the early years, which was an extraordinary, disgraceful and inhumane policy from on high. It is generally believed that although army balloon observers had parachutes to escape when under attack, parachutes were not issued to the aircraft flying crews because it might dull the fighting spirit and reduce their determination to try to save their damaged aircraft. Thus many aircrew perished when their aircraft were disabled or disintegrated in the air during combat, or caught fire.

I have often wondered about the sheer relief he must have felt on the day the First World War ended, because the chances of survival had been so small. However, by Armistice Day 11th November 1918 when peace was declared, Hugh had already been back in England for several months. Following his time on 29 Squadron and the mid-air collision in May 1918 during combat with a German Pfalz aircraft, he was well established at RAF Northolt as the officer commanding flying training. So maybe the relief was less intense in that peaceful environment than if he had still been in France on a front-line squadron.

Nevertheless, it must have been such a relief to have survived the war and for the first time in a few years to be able to look ahead to the real possibility of a full life. But this relief would have been tempered by a feeling of sadness that so many of his friends, colleagues and his brother had died so young. However, even the arrival of peace had its tragedies, because at an airfield far away in France where the pilots were celebrating the end of hostilities by fooling around on the airfield driving fire tenders and firing Verey flares in a mock battle, their squadron commander was killed when he was hit on the head by a flare. Some weeks later, Hugh travelled to France to take over command of this particular squadron (64 Squadron) after that tragic accident.

Around the time of the Armistice on 11th November 1918, his logbook records no flying that month. Was he on leave or was there no longer a need to train new pilots for the time being? Hugh's flying instructing at Northolt stopped abruptly on 31st October after a dual sortie in an Avro with a cadet pilot for 'landings and judging distance'. His next flight was on 2nd December when he recorded in his logbook the flying duties as 'nothing in particular'. The rest of his flying at Northolt through December was solo flying enjoying himself in S.E.5s with aerobatics, formation flying, gun firing against the pond[8], a few air tests and some flights in an Avro with no activities recorded.

On New Year's Eve 1918 Hugh flew from Northolt to the family home at Maidstone, logged as flying solo in a S.E.5 at 100 ft for an hour's flight in strong wind. Presumably he returned the S.E.5 to Northolt and collected his belongings from the officers' mess, but there is no record of this. A few days later he was back in France and airborne again on 8th January in S.E.5a F5460 which he flew during his short time with 64 Squadron.

After this period in command of 64 Squadron at Froidmont at the age of twenty, he moved on 8th February 1919 to Bickendorf near Cologne in Germany to take over command of his previous squadron (29 Squadron). Both of these squadrons had acquired a handful of German aircraft, so it must have been a strange feeling a couple of months after peace was declared to be airborne over Germany trying his hand flying a former German air force aircraft. After flying the Rumpler biplane it was 'not a bad aeroplane, heavy laterally'. Sadly, while Hugh was at Bickendorf his father died on 20th February 1919 aged seventy-three.

Hugh only remained in Germany for a few months before 29 Squadron was reduced to a cadre and he returned to England in August 1919.

Coincidentally, a similar situation arose after the Second World War; because within a year of peace being declared in 1945 he was posted once again to Germany to be on former enemy soil, when he was with the British Air Forces of Occupation at Bad Eilsen.

CHAPTER 8

THE ROYAL AIR FORCE – A NEW BEGINNING

The Creation of an Independent Air Force

Following early trials with military aviation, the Royal Flying Corps was established on 13th April 1912. In parallel, the early naval flying crystallised as the naval air service during 1913, and subsequently became the Royal Naval Air Service (RNAS) as a naval wing of the RFC on 1st July 1914. In time the RNAS became an independent organisation under the Royal Navy on 1st August 1915.

These separate air services operated independently for much of the First World War, during which time the use and significance of military air power increased dramatically. But their overlapping functions and the competition between them for aircraft and spare engines, combined with the failure of the supply organisations to meet their needs, led to a drastic rethinking of the way in which military aviation should be organised.

Although it involved considerable challenges, differences of opinion and resignations, towards the end of the First World War the RFC and RNAS were unified into a single air service, and the Royal Air Force was born on 1st April 1918.

In time the RAF ranks and blue uniform were introduced. Apparently the particular shade of blue came about because of the existence of a large quantity in Britain of blue herringbone fabric which had been ordered for the manufacture of uniforms for Czarist Russian imperial cavalrymen. As the Russian Revolution took place not long after that order had been placed, the material was never delivered and was therefore available immediately for the new RAF uniforms.

But on this potentially momentous day my father told me that the creation of this new independent RAF was the least matter on their minds, as they had a war to fight. In his case he took off from La Lovie in his Nieuport Scout at 7.15 a.m. for his first two-hour patrol of the day at 11,000 ft; and again at 1.15 p.m. for a further two-hour patrol at the same height, each time seeing off enemy aircraft. Thus 1st April 1918 was very much business as usual.

EARLY POST-WAR YEARS

After Hugh had relinquished command of 29 Squadron at Bickendorf on 13th August 1919, and reverted to his new substantive rank of flying officer, he returned to England where he was initially attached to RAF Manston in Kent. He had no formal duties during this short holding posting, so it would have been an administrative arrangement at a convenient location close to his family home at Maidstone. This two-month holding period provided time for him to relax at home and at the nearby seaside at Broadstairs with his mother, with his sister Rita and her future husband Fred Sowrey.

Fred Sowrey was then a squadron leader who had been awarded the Distinguished Service Order and Military Cross during his flying operations in the war. In particular he had gained prominence, and his DSO, for shooting down the second German Zeppelin airship to be brought down. Zeppelin L32 had been on its way to bomb London when Fred Sowrey (then a lieutenant) intercepted it in the dark at 14,000 ft and it crashed near Billericay soon after midnight on 23rd/24th September 1916 killing all twenty-two crew on board.

This event was commemorated at a ceremony a century later on 24th September 2016, when Fred Sowrey's son, AM Sir Frederick Sowrey, unveiled a monument near Billericay at a roadside by the field where L32 came down. This memorable event (where five generations of the Sowrey family were present) was held in a spirit of Anglo-German friendship to commemorate the brave men of both sides who had fought for their nation. Also present was the German nephew of the radio operator on board Zeppelin L32, which added a particular poignancy to the occasion.

During the First World War, Hugh's sister Rita had been a MT driver in the Women's Legion attached to the RFC Flying Training Squadron at Netheravon from August 1916. In time Rita became the driver for the commanding officer of No. 6 (Training) Wing Headquarters at Barming Place, Maidstone; close to the family home. Then during 1918 Rita became the head driver for the Australian Hospital at Joyce Green, Dartford, Kent.

After what must have been a relaxing and enjoyable few weeks spending time with family and friends in Kent, Hugh went up to Jesus College at Cambridge University in October 1919 for a one-year special engineering course.

The reason for Hugh and other officers attending this course (and other such courses) would become apparent during the following weeks as the future structure and disposition of the newly created Royal Air Force was set out in what became known as Trenchard's Memorandum. Although the RAF had been formed by combining the RFC and RNAS during wartime in 1918, once peace arrived the army and Royal Navy wanted the RAF to cease as an independent air force and for the aircraft, officers and men, to be absorbed back into these other two services. AM Trenchard, the chief of the Air Staff, was determined that the RAF should remain independent. Trenchard set out his plan for the future development of the RAF in a White Paper which he signed off to the Secretary of State for Air (Winston

Churchill) on 25th November 1919 and Churchill subsequently submitted the paper to Parliament on 11th December 1919.

A major emphasis of the paper was on training and education. The three pillars of this plan comprised the creation of a cadet college at Cranwell to train officers for a permanent commission; an apprentice school at Halton to provide the core technical expertise in aircraft maintenance for reliability and safety to minimise flying accidents; and a staff college at Andover to provide suitable training for those destined for high rank and responsibility.

Trenchard also placed emphasis on pilots gaining specialist technical training in subjects such as navigation, engines and wireless so that they would be more than just 'chauffeurs' flying aircraft. His paper stipulated that after five years' service officers would be required to select a particular technical subject to study during their subsequent career. Short and long courses would be provided to cater for those wishing to continue primarily in flying with a working knowledge of one or more technical subjects and for those who wished to become expert in a particular branch. Technical knowledge would also qualify an officer for selection to high command. This is why Hugh and many other officers attended engineering courses at Cambridge during this period while the military services were being drastically reduced following the end of hostilities. Hugh's record of service lists this as 'Special Course at Cambridge University'. It would be many years before the technical branch was established in 1940, following the creation of RAF Maintenance Command in 1938.

Whilst Hugh would have been fascinated by what he learned during his year's engineering course at Cambridge, he also found plenty of time for a good social life and sport.

CHAPTER 9

THE EARLY 1920s

A time for flying, national pageants, playing sport, social life

Hugh's early years in England after the horrors of war were marked by what must have been a wonderfully full life of flying, playing sport, participation in major national and social events; and becoming engaged to Joy.

At Cambridge Hugh was in the 1920 Jesus College rugby team, the second tennis team and the second cricket team. In the following three years his sporting activities continued with him being in the RAF Halton Bachelors' polo team in 1921; then in 1922 with his RAF tennis partner they won their doubles match during the RAF tennis championships against the then Duke of York (the future King George VI) and the duke's RAF partner. In January 1923 Hugh and his teammate won the two-man bobsleigh race at Grindelwald in Switzerland. During the 1922/23 season Hugh played fly-half in the RAF rugby team. This was the first season in which the RAF beat the Army and the Royal Navy in the annual inter-services rugby; but as is the way with service life several of the team were posted overseas at the end of that season – including Hugh to India. Other sporting activities through his life included hunting, shooting, golf, skiing, sailing and fly fishing.

NO. 1 SCHOOL OF TECHNICAL TRAINING, RAF HALTON

From Cambridge University Hugh was posted to the staff of No. 1 School of Technical Training (Boys) at Halton from 1st October 1920 for 'admin duties'. It is not clear what his duties entailed or the extent to which these related to the Cambridge engineering course he had just completed. However, following Trenchard's memorandum which was now being developed within the RAF, this was a formative time for the new Aircraft Apprentice Scheme. It is therefore likely that his operational and general service experience, together with the technical knowledge gained from the engineering course, would have been put to good use. Moreover, during his time at Halton Hugh would have learned much about the practical issues of technical training in the RAF through the activities in the trainee workshops.

There were a number of other young pilots at Halton during this period, some of whom were destined to become technical officers in later years, so it may have also been an interim 'holding' posting for them while the shape and size of the future RAF was settling down. This year at Halton was also highly relevant for Hugh's future career when some twenty years later he would hold a senior position at Technical Training Command before returning to Halton as the commandant.

The military site at Halton had been created during the First World War on land made available by Alfred Rothschild in response to Lord Kitchener's appeal to landowners in 1914 to make land available for military use. Rothschild had been one of the first to support this scheme and some 20,000 troops then moved into the Rothschild estate at Halton where they lived in tents during their training through the wet and muddy winter of 1914/15. These unsatisfactory conditions provided the impetus to construct more durable buildings and by 1916 RFC personnel were able to move into a semi-established camp at Halton after outgrowing the capacity of Farnborough to train sufficient air mechanics.

The officers' mess at RAF Halton. Rothschild's Halton House, built in 1883, had been modelled on the lines of an elegant French chateau.

During 1917 new workshops were built and the grass airfield established at Halton. By the end of the war in November 1918 there were some 6,000 British and Australian male mechanics at Halton, together with 2,000 female air mechanics and 2,000 boy air mechanics, being trained by some 1,700 staff. This sprawling camp with its grass airfield and workshops for training air mechanics, together with wooden hutted accommodation, had been constructed with the aid of German prisoner of war labour. Following the death of Rothschild in 1918 the Air Council bought the estate.

By April 1918 the Training Depot at Halton for air mechanics had been renamed as the School of Technical Training (Boys). Then in April 1920 the name was changed again to become the No. 1 School of Technical Training (Boys). In parallel, No. 2 School of Technical Training (Boys) was established at Cranwell (and Hugh spent a month there immediately before his posting to Halton). The creation of these technical training schools for boys was part of Trenchard's vision to consolidate the RAF's position as a single, independent service, which included training a permanent core of technicians during a three-year course to be the backbone of the RAF.

In Trenchard's memorandum 'Permanent Organisation of the Royal Air Force', which had been presented to the House of Commons as a White Paper by Secretary of State for Air Winston Churchill in December 1919, Trenchard had placed great emphasis on the importance of training, particularly of skilled ground crew.

He had emphasised that the way to achieve the best training of mechanics in the multiplicity of trades required by a highly technical service would be to enlist the bulk of the skilled ranks as boys, and train them within the RAF. This would have the added benefit of fostering the air force spirit on which so much would depend.

Later in the memorandum, Trenchard noted that the training of all those boys would eventually be carried out at Halton. The first entry under the scheme would take place early in 1920 at Cranwell and then move to Halton as soon as permanent accommodation there was ready.

Trenchard had already provided more detail about his intentions for the scheme in a letter to Churchill in November 1919, writing that it would be necessary to enlist the bulk of the technical tradesmen as boys, because the Royal Air Force could not hope to compete in the recruitment of men who had served full apprenticeships in civilian life and could therefore command high wages. He went on to say that apprentices would form forty per cent of all ground crews in the Royal Air Force, and sixty-two per cent of all the skilled tradesmen.

It was clear that Trenchard wanted highly skilled men at a price the service could afford from its meagre budget, as men who would foster an 'Air Force spirit'. Thus in late 1919 the Halton Apprentice Scheme was promulgated to local education authorities and entrance examinations held in London and the provinces.

The rigorous selection procedure ensured that recruits would be of the highest quality. Moreover, because of their resourcefulness and intelligence, they could be expected to complete their apprenticeships in three years rather than the five normally served by civilian engineering apprentices. A shorter course would be a cheaper one, which would no doubt please the Secretary of State for Air – Winston Churchill.

In February 1920, still known as Boy Mechanics, the first intake of 235 was accepted at Cranwell for a three-year apprenticeship. The first four intakes trained at Cranwell, and it was not until January 1922 that the first group arrived at Halton as the fifth entry. This move coincided with the adoption of the rank of aircraft apprentice. Two entries a year were planned.

This scheme continued for over seventy years from 1920 to 1993, when it was eventually discontinued following the end of the Cold War. In parallel with the apprentice scheme the RAF College Cranwell had been created in 1920 for flight cadets to complete a three-year course for officer and flying training to provide a core of potential future leaders for the RAF. This flight cadet scheme would continue until 1971 when the new Graduate Entry scheme was introduced; with HRH Prince Charles as one of the student officers on the first course. (I was a flying instructor at the RAF College Cranwell when this change took place and instructed student pilots during four of the final flight cadet entries and the first graduate entry.)

The arrival of the first RAF commandant at Halton, Air Commodore Scarlett, in December 1919 heralded many improvements to all aspects of boy training. Scarlett remained in post until 1924 which enabled him to oversee the transformation of a temporary wartime military camp into the permanent RAF station. He therefore established the firm basis for building up Trenchard's aircraft apprentice scheme. Scarlett was the commandant throughout Hugh's year on the staff at Halton.

When Hugh arrived at Halton in October 1920 he had been away from flying for eighteen months and was then able to make use of the airfield at Halton to keep his hand in flying the Avro 504K, Bristol Fighter and single-seat Martinsyde F.4 Buzzard (which he had not flown before) with a total of thirty-seven flights during the year. This flying was mostly short local solo flights; but he also carried out some flying instruction and flew air experience flights for airmen, as well as flying demonstrations in the Martinsyde F.4 for relatives of the boy apprentices. The fast and manoeuvrable Martinsyde fighter had first flown in mid 1918 and was soon ordered for the RAF in large numbers, but deliveries were still at an early stage when the Armistice was signed and the remaining orders were cancelled. Although various units such as the Central Flying School and Halton received some of the fifty-seven aircraft delivered to the RAF, none reached the operational squadrons. The sight and sound of the aircraft flying from the grass airfield at Halton would have helped to establish the all-important 'air mindedness' in the boy apprentices.

After a year at Halton, Hugh returned to full-time flying on 1st October 1921, beginning with a five-month course at the School of Army Co-operation at RAF Old Sarum on the edge of Salisbury Plain in Wiltshire. Later that month Hugh was away for a few days in Sussex for the wedding of his sister Rita. As Hugh and Rita's father had died in 1919 it was

Hugh chasing the polo ball during a match at Halton in 1921.

Hugh's lifelong friend Quintus Studd in 1921 – probably taken at Halton (see page 205).

Hugh and Rita (Margarita) with their mother and a bridesmaid before the wedding, 18th October 1921.

Hugh's duty to give away his sister at her wedding to Sqn Ldr Fred Sowrey at St Peter's Parish Church, Bexhill-on-Sea.

THE SCHOOL OF ARMY CO-OPERATION, RAF OLD SARUM

In the years after the First World War Hugh's RAF career had two main threads running through it. His flying career was now mainly involved with army co-operation, flying the Bristol Fighter and later the Westland Wallace, while the direction of his overall career moved progressively into the engineering sphere. As he once explained to me, in the early days of the RAF it was necessary for an officer to have a specialisation in order to progress, and his was engineering.

But it was the Bristol Fighter (known as the 'Brisfit') which played an increasing part in Hugh's life for much of the 1920s. Although Hugh had already flown the Bristol Fighter on occasions in previous years, this marked the beginning of seven continuous years flying this aircraft type.

The Bristol F.2B Fighter was a highly successful aircraft which was constructed in large numbers. A total of over 5,000 were built for seventeen air forces. Of these, the 1,600 Bristol Fighters for the RAF were active for a decade on thirty-nine different squadrons. With a maximum speed of 123 mph and ceiling of 18,000 ft, the crew comprised a pilot in the forward open cockpit and the observer/gunner in a separate open cockpit behind the pilot. The air gunner's duties included photography, message dropping and pick-up, gunnery (a Lewis machine gun was mounted on a curved 'scarf ring' around the edge of the cockpit) and occasionally bombing.

The prime task of the army co-operation course was to train and continue developing efficient air-to-ground procedures and communication, under operational conditions, between army units on the ground and the crews of the aircraft supporting them. The tasks included spotting fall of shot for the artillery, bombing and gunnery, and various forms of communication between land and air. Communication was achieved by a mix of aircrew recording and decoding messages displayed on the ground using Popham Panels; message-dropping in weighted bags and message pick-up using a hook beneath the aircraft to pick up a bag on a line slung between two poles fixed in the ground (or sometimes rifles stuck in the ground by their bayonets); and developing the new W/T (wireless-telephony).

The flying activities during this five-month course involved RAF aircraft operating with army units on the ground, and army officers being given flying experience to gain a good understanding of the issues from an air perspective. Hugh and his fellow students were assessed under the four headings of army co-operation, infantry co-operation, photography, reconnaissance – and their suitability to be future instructors on the staff at Old Sarum.

Following the course at Old Sarum Hugh was posted as a flight commander on 4 (Army Co-operation) Squadron at Farnborough, as he recorded over forty years later in a letter to a researcher looking into the history of 4 (AC) Squadron. Hugh wrote:

No. 1 Army Co-operation Course, Old Sarum October 1921–March 1922.

Back row: Swanton, Cook, Keeping, Mullette, Dipple, Jameson, Bragg, MacMillan, and Dufty.

Front Row: Clemens, Walser, Gossage, Stevenson, and H G White.

'After attending the 1st Army Co-op course at the School of Army Co-op at Old Sarum (five-month course), I joined No. 4 Squadron as a flight commander and was detailed with my flight to co-operate with the local brigade commander and his men and be bosom pals. But all I got were blank refusals to co-operate in any way at all coupled with complaints about breaking his men's bayonets trying to pick up messages with our hooks from ropes strung between rifles stuck in the ground by their tooth picks [bayonets].

'Also, refusal to allow any other or more enlightened demonstrations of means of communication between air and ground and vice-versa. Anyway, he said his brigade was engaged on its annual musketry. Plus preparations for inspection by HM King George V (after he had done us on 20th May 1922) and during which I not only took an air photo of his arrival for giving to him shortly after, but also shook hands with him and talked to him in front of my aircraft, and then led a mock bomb raid for HM's benefit with flour bags thrown out by our observers who were told to simulate the real thing.

'I see I took quite a lot of army types into the air (including a Brazilian Major General Fernandez) while with No. 4 Squadron. I also flew to Netheravon on two separate occasions to act as a member at a couple of Courts Martial. All of which is not very exciting, but perhaps somewhat different from life in the RAF today.'

Coincidentally when my father wrote this letter in 1966, I was a pilot on this same 4 (AC) Squadron then based in Germany where one of our main roles was still army co-operation, by then termed as close air support.

After an action-packed month with 4 Squadron during which he flew thirty-two times, Hugh returned to Old Sarum in May 1922 to be on the staff as an instructor pilot flying Bristol Fighters with the army co-operation courses.

In addition to his routine army co-operation activities, Hugh's flying during this period included visits to other RAF airfields in the area which were involved with army co-operation, including Upavon, Netheravon, Andover, Northolt and Farnborough. He also flew further afield to the RAF airfields at Biggin Hill, Hawkinge and Shotwick (south of Liverpool at the head of the River Dee estuary as one of a pair of airfields with nearby RAF Sealand).

Hugh flew many engine and rigging air tests; and on some occasions flew spares to aircraft which had forced-landed in the countryside with engine problems – and sometimes flying these aircraft back to Old Sarum. With his earlier experience as

Top left: Looking back over Hugh's shoulder at Fg Off Pratt, airborne in the Bristol Fighter while searching for a landing ground near Elstead (Farnham), 25th April 1922.

Right: View of Hugh from the rear cockpit of a Bristol Fighter.

Bottom left: No. 4 Squadron Farnborough April-May 1922. Hugh and Fg Off Pratt (left of picture) with their pipes.

a flying instructor he flew dual instruction with new pilots. He also flew several set-piece army co-operation flying demonstrations for the army and sometimes for the public.

One such occasion was in November 1922 when he flew a demonstration for the Kings Own Scottish Borderers and South Devonshire Regiment at Devonport, Plymouth. Ahead of this he flew from Old Sarum to the downs at Staddon Heights above Plymouth Sound where a small ground party of their technicians would have positioned petrol cans, tools and spare parts. Hugh's passenger/crew for this one-hour and forty-five-minute flight from Old Sarum was Wg Cdr Gossage (the CO of the School of Army Co-operation) who probably continued to Devonport by road to watch the demonstration.

Once on the downs at Staddon Heights, Hugh and Flt Lt Dowling (his observer) waited their time to take off for the demonstration a few miles away. This demonstration included dropping a box of ammunition by small parachute and picking up a message bag with the hook under the aircraft, before flying direct back to Old Sarum without the need to land again at Staddon Heights – with a total flight time of two hours and twenty minutes. Photographs of the ammunition drop and message pick-up were subsequently published in the *Daily Mirror*.

THE HENDON AERIAL PAGEANT

The annual RAF Aerial Pageant at Hendon had begun in 1920 with the purpose of instilling air mindedness in the public. This was a hugely popular event and would continue until 1937. For the pageants held in 1920 and 1921, the theme for the finale 'event of the day' had been based on typical events in the First World War, with an RAF aircraft downing an observation balloon one year and attacking a simulated German headquarters in a village the following year. By 1922 the theme for the finale had moved on to be a demonstration of the use of RAF air power in an eastern setting with a simulated attack on a 'desert stronghold' to illustrate the work of the RAF in air policing. This theme was continued in 1923; demonstrating co-operation of air and ground forces as the RAF came to the aid of a besieged garrison.[9]

The 1923 pageant held on Saturday 30th June was attended by King George V and Queen Mary. Hugh's participation was to fly a Bristol Fighter in an inter-station relay race with Leading Aircraftman Millward as his crew. As reported in *Flight* magazine on 5th July, the heats were flown in the morning with the final between six RAF stations during the afternoon. Each team comprised an Avro, a Bristol Fighter and a Sopwith Snipe. The first lap was flown by the Avros; followed by the Bristol Fighters; before the Snipes flew the final lap. Each team had a tally disc, to be handed on to the next crew in their team, before the final lap with the finishing line opposite the Royal Box. The six finalists were Farnborough, Netheravon, Halton, Spitalgate, Northolt and Upavon – so Hugh's Old Sarum team must have been knocked out during the heats. No information was found on which station won.

It is likely that Hugh and Joy met towards the end of 1921 or early 1922. The first pictures of Joy in his photograph album look to be around this time, together with photos of Joy with her brothers and sisters at their parents' farm. Hugh's sister Rita had been friends with Joy's eldest sister Rene (perhaps at school) and one day Rita and Hugh had visited their family home in Hastings where Hugh had met Joy.

Joy was the sixth of eight children (Rene, Jack, Isobel, Nell, Frank, Joy, Charles, and Sybil) born to John and Daisy Hickman who farmed at Hole Farm near Hastings.

School of Army Co-operation Bristol Fighter and B Squadron crew at the Hendon Aerial Pageant on 30th June 1923. Sqn Ldr Durston (OC B Squadron) is in the cockpit. Hugh (standing by roundel) flew in the relay race with LAC Millward (sitting in rear cockpit) as his crew.

King George V and Queen Mary accompanied by AM J F A Higgins (Air Officer Commanding Inland Area) at the Hendon RAF Aerial Pageant on 30th June 1923.

Sledding winners Hugh and Guy at Grindelwald, Switzerland on 5th January 1923.

Top: RAF Tennis Championships at the Queen's Club 1922. Third round of RAF Doubles. From left to right: far side of net HRH The Duke of York (later King George VI) and Wg Cdr Louis Greig versus Flt Lt HM Fraser (nearest to camera) and Flt Lt Hugh White on the right (winners).

Middle: 1922-23 RAF Rugby victorious inter-services team. Team members: A C Collins, Flt Lt H G White (fly half), P/O Coventry, Padre Stevens, F/O Adams, Carter, Rose, Flt Lt Riddle, Sqn Ldr Russell, Flt Lt Simpson, Lowe, Flt Lt Wakefield (Capt), Flt Lt Usher, LAC Runham and Flt Lt Bryson.

Bottom: Hugh with his fiancée Joy at the Hendon RAF Aerial Pageant on 30th June 1923.

The eldest of the boys was Jack, who tragically was killed during the First World War. Joy was only thirteen years old then and she remembered Jack arriving in uniform at the farm before he sailed for France. Jack had been a nineteen-year-old second lieutenant in the Royal Field Artillery and apparently during the evening of 4th October 1917 he was one of three officers, together with three sergeants, who had gone forward under cover of darkness to check on the German lines. They had all been killed except for one of the sergeants who later visited Jack's parents at Hole Farm to tell them what had happened. Joy's other two brothers were too young to be involved in this war and both became farmers as their father.

Along with the other children (apart from Isobel who had been born with a dislocated hip) Joy was an enthusiastic pony rider with secret ambitions to become a race jockey. Indeed, one day her father was just in time to stop her loading her pony (with help from the family groom) into a horse box trailer to go off to ride in a race.

Hugh and Joy became engaged towards the end of 1923 when Joy was nineteen. However, by this time Hugh was due to leave for India so the wedding was planned for his mid-tour leave some two-and-a-half long years away.

HMT *Glengorm Castle* in the Persian Gulf to disembark RAF personnel on posting to Iraq. Hugh remained on board for the onward journey to Karachi.

CHAPTER 10

INDIA 1924-1928

Air Control / Air Policing and Army Co-operation

Following Hugh's two years at Old Sarum, on 22 November 1923 he embarked on HM Troopship *Glengorm Castle* at Southampton for the five-week journey to India. The sea voyage routed via Malta, Port Said, Aden, the Persian Gulf (to drop off servicemen destined for Iraq), with Christmas onboard before arriving at Karachi on 28th December 1923. This was followed by a lengthy overland train journey of some 800 miles to Peshawar where Hugh joined 28 (Army Co-operation) Squadron as a flight commander to fly Bristol Fighters for a five-year posting. But why were RAF squadrons based in India during the 1920s and 1930s and what were they doing there?

THE HISTORICAL SETTING FOR THE RAF IN INDIA DURING THE INTERWAR YEARS

The First World War was seen by many as the war to end all wars. Once it was over there was considerable uncertainty about what lay ahead for the British armed forces. With no obvious threat in sight the role of the armed forces was mainly directed at Imperial peacekeeping to hold the massive British Empire intact. While the army considered that it was their responsibility to keep warring tribes under control in the Middle Eastern areas of the Empire, in Mesopotamia (now Iraq), Trans-Jordan, Aden, and the Afghan frontier with India, the RAF considered it could do the job from the air more effectively and in a shorter time, as well as at lower cost. This expanding role for the RAF and therefore its share of the peace-time budget brought about a fierce dispute between the army and the RAF which rumbled on through much of the 1920s, and to a lesser extent into the 1930s.

RAF aircraft were first used in tribal areas in January 1920, when a force of ten D.H.9 reconnaissance bomber aircraft were sent to support the Camel Corps in dealing with the 'Mad Mullah' in Somaliland; successfully dispersing his forces. The success of this venture was reported in the *London Gazette* of 1st November 1920, in which the British Governor of Somaliland, Geoffrey Archer recorded:

'For this the credit is primarily due to the Royal Air Force, who were the major instrument of attack and the decisive factor. They exercised an immediate and tremendous moral effect over the dervishes, who in the ordinary course are good fighting men, demoralizing them in the first few days.'[10]

Subsequently, at a pivotal meeting in Cairo in March 1921 Churchill and Trenchard agreed to hand over the garrisoning of Mesopotamia to the RAF. The RAF was also active in Trans-Jordan following the accession of King Abdullah in 1921. Later, in 1928, the RAF also took over the territories of Aden from the army.

The advent of air control / air policing by the RAF throughout the Middle East and India really came of age in 1923, the year Hugh sailed for his posting in India. A major issue for this military concept was to ensure that the public would be convinced that the RAF was not using excessive force to maintain the Empire. Therefore, throughout the interwar years the RAF was careful to moderate its policy and activities to maintain this public support, thus avoiding excesses which might otherwise have occurred. During such operations every effort was made to avoid civilian casualties. Leaflets were dropped before a village or a particular house was planned to be bombed, to allow the inhabitants to get clear and watch the show from a safe distance.

This practice was still in being when I arrived in Aden four decades later in 1963. With our Hunter aircraft the leaflets were loaded between the two surfaces of the split flaps and then the flaps raised (closed) to keep the leaflets squeezed in place. We then overflew the area being troublesome and lowered the flaps to release the leaflets into the slipstream. In some cases the locals were deliberately troublesome so that they could create a situation which would require a cautionary demonstration of fire power from the air. The Hunters would be tasked to fire their 30-mm calibre cannons at a particular area or a building. The tribesmen would watch this display of power and then go out to collect the empty brass cartridge cases which were ejected from the gun bays. This provided them with a valuable supply of brass for various purposes.

At the time of Trenchard's memorandum in late 1919 he envisaged there being eight RAF squadrons in India; three squadrons in Mesopotamia; seven squadrons in Egypt (which he viewed as the 'Clapham Junction' between the east and the west); a seaplane squadron in Malta and another in the eastern Mediterranean. Back home in Britain there would be just four squadrons. With no evident air threat to Britain after the First World War, and no significant threat to aircraft in the overseas tribal territories (apart from rifle fire) there was no need for more advanced aircraft than those already in service. Thus the Bristol Fighter and the D.H.9A (known as the 'Ninak') became the backbone of the RAF for much of the

1920s, together with Vickers Vernon transport aircraft.

In India the majority of RAF squadrons were based in the North-West Frontier Province (NWFP) which was divided into three areas for the RAF. The northern area comprised the region to the north of the Khyber Pass up to the foothills of the Himalayas – referred to as the 'Roof of the World'. The second or central area lay south-west of the Khyber Pass roughly between the rivers Kabul and Kurram. This was a mountainous area, criss-crossed by deep valleys and dried-up water courses. The third region was the southern area which lay to the south-west of Kohat, from the Kurram river down towards Fort Sandeman and Baluchistan. This was dominated by Waziristan, the storm centre of the frontier and stronghold of tribal resistance.

At the time Hugh arrived in India on New Year's Day January 1924 (aged twenty-five) to join 28 (AC) Squadron there were six RAF squadrons in India operating Bristol Fighters or the D.H.9A, mostly based in the NWFP.

RAF Headquarters, Ambala
No. 5 (AC) Squadron Bristol Fighters

No. 1 (Indian) Wing, Peshawar
No. 28 (AC) Squadron Bristol Fighters, Peshawar
No. 31 (AC) Squadron Bristol Fighters, Dardoni

No. 2 (Indian) Wing, Risalpur and Nowshera
No. 27 (B) Squadron D.H.9A
No. 60 (B) Squadron D.H.9A

No. 3 (Indian) Wing, Quetta
No. 20 (AC) Squadron, Quetta

In addition there was a Port Detachment at Karachi; and an Aircraft Park at Lahore.[11]

Since arriving in India in 1920, 28 Squadron had already been based at Ambala; then at Kohat, Parachinar, Dardoni and Tani – all in the central and northern areas of the NWFP; before moving to Peshawar where Hugh joined them. The squadron would continue to move every year or two during the interwar years to Quetta, Ambala, Risalpur, Ambala, Manzay, Ambala and Kohat. Some changes in location may have been for operational reasons, but the regular two-yearly moves were planned to give squadron personnel broader experience of the differing regions in India which enhanced their operational flexibility and effectiveness. It also balanced out the time spent in the more or less attractive locations and climates during the long tours in the region of up to five years.

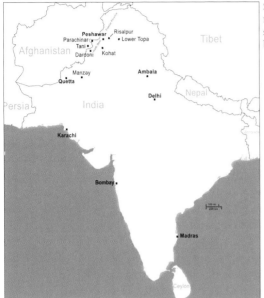

Some of the major cities in India mentioned in this chapter and RAF stations where 28 Squadron was based during the 1920s.

NO. 28 (ARMY CO-OPERATION) SQUADRON

Hugh's years in India with 28 Squadron must have been a happy and perhaps even a relatively carefree time. Against the odds he had survived the Great War, and after four years back in England, first at Cambridge University, then a year at Halton, followed by two years flying Bristol Fighters from Old Sarum on army co-operation, he was once again on a front-line operational squadron. When Hugh joined 28 Squadron it was commanded by Sqn Ldr H. S. Powell MC.

An RAF squadron is a close-knit community so there would have been a group of fellow officers of a similar age with whom to enjoy recreational, sporting and social activities. Sporting activities included tennis, cricket, polo, hunting and watching horse racing. Also, in the days before there was a concern about preserving the lives of wild animals, shooting game. With the squadron's task there was an abundance of interesting flying over majestic mountain and desert scenery, which provided the opportunity to see many parts of India (and what is now Pakistan) during the squadron's routine flying and operational activities. Moreover, for the second half of this posting Hugh was newly married and living with his young wife Joy. Their first child John was born at Ambala during 1927.

When Hugh joined 28 Squadron at Peshawar it had been located there for some eight months. A year later the squadron would move to Quetta for two years, about 400 miles to the south-west. The mountainous tribal regions around Peshawar and Quetta near the border with Afghanistan were troublesome then, and continue to be so today. The only difference is that following the partition of India in 1947 these tribal areas are now a part of Pakistan. After two years at Quetta, 28 Squadron moved to Ambala for Hugh's final eighteen months in India.

Hugh's four-and-a-half years in India flying the Bristol Fighter was mainly working with the army for training and to quell tribal difficulties. The Bristol Fighter had entered service with the RFC in 1917 as a scout aircraft and fighter; and after the First World War continued as a rugged and trusty army co-operation aircraft until September 1931. Hugh flew the Bristol Fighter on and off throughout this fourteen-year period, from a ten-minute evening check-out flight on 2nd July 1917 when he was a flying instructor at Yatesbury, to his final air test of a Bristol Fighter at Cranwell on 16th June 1931.

No. 28 Squadron comprised twenty-four officers/pilots divided into A, B and C Flights; together with the senior NCOs and airmen technicians for each flight – some of whom flew as observer/gunners. Hugh's life as B Flight commander was active and varied. Their diverse activities included exercises or operations in the North-West Frontier Province and on the Persian border; and detachments to other regions of India for army co-operation training or operations with British and Indian Army units, during which they sometimes flew low over specified areas to 'show the flag' to troublesome tribesmen. There is the occasional mention of 'raid on enemy' in Hugh's flying logbook but there are few details and it is difficult to detect which were training flights and which may have been operations. Although there were operations involving RAF squadrons to quell tribal unrest in India throughout the 1920s and 1930s there are few indications of active operations in Hugh's India flying logbook; although he was certainly involved in aerial reconnaissance and providing a visible 'presence' over potentially troublesome tribal areas.

The squadron's flying activities included the use of out-lying landing grounds for operations or exercises, as well as for liaison meetings with army units in an area. The aircraft were sometimes used to provide an informal air taxi to transport army officers or district commissioners to or from these landing grounds and for air experience or area reconnaissance flights for British (and occasionally Indian) army personnel, district officials or regional dignitaries. Other tasks included delivering aerial photographs or official correspondence to RAF or army units. In addition, as a flight commander, Hugh was involved in leading flypasts and as an individual activity carrying out aerobatic displays for ceremonial occasions. As in earlier years he carried out air tests and dual checks or instruction for newly arrived pilots (some of whom had no experience of flying the Bristol Fighter for which there was no central conversion unit).

Hugh seemed to have particularly enjoyed surveying and inspecting the many austere landing grounds spread across India and sometimes identifying potential locations for new landing grounds. While doing this he landed at a total of sixty-seven airfields or landing grounds, many of which were used during various exercises with the army and operations in the mountainous areas or down on the plains, each carefully recorded in the back of his logbook. His visits to landing grounds often included oblique and vertical aerial photography, sometimes visiting several locations over a few days.

Frequent air tests were carried out after engine maintenance or replacement, repairs or adjustment to the tensioned wire rigging which ensured the aerodynamic qualities of the aircraft. His logbook is dotted with comments such as 'engine running rough', 'flying left wing low', 'machine nose-heavy – to be re-rigged', 'nose of aircraft dropped and requires re-rigging', 'engine test – popping slightly', 'oil pressure OK', 'engine running rough below 1850 rpm', and so on. Such comments might be followed a day or so later by 'engine and rigging test OK'. Several air tests were flown after heavy landings or mishaps by himself or other pilots, as for example on 10th December 1924 his logbook records: 'Co-op with 18 Infantry Brigade. Forced landing owing to running out of tank whilst dropping a message, propeller and wheels broken.' This sounds as though the engine had stopped after he left it too late before changing to the next fuel tank.

Two days later, the aircraft was repaired and he air-tested it during the twenty-minute return flight to the landing ground they were using, noting in his logbook 'engine and rigging test after re-erection'. There are several flights when he was searching for other squadron 'machines' which had force-landed in some remote area.

'One of my forced landings – propeller and wheels broken.' 10th December 1924.

Flypasts and similar activities for ceremonial occasions added extra colour. For example 'Flypast for the annual Proclamation parade on New Year's Day'; 'Flypast for HE Governor of Madras'; 'Night-flying for torchlight tattoo'; 'Aerobatics during garden party Kapurthala Jubilee celebrations'. There was also a sombre entry of 'dropped wreaths by parachute at military funeral'. Hugh also flew successive air officers commanding India, the commander of the Afghan air force, and a number of local army commanders and district commissioners.

Hugh's years in India were characterised by the various operating areas which were the focus during his time at each of the three successive RAF stations of Peshawar, Quetta and Ambala where 28 Squadron was located.

Peshawar 1924

Peshawar is some thirty miles from the border with Afghanistan, situated in a large valley leading from the eastern end of the Khyber Pass. Known as the 'City on the Frontier', Peshawar's strategic location at the crossroads of central and south Asia has made it one of the most culturally vibrant and lively cities in the region. The area is irrigated by various canals of the Kabul river and by a tributary named the Bara river. It has a semi-arid climate, with very hot summers and mild winters. The airfield is at an elevation of 1,158 ft.

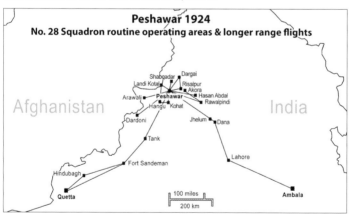

RAF Peshawar was then the headquarters of the RAF's No 1 (Indian) Wing, where 28 Squadron was the resident squadron. In addition there were various outlying airfields and austere landing grounds within the region which were activated when required.

During 1924 when Hugh was stationed at Peshawar the focus for their flying was army co-operation with military units in the northern area of the North-West

Frontier Province, including with the 131st Indian Cavalry Brigade. These activities took place over a wide region with army units at main garrisons and at outposts in remote mountain areas. This included the rugged mountainous area of the nearby Khyber Pass to the north-west of Peshawar and the border with Afghanistan; the mountainous area to the north of Peshawar; and the busy area along the main route to Rawalpindi 100 miles to the east. Such co-operation involved flying from the many landing grounds located in valleys in the mountainous areas or along the foothills.

On many occasions ahead of exercises Hugh flew to a landing ground to meet army officers to co-ordinate the involvement of 28 Squadron aircraft and crews. These exercises would typically involve reconnaissance and aerial photography of the operating areas, observing artillery shoots and flying army officers to give them an aerial perspective of the activities and to improve their understanding of RAF capabilities. There were many occasions when Hugh took a passenger or delivered official correspondence to other RAF airfields or army headquarters, sometimes in remote forward areas near the Afghan border such as the RAF stations of Arawali and Dardoni. Arawali was a forward RAF airfield some seventy miles south-west of Peshawar on a natural rock plateau 4,000 feet above sea level, while Dardoni with its resident RAF Bristol Fighter squadron was a hundred miles to the south-west of Peshawar in a valley near Miranshah. In addition to army co-operation flying there was also a frequent need for Hugh to fly engine and rigging air tests and (as a former flying instructor) to give dual instruction.

A few months after joining 28 Squadron Hugh was detached to Quetta to attend a six-week course at the School of Army Co-operation during which he flew only nine flights – each with an army officer as observer.

Once back at Peshawar, June was a busy month with a mixture of army co-operation flying, giving dual instruction, flying air tests, air gunnery and bombing practice – and flights to Dardoni and Risalpur. Then in July Hugh took his crews on a long-range flight from Peshawar to Ambala with refuelling stops at Jhelum and Lahore – a total of seven hours flying during a single day. This was not a straightforward trip because, as happened all too often, Hugh had a technical problem soon after leaving Jhelum and had to make a forced landing ten minutes later at Dana Musa. Presumably another of their aircraft also landed there because Hugh and his air gunner Leading Aircraftman Williams continued their flight the same day in another aircraft. After spending the next day at Ambala the flight returned on the following day to Peshawar by the same route.

Flying in India at that time was often a hazardous occupation, in particular in the mountains which were above 10,000 feet in places. Although the Bristol

Fighter had a maximum ceiling of 20,000 feet (and the D.H.9A aircraft of other squadrons in India could reach nearly 17,000 feet) in reality this depended on what equipment or weapons were being carried. There were many instances of pilots flying in mountainous valleys when the rate of climb of their aircraft was less than the angle of the rising ground and they were faced with the decision of how far to continue up a narrowing valley and whether they would be able to turn back. With no escape route this sometimes meant that there was nothing which could be done other than to make a forced landing straight ahead or turn as hard as was possible in the thin mountain air (with the larger turn radius) and hope for the best.

Flying into and out of landing grounds in the mountains was also hazardous with the longer take-off and landing distances at the airfields and landing grounds which were a few thousand feet above sea level. Here the combination of reduced engine thrust at higher altitude and the need to travel faster across the ground to achieve flying speed through the thin air (and faster speeds over the ground when landing) added to the hazards – especially as aircraft such as the Bristol Fighter had no brakes. Parachutes would not have been much help in many such situations and these were not generally issued to aircrew until December 1928. Even then some pilots resisted wearing parachutes because the additional weight would reduce the amount of fuel or weapons which could be carried. However regulations soon came in which made wearing them compulsory.

No. 28 Squadron had its share of flying accidents along with the other squadrons in India. For example, on 28th July 1924 (while Hugh was away on leave) six aircraft of 28 and 5 Squadrons were undertaking operations in a valley in the Razmak area some 120 miles south-west of Peshawar when cloud formed on the mountains. Two of the aircraft of 28 Squadron crashed while trying to land at Razmak. The crew of one aircraft, Fg Off Ian P Anderson and AC1 Kenneth R Taylor (rigger aero), were both killed. In the other aircraft Fg Off Edward Bell was killed, but there is no information on his crew.[12] A third 28 Squadron aircraft crashed on higher ground further up the valley killing the pilot with his air gunner dying later from his injuries. One of the 5 Squadron aircraft crashed and the other landed in enemy territory and the crew was captured. The pilot of the captured aircraft was the CO of 5 Squadron (Sqn Ldr A J Capel) who together with his crew (LAC Bell) was released unharmed after a few days of haggling over an agreement of political terms – despite the bombing continuing. They were extremely fortunate.[13] Sadly, just over a week later (4th August 1924) there was another fatal accident with a 28 Squadron aircraft at Peshawar when Fg Off Douglas McG Morphy crashed in Bristol Fighter D8057 after engine failure – dying from his injuries. It is unclear whether Morphy was flying solo or with Aircraftman Benjamin Cook as crew/ passenger (from No. 2 Wireless Station), who also died that day.[14]

Surprisingly, only six months after joining 28 Squadron, Hugh was able to take a three-month leave break (1st July to 18th October) with a fellow RAF officer for an extensive trip to Kenya for big game hunting. For such a long leave to be possible for a flight commander on an operational squadron this would have been at a time when his B Flight was at the Hill Station of Lower Topa for their periodic two-month summer rest and recreation away from the heat on the plains.

Hugh's initial journey by train from Peshawar to Bombay (now Mumbai) took four days, which included a twenty-four-hour stopover at Delhi. From Bombay it was then a ten-day sea passage to Mombasa (including a twenty-four-hour stop at the Seychelles) – a total of two weeks travel to Kenya. His companion, Flt Lt Walser, had been on the same army co-operation course as Hugh in 1921 and was now flying Bristol Fighters with 31 Squadron at Dardoni.

Hugh's time in Kenya must have made a significant impression on him because in later years he said that he had considered a possible move to Kenya to start a new life there, perhaps as a coffee grower.

While Hugh was away in Kenya his squadron commander was posted away and was succeeded during September by Sqn Ldr C S Wynne-Eyton DSO who would be Hugh's CO until early in 1926. Hugh already knew Wynne-Eyton who had been his station commander at Northolt during the second half of 1918.

Flt Lt Walser and Hugh at the Khyber Pass, 1924.

Once back in India after his four months away, the flying from Peshawar in late October and through November 1924 was mostly in the Risalpur area with Hugh inspecting the landing ground at Akora (forty miles east of Peshawar) and meeting the army commandant there ahead of an artillery practice camp which would run through much of November. This exercise involved watching artillery shoots from the air to observe fall of shot while flying from a tented camp at the Akora landing ground. Hugh also flew to the landing grounds at Hassan Abdul and Hatti, and to the district headquarters at Rawalpindi (about fifty miles further to the east).

Later in November, army co-operation flying took place to the west and north of Peshawar which included Hugh taking vertical photographs from 10,000 feet of a section of railway between Jamrud and Sultan-Khel and inspecting the landing ground at Shabkadr in the mountains to the north. He also air-tested one aircraft after the rigging had been adjusted and another which had a rough-running engine. November finished with him taking the Nowshera district commissioner (DC) Capt Kirkbride from Peshawar to Arawali (elevation 3,000 ft above sea level) and back later that day. During this busy five-week period Hugh flew thirty-seven times.

The first half of December 1924 was taken up with a detachment to Hassan Abdul (sixty-five miles east of Peshawar) in the area between Risalpur and Rawalpindi for army co-operation flying with an infantry brigade. This included dropping contact maps, flying low to pick up messages and visiting the army headquarters at Rawalpindi. Hugh's flying later in December (with just a two-day break for Christmas Day and Boxing Day) included air experience flights for army officers and dual instruction for new squadron pilots. His year finished on 29th December with him taking the Nowshera DC to the airfield at Kohat and back.

During his first year in India Hugh had visited, inspected or operated from seventeen airfields and landing grounds away from Peshawar, namely: Risalpur, Dardoni, Dargai, Quetta, Dana, Jhelum, Lahore, Nr Jhelum, Ambala, Shabkadr (now Shabqadar), Akora, Rawalpindi, Hassan Abdul, Hatti, Arawali, Nr Hassan Abdul, Kohat.

After Christmas at Peshawar the new year of 1925 at Peshawar began as usual for the RAF in India with a flypast over a Proclamation Day parade.

Three 28 Squadron Bristol Fighters taxying out at Peshawar against the mountainous back-drop for the annual New Year Proclamation Day parade flypast, 1st January 1925.

After Proclamation Day it was time for 28 Squadron to move from No. 1 Wing at Peshawar to join No. 3 Wing at Quetta, some 400 miles to the south-west and about fifty miles from the border with Afghanistan. While the ground crews would have travelled to Quetta by train with the ground equipment, the Bristol Fighters were flown to Quetta during three days 4th-6th January. On 4th January they flew to Tank to refuel before continuing to Fort Sandeman (4,200 ft elevation) for the night. Next day they flew on to Hindubagh (6,000 ft elevation) where a dust storm prevented them from landing so they returned to Fort Sandeman. The following day they flew on direct to their new home of Quetta.

Following this rotation of the squadrons, these were the locations during 1925:

RAF Headquarters, Ambala
No. 31 (AC) Squadron Bristol Fighters

No. 1 (Indian) Wing, Peshawar
No. 5 (AC) Squadron Bristol Fighters, Kohat
No. 20 (AC) Squadron, Peshawar

No. 2 (Indian) Wing, Risalpur and Nowshera
No. 27 (B) Squadron D.H.9A
No. 60 (B) Squadron D.H.9A

No. 3 (Indian) Wing, Quetta
No. 28 (AC) Squadron Bristol Fighters

Port Detachment at Karachi[15]

Quetta 1925

Quetta is the provincial capital of the Baluchistan province and is known as the fruit garden of Baluchistan because of the diversity of its plant and animal wildlife. Located near the border with Afghanistan, the city lies on the Bolan Pass route which was once the only gateway with South Asia.

With the airfield at Quetta situated at an elevation of 5,265 ft it would have been a much more pleasant climate than Peshawar. Although Quetta has an average summer temperature from May to September of around 25°C, summer temperatures can reach up to 40°C. However, with its high elevation Quetta was probably a more pleasant and popular posting for RAF personnel within India than being down on the sweltering plains.

Once established at Quetta, the pilots of 28 Squadron spent the rest of January familiarising themselves with the local area to the north-west of Quetta towards the border with Afghanistan, flying to the landing grounds at Gulistan, Pishin and Chaman – and to Sibi to the south-east.

Apart from routine local training flights, the focus during the squadron's

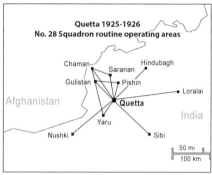

No. 28 Squadron routine operating areas while based at Quetta.

two years at Quetta was army co-operation flying over the nearby mountainous area to the north-west towards the border with Afghanistan some fifty miles distant; and further afield to the Persian border some 400 miles to the south-west. In addition there were occasional long-range flights including to far-off Madras on the far side of southern India.

During the following weeks the squadron pilots flew to other landing grounds including Hindubagh to the north-east of Quetta and Loralai to the east. During March Hugh and his observer/gunner Flt Sgt Dye flew 400 miles south to Karachi, with a refuelling stop at Pad Edan (now Pad Idan). On the way they landed briefly at Jacobabad and Hyderabad for familiarise himself with these landing grounds. Two days later they returned by the same route with a refuelling stop at Pad Edan while flying as 'escort to AVM' who was travelling from Karachi to Quetta – perhaps by train.

During the weeks between late April and June 1925 Hugh spent time flying to an area some 350-400 miles south-west of Quetta, close to the Persian border. This flying was in two distinct areas and mostly with army officers as passenger in his aircraft. A second aircraft would have flown as Hugh's wingman so that in the event of one aircraft having to make a forced landing for technical reasons the other crew would know the location of the stranded aircraft.

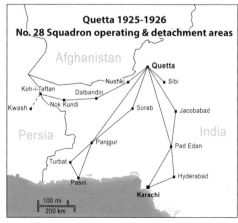

No. 28 Squadron flights to Karachi and Persian border areas.

The first area they flew to (22nd-23rd April 1925) was 300-400 miles to the south-west of Quetta between the southern part of the Persian border and the Arabian Sea. During this flight from Quetta, with Capt Barn as his passenger, Hugh refuelled at the landing ground of Sorab with the intention of continuing to Panjgur, but turned back to land fifteen minutes later. The reason for this is not given in his logbook and Hugh returned solo to Quetta next day flying with ballast.

Then after a busy month of routine flying at Quetta through May, Hugh's next venture towards this area of the Persian border came during a five-day period in late May. On this occasion he continued further to the south-west. On 27th May he flew with his usual observer/gunner Flt Sgt Dye from Quetta direct to Panjgur in three hours and thirty minutes. At Panjgur he was joined by Col Keyes as his passenger and on 29th May they continued to Diz Perom (precise location unknown) with a forty-minute flight. After refuelling they took off for a long triangular flight overflying Turbat and Pasni (Pasni being on the coast of the Arabian Sea), before landing back at Panjgur after a little over three hours. Two days later on 31st May Hugh and a Col Hobart flew back to Quetta via Sorab.

After this busy month during which Hugh had flown thirty-five hours, he was off again four days later for a further ten days to a slightly more northerly area of the Persian border with Flt Lt Murray as his wingman. On 4th June Hugh flew with Col Keyes direct from Quetta to Nok Kundi in three hours and forty minutes, then after refuelling they flew for a further hour to land at Koh-i-Taftan at the border. During the following days Hugh flew sorties to Kwash and back to Koh-i-Taftan; with flights of typically one hour and forty minutes with his successive passengers being Col Keyes, Flt Lt Murray and Major Betham. Finally, on 13th June he flew with Col Keyes back from Koh-i-Taftan to Quetta with a refuelling stop at Dalbandin – a total flying time of four hours and thirty-five minutes for the two flights flown at 10,000 ft.

A few days after completion of this deployment, Colonel Keyes wrote to Hugh on government of India writing paper:

'Dear White. The A.G.G. [acting or assistant governor general] has wired to the Gov't of India asking that the squadron should be thanked for the assistance given in the Sarhad show. I am very grateful for all you did, and am afraid you had a rotten time. I hope that Murray got in all right.'

In his photo album for this flying, Hugh used the heading 'Operations on Persian Border'. It is not clear what these operations with army officers might have been – with the only clue being in the term 'show' used in Col Keyes' letter. On balance it seems likely that this may have been a routine operation of 'flag wave' sorties or 'showing the flag' to tribesmen in a potentially troublesome area. I recall Hugh telling me that he had flown a 'flag wave' flight in Persia as a single aircraft, making a number of passes over a particular area from behind hilly terrain to give

'Kwash Fort, Sarhad' June 1925. The location of Kwash could not be found. However, as spelling can vary in this part of the world, Kwash Fort looks likely to be Khash Fort (Heydar Abad Castle) located some fifty miles inside the present Iranian (Persian) border.

the impression that there were several aircraft in the area.

After this detachment Hugh did not return to the Persian border area until more than a year later, when his flight would deploy to Nok Kundi for eleven days during August 1926 for a major exercise in the border area around Koh-i-Taftan.

Meanwhile, for the second half of 1925 Hugh's flying was a mix of air tests, dual instruction for new pilots and exercises in the local area around Quetta using the landing grounds of Chaman, Pishin, Nuski and Yaru. On 29th November he flew to Hindubagh to refuel before spending two hours and thirty minutes flying towards Fort Sandeman and back searching for a machine which had forced-landed. He then refuelled again at Hindubagh before returning to Quetta, presumably after the missing aircraft had been found.

There were some innovative ideas tested, such as the potential use of a Bristol Fighter as a rudimentary air ambulance with the casualty stretcher strapped on the fuselage over the observer's cockpit. By flying without the observer this would have ensured that the overall weight and centre of gravity stayed within safe limits. On 14th September 1925 Hugh flew a fifteen-minute 'trial' with an empty stretcher (25 lbs), ballast (105 lbs) and a full third fuel tank; followed by two fifteen-minute 'demonstration' flights with the squadron medical officer, Flt Lt B F Haytherathwaite, and then a Colonel Cruddas on board. This technique had already been used as early as 1920 with a modified D.H.9, when a casualty had

No. 28 Squadron Bristol Fighter with a stretcher strapped over the rear cockpit during the air ambulance trial.

Top: Hugh's B Flight at Quetta with his observer/gunner Flt Sgt Dye sitting next to him in the centre.

Bottom: No. 28 Squadron officers at Quetta in 1925. Hugh is sitting in the front row second from left.

been air-lifted on a stretcher inside a hatch behind the pilot during the evacuation of the port of Berbera.[16]

As 1925 drew to a close, on Boxing Day Hugh flew Major Betham (a regular army co-operation colleague) to Nuski and back the next day. After this it was time for the annual formation flypast practice ahead of the Proclamation Day celebrations on New Year's Day 1926.

Quetta 1926

Apart from squadron moves for 5 and 60 squadrons, which swapped their locations between Kohat and Risalpur or Nowshera, the other squadron locations remained unchanged for 1926.

From time-to-time a flight of aircraft would depart for a few days or weeks to fly to distant areas where there was no regular RAF presence, for exercises, operations, or to take part in a tournament or ceremonial occasion. Flying activities would usually include army co-operation training with the units in the area. These detachments also provided an opportunity for the pilots and air gunners to become familiar with more distant regions of India away from their home airfield and local area; and once in the new area to give air experience flights to locally based military personnel or local officials for them to gain an aerial perspective of an area or situation.

As an example of such detachments, Hugh's logbook and photographs record an extensive itinerary during a five-week period from 20th January to 25th February 1926. This involved him flying Bristol Fighter F4916 with Flt Sgt Dye as crew leading four aircraft of his B Flight on a succession of 'travelling flights', typically of two to three hours' duration flying at 3,000 ft – 5,000 ft. The other pilots for this Madras flight were Milne, Murray, Vetch and Rodwell – so with five pilots total during this trip one of the aircraft was manned with two pilots. They flew in eleven stages of up to 230 miles each from Quetta in the north-western area of India to Madras located three-quarters of the way down India's eastern coast. The logistics of such detachments must have been challenging with petrol being transported to the landing grounds in barrels.

When going away like this for days or weeks with no spare room for luggage in the cramped cockpits of the pilot and observer/gunner their kit was carried in rolled-up bags (known as sausages) lashed into a pannier frame mounted under the lower wings. As well as adding weight to the aircraft, this would have added considerably to the aerodynamic drag. The result was a much longer take-off run, a reduced rate of climb and altitude obtainable, as well as reduced cruising speed and range for the aircraft. With the light airframes of that era, with simple lightweight wicker seats for the crew, any increase in weight and drag had a considerable impact on flying performance.

Sitting (and standing for many of the operational tasks) in the open cockpit behind the pilot, the second crew member in each aircraft carried out a myriad of roles and tasks. At this time the only recognised non-pilot aircrew specialisation was aerial gunner; but in practice the gunner acted in a variety of roles including wireless operator (when this was carried), photographer and bomb-aimer for which there were no formal courses. It was also customary for ground crew fitters, riggers and some armourers to be included within the aircrew complement of a squadron. An Air Ministry Weekly Order (AMWO 624 dated 4th August 1921) had recognised the need to start training volunteer airmen as air gunners. As there were no dedicated armaments training facilities overseas, this training was carried out on squadrons as a local task. This use of technical ground crew for flying tasks also provided the essential technical expertise for rectifying the many airframe and engine problems which would inevitably arise during the 'travelling flights' over several days. During these deployments to distant destinations the intermediate refuelling stops were often at rudimentary landing grounds with an uneven or stony natural surface and no technical support.

Although Hugh flew with a wide variety of crews, the two names which crop up regularly in his logbook are Healy and Dye. He first flew with Aircraftman First Class (AC1) Healy for an engine air test soon after arriving at Peshawar in January 1924. Healy subsequently flew as Hugh's crew for many engine air tests during the following months so it is likely that he was an engine mechanic (engine fitter) by trade. In time Healy flew as crew during some routine squadron flying and by December 1924 had been promoted to leading aircraftman; and in August 1926 to corporal. Healy continued to feature in Hugh's logbook, including later on during photographic flights when working with the army or surveying landing grounds, when Healy would have been standing in the rear cockpit leaning over the side with the camera. Meanwhile from November 1924 Flt Sgt Dye was Hugh's regular crew for most of the long-range 'travelling flights' during a two-year period; including during the squadron move to Quetta in January 1925. Dye continued in this role until October 1926 when he was presumably posted away and Cpl Healy took on a more prominent role including the long-range flights. Healy's final flying as Hugh's crew was in December 1927 during seven flights over three days from Ambala to Ahmadnagar – nearly four years after they had first flown together.

The first nine days of the outbound Madras flight were spent flying in stages from their airfield at Quetta to Jacobabad, Hyderabad (Sindh), Uttarlai, Jodhpur,

Ahmedabad, Deolali, Poona (now Pune), Sholapur (now Solapur), Bellary (now Bullari) and Bangalore (now Bengaluru). After taking off from Ahmedabad on the leg to Deolali, Hugh noticed oil overflowing from his engine, so landed again to check whether there was a problem – before taking off again. During the flight from Poona to Sholapur there was some low cloud and rain so they flew at the lower height of 1,500 ft and on arrival had to hold off for half an hour before landing because there were an estimated 8,000 Indians with carts on the landing ground.

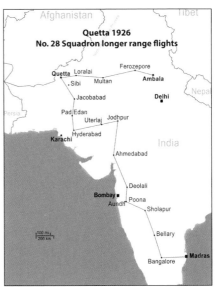

No. 28 Squadron Madras flight (January-February 1926) and move to Ambala (December 1926).

Once at Bangalore they spent a week carrying out army co-operation training with artillery and infantry units and taking army personnel for air experience flights. During this week Hugh flew the Royal Artillery Brigade commander (Col Johnson) and Col Geary to watch artillery shoots. He also flew the district commander (Col Jackson) for air experience and Col Segrave to watch infantry formations – plus flying another ten army personnel in addition to his share of the army co-operation flying.

From Bangalore the flight continued to Madras taking two hours and forty minutes, with Hugh flying AVM Sir Edward Ellington, the air officer commanding (AOC) of RAF India as his passenger. By then AVM Ellington had been successively AOC RAF Middle East, AOC RAF Iraq and AOC RAF India during 1922-1928. He later became chief of the Air Staff in 1933. A few days after arriving at Madras the aircraft took part in a night-time torchlight tattoo over a tournament ground. This was followed by day-time flypasts for His Excellency the Governor of Madras; for the British admiral during which they flew over his Royal Navy cruisers HMS *Effingham* and HMS *Cairo*; and for the British general officer commanding India Southern Command which culminated in a simulated attack on a fort. After the week in Madras which also included air experience flights for some Royal Navy officers, they returned during the next eleven days to Quetta using the same route (except for landing at Aundh instead of Poona).

The usual routine when flying to and from these lengthy detachments was to fly two stages during each of the flying days, but with a spare day and a weekend off during the route out and back. During the five weeks of this particular detachment they flew a total of forty hours. Judging by Hugh's photo albums they had some superb sightseeing opportunities during their days off, with visits to palaces and official residences, often with expensive cars laid on for their use. This was certainly an impressive way for them to see the sights of India while carrying out their RAF duties. This long-range deployment appears to have been highly successful, during which the only mishap recorded was on 27th January of Milne's 'crash' at Sholapur on the outbound flight in aircraft F4599. Although Hugh took a photograph of Milne's aircraft with the wings removed, the damage must have been minor because a photograph ten days later shows this same aircraft in use at Bangalore (see page 106).

Some months ahead of the Madras flight, Hugh had prepared a flight plan of the most suitable airfields and landing grounds along the route. This plan was submitted to the RAF Headquarters and confirmed by a staff officer in a letter of 5th October 1925, which stated:

'I am directed by the Officer Commanding, Royal Air Force, in India, to send his congratulations to Flight Lieut. H.G. White on the very excellent and careful report which he has rendered. The necessary action is being initiated from these Headquarters to have the Madras route put in preparation for the proposed flight in the beginning of next year.'

This long-range deployment was a considerable improvement on the first such venture a year earlier when a flight of six D.H.9As of 27 and 60 Squadrons set out from Risalpur to Calcutta. They suffered technical problems along the way which led to some aircraft having to make forced landings. Only four of the six aircraft

Over the Sindh desert in the area of Hyderabad during the second outbound leg with one of the baggage panniers visible under the port wing of Hugh's aircraft F4916 on 20th January 1926.

Top: Deolali landing ground on 24th January 1926 with the usual white circle in the centre and the tented lines of the transit camp.

Bottom: Topping up the radiator water at Bellary on 28th January 1926. During travelling flights this task was often carried out by a local Bhisti – the term for a traditional water carrier in India and the Middle East with skin water bags.

which set out made it to Calcutta and only two of these flew back to Risalpur. There were no casualties and two dismantled aircraft and their crews travelled back to Risalpur by train.

Deolali was a transit camp for British soldiers, notorious for its unpleasant environment, boredom, and the psychological problems of soldiers who stayed there

Top: 'The Last Lap – passing Nudar near Quetta' during the return from Madras, 25th February 1926.

Middle left: Murray, Vetch, Hugh and his observer/gunner Flt Sgt Dye at Bellary.

Middle right: Over Madras with the Royal Navy cruisers HMS *Effingham* and HMS *Cairo* at the far end of the harbour.

Bottom: Local interest at Bellary landing ground on 16th February 1926 during the return to Quetta.

while waiting for passage on a trooping ship back to Britain after finishing a tour of duty in India. It is also the source of the British slang term 'Doolally' meaning 'camp fever', when referring to the dispirited morale of the men there.

In the summer of 1926 Hugh was away from the squadron for four months (16th March to 22nd July) when he returned to England for his mid-tour leave and marriage to Joy Hickman. Hugh and Joy had become engaged before Hugh left for India at the end of 1923, when Joy was only nineteen years old. Hugh arrived back in England during mid April 1926, some six weeks before they were due to be married. This was to be their first meeting for two-and-a-half years since they had become engaged. Hugh and Joy were married in Hastings on 1st June 1926 and married life in India would be a big change for both of them. However, they were not to be together in India immediately because although Hugh returned direct to India by sea at the end of their honeymoon in the south of France and

Left: Hugh and Joy's wedding at Christ Church, Blacklands Hastings close to Joy's parents' home at Hole Farm, 1st June 1926.

Above: John Osborne (best man), sisters Sybil (left) and Isobel (bridesmaids) and Freddie Sowrey (page boy – who wrote the foreword for this book).

Venice, Joy travelled home alone to Sussex until the summer weather in India would be less oppressive and because Hugh would be away on exercises from late August until October.

Finally, on 15th September 1926 (a month after her twenty-second birthday) Joy embarked from Liverpool on the *City of Exeter* for the long sea voyage to India. It is likely that she left the ship at Karachi for overland travel by rail to Quetta (about 400 miles by train to the north). Hugh's logbook shows him flying one way from Quetta via Pad Edan to Karachi on 10th October and not flying again until 16th October. It is likely that his passenger to Karachi (Sqn Ldr Bailey) flew the aircraft back to Quetta so that Hugh could meet Joy from her ship and travel with her by train to Quetta and have a week there together before he returned to flying.

Meanwhile, Hugh had already been back in India since late July ahead of three important deployments during the second half of 1926. The first of these took place towards the Persian border and the second and third towards the border with Afghanistan.

The first of these major deployments was during an eleven-day period in August with seven aircraft operating from the landing ground at Nok Kundi some 300 miles south-west of Quetta and seventy miles from the Persian border. From there they would be operating in the border area of Koh-i-Taftan.

Although Nok Kundi is just over 2,000 ft above sea level, the August midday temperature would have been up to 41°C and only reduced to 26°C at night. Ahead of this, in late July Hugh had flown Major Betham from Quetta via the landing grounds at Dalbandin and Nok Kundi to Koh-i-Taftan on the Persian border (a total of just over five hours flying). After staying there overnight they returned via Dalbandin to Quetta. This is likely to have been a pre-deployment visit to check things over.

The exercise proper began during really hot conditions in mid August 1926. First the RAF ground party, with tents, cook house and aircraft equipment, deployed by train from Quetta to Nok Kundi. There they set up camp in preparation for seven Bristol Fighters to fly in from Quetta ahead of their flying activities at the Persian border. As the detachment commander, Hugh spent much of the time shuttling between Nok Kundi and Koh-i-Taftan. Thus on 10th August he flew with LAC Tipper as crew from Quetta to Dalbandin and on to Koh-i-Taftan where he stayed for two days before flying back to their deployment site at Nok Kundi.

During the following days he flew Major Betham from Nok Kundi to Koh-i-Taftan and collected him three days later – having flown back solo with ballast in the rear cockpit while Betham remained at Koh-i-Taftan. Meanwhile, the other pilots (Murray, Milne, Fisher, Bennett, Chisman and Jordan) were engaged with the exercise flying activities at the Persian border area around Koh-i-Taftan. During the following days Hugh made one more flight from Nok Kundi to Kohi-i-Taftan and back, before returning to Quetta via Dalbandin on 21st August.

The ground party had travelled the 300 miles from Quetta to Nok Kundi by train in the sweltering heat, returning after the exercise finished on 21st August. By contrast the pilots and their observers could enjoy the cooler air in their open cockpits for their faster journey via a refuelling stop at Dalbandin.

Only a week after the Nok Kundi deployment it was time for a further week's deployment (28th August to 4th September 1926) to the landing ground at Yaru (twenty

Top: Some of the ground party who had arrived at Nok Kundi railway station – including sheep as live rations for attention by the camp cook Aircraftman Cain.

Middle: Landing at Nok Kundi; Middle right: Bringing up the petrol at Nok Kundi.

Bottom: General Sir George Kirkpatrick, GOC-in-C, India Western Command, at Nok Kundi (standing by the wing) while others shelter in the shade under the aircraft. The exercises had been taking place within the general's area of responsibility.

miles south-west of Quetta and midway between Quetta and the Afghan border) for an artillery practice camp to spot the fall of shot for the 61st and 88th Field Batteries.

Then a further major deployment took place in late September and early October, with a busy two weeks' flying in support of army inter-brigade manoeuvres in the mountainous areas between Quetta and Afghanistan. On 21st September and again the following day, Hugh flew from Quetta to inspect the landing ground at Gulistan (to the north-west of Quetta and halfway to the Afghan border) and to carry out some landings there. The following day the rest of the detachment aircraft were flown from Quetta to Gulistan from where they supported army manoeuvres for a week, including army co-operation with the 16th Indian Infantry Brigade.

From Gulistan they flew onwards to operate for two days at Chaman on the Afghan border, followed by two days back at Gulistan and at Yaru. Hugh also flew transit flights between Gulistan and Saranan (north of Quetta halfway to the Afghan border). The flying during this period involved reconnaissance utilising two-way W/T and there were some simulated bombing raids against transport vehicles and the brigade headquarters – and against Quetta aerodrome. There was certainly plenty of activity during this time, with Hugh flying eight times on 3rd October with a total of four hours and thirty-five minutes airborne that day. They returned to Quetta on 5th October and the following day Hugh flew the commander of the Afghan air force, General Hisan Khan, in a Bristol Fighter. At that time the Afghan air force operated three Bristol Fighters. General Khan, together with the Afghan army commander (General Syed Khan) and the Afghan Under Secretary (Habibullah Khan) had spent some at Gulistan during the exercise and would have taken a keen interest in the activities close to their border.

Hugh and Joy's bungalow at No. 430 Lytton Road, Quetta, their first home together – but for just two months.

A few days after the end of these two busy months of deployments and exercises, on 10th October Hugh flew to Karachi to meet Joy when she arrived by sea and to bring her by train to Quetta where they moved into their bungalow.

By the time Hugh returned to work after Joy's arrival there were only a few more weeks remaining for the squadron at Quetta. Most days he was busy air testing

No. 28 Squadron Quetta November 1926. Hugh in front row sitting eighth from left. The squadron commander was then Sqn Ldr A W Mylne since 1st February 1926.

aircraft after oil or water leaks, engine changes or rigging adjustments – flown with a technician airman in the rear cockpit or flying solo with ballast. Other than the air tests, the only flights of note during the rest of October and through November was Hugh taking an army Captain Winter to the political administrator's camp at Zungi Nwar thirty minutes flying time from Quetta and bringing him back two days later. Hugh also flew in a farewell formation flypast for General Sir Hastings Anderson the outgoing general officer commanding of the Baluchistan District.

At the beginning of December 1926, after two years at Quetta, it was time for 28 Squadron to move again, this time to Ambala some 600 miles to the east and about thirty miles from where the Himalayas begin to rise up from the plains. While the ground personnel would have travelled by train, the aircraft were flown to Ambala during 1st-2nd December; with refuelling stops at Loralai, Multan (night stop) and Ferozepore – with Corporal Healy flying in the rear cockpit of Hugh's aircraft. A few days later on 6th December Joy travelled by train to Ambala with her friends Foddie and Kitty and probably some of the other wives. It is likely that Hugh and Joy's car 'Henry' was also transported by train. At Ambala Hugh and Joy moved into a spacious bungalow No. 17 as their married quarter.

Following this rotation of the squadrons, these were the locations during 1927/1928.

RAF HQ, Ambala
No. 28 (AC) Squadron Bristol Fighters

No. 1 (Indian) Wing, Peshawar
No. 20 (AC) Squadron, Peshawar
No. 60 (B) Squadron D.H.9A, Kohat (with a detached flight at Miranshah in 1928)

No. 2 (Indian) Wing, Risalpur and Nowshera
No. 27 (B) Squadron D.H.9A
No. 5 (AC) Squadron Bristol Fighters

No. 3 (Indian) Wing, Quetta[17]
No. 31 (AC) Squadron Bristol Fighters

Ambala 1927

During the 1920s Ambala was in the state of Punjab, in the days before changes were made to state borders in 1966. At that time Ambala featured a large British military cantonment which had been established in 1843 during the British Raj. Today Ambala still has many colonial bungalows and wide tree-lined roads typical of British cantonments. The city of Ambala separates the Ganges river network from the Indus river network with the Ghaggar river to the north and the Tangri river to the south. Ambala airfield is at an elevation of 900 ft.

After the unsettled months since their marriage six months earlier, Joy may have been looking forward to a more stable married lifestyle – but any such optimism was probably not compatible with the reality of Hugh's commitments with 28 Squadron. After a week settling in at Ambala, Hugh was off again in mid December to Lahore for an overnight stop ahead of army co-operation flying with the Lahore Brigade area. When he returned it was a week before Christmas and time for Hugh and Joy to have their first Christmas together as a married couple in their new bungalow. Judging by their photographs it looks to have been a very sociable time.

The Christmas break for 1926 was brief, because immediately after Boxing Day Hugh was back flying with practice formation flypasts each day ahead of the annual Proclamation Day parade on New Year's Day. However, disaster struck during the rehearsal on 29th December when one of the Bristol Fighters crashed killing the pilot and observer.

After a sixth rehearsal on 31st December the flypast went ahead next day as planned. Joy wrote in her diary for New Year's Day 1927: 'Went up to the Parade Ground to see the New Year's Flypast – rather a subdued one because of Mac's death.'

The *London Gazette* published this statement:

'The Air Ministry regrets to announce that Flying Officer (Hon. Flight-Lieut.) Alastair Neil Macneal, the pilot of the aircraft, and No. 362102 LAC Cyril Arthur Overy, died of injuries on December 29, 1926, as the result of an accident at Ambala, India, to a Bristol fighter of No. 28 Squadron.'

This must have hit Hugh and Joy hard because Mac had been with Hugh on 28 Squadron since he first arrived at Peshawar three years earlier.

Decades later, after I had experienced the grim reality of being a pall bearer carrying the coffin at the funeral of one of our squadron pilots in the Middle East, Joy told me how shocked she had been that the funerals of Mac and Overy had taken place later in the day and only a few hours after the accident. This was a harsh introduction for her to RAF life in that era.

Despite the tragic accident, Hugh and Joy had gone ahead with a dinner party planned for New Year's Eve when they entertained nine of their friends and colleagues. This would have been typical with such a close-knit community in a distant land.

January 1927 was to be another busy month. Following the Proclamation Day flypast, Hugh flew to Delhi on 5th January to carry out oblique photography before returning later in the day. Then on 11th January he flew five times, beginning with giving some dual instruction; a short flight to test the rigging of an aircraft; then further short flights with three successive airmen for them to gain experience testing and using the W/T system in preparation for the forthcoming deployment to Kutwa.

In mid January Hugh's B Flight headed off to Kutwa (now Khutwa) some 450 miles to the south-east of Ambala. This was achieved during two days with refuelling stops at Delhi, Agra (night stop), Cawnpore (now Kanpur) and on

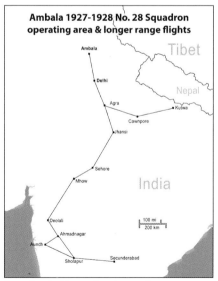

Route for the Kutwa detachment January – February 1927. Routes during the Aundh (Poona) detachment December 1927- February 1928.

to Kutwa. Kutwa is located towards the Nepal border, about sixty miles short of the Himalaya mountain range with Kathmandu another ninety miles further on.

At Kutwa they spent two weeks flying army co-operation exercises using W/T, spotting fall of shot for the artillery and giving air experience flights to Royal Artillery personnel. Judging by the many photos of Benares and Mirzapur in Hugh's albums around this time, it seems possible that from Kutwa a few of them may have found time for some weekend sightseeing and photography at Benares (now Varanasi) about a hundred miles to the south of Kutwa and at Mirzapur on the south bank of the Ganges forty miles west of Benares.

By early February 1927 the army co-operation exercises at Kutwa were completed and Hugh flew back to Ambala with his flight during two days, using the same refuelling stops at Cawnpore, Agra and Delhi.

While Hugh and other squadron personnel were away at Kutwa, Joy moved in with the wife of one of the other pilots and spent her days playing tennis and meeting other wives for tea at the club. She also helped at a child welfare clinic and dined out most evenings at the homes of army or RAF couples. One evening some of them went to a concert at the nearby army fusiliers' mess. Joy visited the wives of the squadron NCOs while their husbands were away and invited them all to tea one day at the bungalow. During this time Joy and one of the other wives were driven by one of the pilots in his car to Lahore for dinner and a polo dance. Meanwhile Joy noted in her diary her delight at receiving a letter every day from Hugh.

A week after Hugh's flight returned to Ambala, in mid-February 1927 the squadron aircraft were flown to Delhi New Court Aerodrome as their temporary base for a RAF Air Pageant. This was a major event during which their participation included Hugh representing the squadron when flying in a mixed aircraft flypast with other RAF aircraft types. This was followed by a 28 Squadron flypast in squadron 'V' formation. Joy travelled to Delhi by car for the pageant where she and Hugh had impressive tented accommodation.

Top: Vickers Victoria taking off for the RAF Flypast of Types.

Bottom: Hugh about to take off in his Bristol Fighter from the New Delhi racecourse during RAF Air Pageant.

Looking down on a Bristol Fighter over Jami Masjid at Delhi during the RAF Air Pageant in February 1927.

For the rehearsal day on 19th February the participating aircraft were first flown the short distance from the New Court Aerodrome to the New Delhi racecourse. From there they took off in turn for a full rehearsal, landing back at the New Court Aerodrome. This rehearsal must have gone well because there was no flying on the following day. After completion of the Air Pageant on 21th February the 28 Squadron aircraft were flown back to Ambala on 23rd February.

In mid March, a couple of weeks after returning from the Delhi Air Pageant, Hugh and Joy went riding together for only the second time. Hugh had ridden Major Duncan's horse and Joy was on 'Chance'. Joy recorded in her diary that they had had a 'topping ride' and came back over the sand hills. The following day Joy rode 'Chance' in the Ladies Hack at the Ambala Horse Show and the day after she won the Ladies Race at the RAF Gymkhana Race

Joy on 'Chance' after winning the three-furlong Ladies Race by four lengths (five runners) at Ambala RAF Gymkhana on 15th March 1927.

meeting. Mrs Deane, the RAF 'senior wife' wasn't at this event so at the tender age of twenty-two Joy was the hostess and gave out the prizes.

That evening Joy went up to Ambala aerodrome at dusk with Hugh where the squadron would be night flying – which she loved watching. But this would be his last flying for a while because he was then detached for four months (28th March to 15th July 1927) accompanied by Joy, to be the adjutant of the RAF Hill Depot at Lower Topa.

Lower Topa 1927

The RAF Hill Depot at Lower Topa was located in the mountains some 300 miles to the north-west of Ambala. This unit, and at least one other RAF hill depot in the area, was opened during the summer months to give airmen a period of recreation away from the heat of the plains. Most squadrons comprised three flights and each flight would go in turn to Lower Topa for two months where they did some drill, education and plenty of sport. Every effort was made to make their stay as pleasant as possible with the help of events such as inter-squadron sports and tennis, officers and sergeants' tennis matches and a sports day. In addition there were dances in the various messes, home-grown concerts and other entertainment.

Lower Topa was commanded by a squadron leader, probably supported by a small permanent staff. Other supervisory staff would have been provided by the officers and sergeants of the visiting flight. It is evident that Hugh's B Flight airmen were at Lower Topa during half of his time as adjutant because Joy noted in her diary that Cpl Healy (one of Hugh's regular flying crew) excelled himself during a camp concert. It is likely that either A Flight or C Flight of 28 Squadron was there for the other two months of Hugh's stay. One or two of his pilots and their wives were also at Lower Topa and others visited on their way to holidays in the Srinagar area of Kashmir.

Hugh and Joy drove to Lower Topa in 'Henry' which would have been a challenging journey for the 1920s in such a small car with their luggage in the back together with their bearer Chokra and dog 'Dinah'. This was achieved during a leisurely week with overnight stops at Lahore (188 miles) and Rawalpindi (a further 168 miles), where as usual when staying in hotels they met other British military officers and their wives.

During this journey Hugh had to leave Joy at Rawalpindi for a few days while he went on official business to Risalpur. Fortunately, at the Flashman's Hotel where they were staying, they had met up with Major Davies and his wife whom they had known at Quetta. The Davies's were then living in the hotel which enabled Joy to go shopping with Mrs Davies and to make up a four for tennis at the club while Hugh was away. She also met two single women who had been on the *City of Exeter* with her when she had travelled out to India and one of the 28 Squadron pilots who was also passing through Rawalpindi on his way to Lower Topa. After a few days Joy received a telegram from Hugh giving his arrival time back by train that afternoon and she took a small horse-drawn 'Tonga' carriage to the railway station to meet him.

On 28th March they continued their onward journey from Rawalpindi for the final forty-nine miles to Lower Topa. Joy recorded in her diary that it was 'a marvellous drive climbing the last twenty miles to 7,000 feet and the scenery was simply marvellous'. At Lower Topa they moved into a tiny bungalow which would be their home for the next few weeks.

There was much frustration with this move because the lorry with their luggage had been delayed while the road was closed for two days as the Viceroy was travelling

Hugh and Joy travelled with their bearer 'Chokra' in 'their car 'Henry' on the Grand Trunk Road during the journey from Ambala to Rawalpindi in March 1927; during which Joy noted that they only had this one puncture!

through to Kashmir. Furthermore, Joy was suffering days of feeling unwell as by now she was in the early weeks of her first pregnancy. However, their belongings eventually arrived and a few days after arriving at Lower Topa Joy was presented with the silver cup by Major Duncan for winning the Ladies Race on 'Chance' at Ambala – and Joy's daughter Diana still has the cup. Later that day Joy drove into Murree which she described as 'a quaint little place and fearfully steep'.

There were many sporting competitions and social activities at Lower Topa; but while Hugh was busy with the organisation and activities for the airmen, there seems to have been relatively little for Joy to do on many days other than socialising with the few other wives there and going for long walks until the tennis courts were ready. These walks during the cool weeks in April might take her 1,000 ft up the hills to the Royal Signals Hill Depot at Upper Topa, with the opportunity on the way to pick (as she recorded in her diary) maidenhair fern, violets and wild peach blossom. Another favourite walk was down to a waterfall or into Murree for shopping. During the early weeks Joy sometimes went riding with Hugh.

Joy also spent time writing to family and friends in England, in particular to her close friend Flora. Joy and Flora had first met at their junior school as they walked together in the school 'crocodile' when going from place to place and had become best friends – as they would continue to be throughout their long lives. They were both from farming families in the adjoining counties of Sussex and Kent and both horse-mad. Indeed, Flora would be lucky in the years to follow to survive being kicked in the stomach by a horse. But even this didn't stop her riding. Flora would have been a strong home-link for Joy during this period of her early married life while living in a far-off land. Joy and Flora continued to meet, write and telephone each other into their nineties, with Flora as the slightly older of the two dying only a few months before Joy.

Three weeks into their time at Lower Topa, on 19th April Joy heard unofficially from one of the wives that they wouldn't be going home at the end of the year and were likely to be in India until the end of 1928. Joy wrote that she was 'heartbroken' by this news and the thought of this extra time in India. However, she was a determined and loyal young woman who would simply get on with it. On 4th May she wrote to tell her family that she was expecting a baby later in the year. The letter reached home towards the end of May and Joy noted in her diary that she had received a cable from her mother who seemed to expect that she would return to England for the birth. But Joy commented that she wouldn't go home without Hugh for anything in the world.

From mid May the weather had became very hot and thundery with the start of the monsoon season and Joy continued having days of feeling unwell. Although there were riding opportunities and tennis, she was becoming limited in what she could and should sensibly do. Indeed, after being talked into running in the ladies race at the sports day on 19th May she realised that she had done too much that day and the time had come to stop playing tennis.

On 1st June (their first wedding anniversary) Joy organised their move from the tiny bungalow into an upstairs flat in a large house for the second half of their four months at Lower Topa. Their bearer had wanted to be on leave that day so was resentful and unhelpful. Joy wrote in her diary that 1she 'hoped sincerely that she would never have another wedding anniversary like it'.

Some weeks later during mid July Hugh went into Murree hospital to have an operation on his nose carried out by a British Army surgeon. By the time he returned to Lower Topa there was only one more week remaining of this four-month detachment. But before leaving the area Hugh and Joy took the opportunity for a ten-day holiday in the picturesque area near Srinagar in Kashmir which was a popular destination for the British.

Joy's diary records that they left Lower Topa at 7.30 a.m. on 20th July 1927 – the day after Hugh was discharged from hospital:

> 'Pretty hot going along. Dropped 6,000 ft into a valley and followed the River Jhelum for about seventy-five miles, wonderful country all the way – the last twenty miles into Srinagar is an avenue with tall Poplar trees either side of the road. Became rather lost finding our way out to Ganderbal but we arrived about 5.45 p.m. after 170 miles. A weary dinner and to bed early.'

They stayed on a houseboat (a Doonga) on the River Jhelum and spent their time sightseeing in the local area, visiting Ganderbal and Srinagar and taking a trip in a small paddle boat to see Lotus Lilies along the river. Hugh also had a day of trout fishing. Other British couples they knew were also staying in the area so it was a typically sociable time.

Once back from their holiday, Hugh and Joy loaded up 'Henry' and left Lower Topa for good. In the years ahead this hill depot would continue in use with the RAF until after the end of the Second World War. Then at some time after partition in 1947, with the birth of Pakistan, Lower Topa became a Pakistan Air Force school focused on developing potential future leadership for the Pakistan Air Force. It continues in this role today.

Back to Ambala

Upon leaving Lower Topa on 31st July 1927, Hugh and Joy drove the 415 miles to Ambala during three days (with night stops as before at Rawalpindi and Lahore) to rejoin 28 Squadron. They arrived at Ambala on 2nd August, but Joy was only there for a few days because it was time for her to join the other wives who were already at the Summer Hill Station of Simla (now Shimla) – some seventy miles north-east of Ambala.

Very early on 5th August Hugh took Joy to the railway station to catch the 4.20

a.m. pre-dawn train to Kalka at the foot of the mountains from where she travelled by car up to the Simla car stop and thence by rickshaw to her hotel at No. 8 The Park. Meanwhile, having taken Joy to the railway station, Hugh returned to flying duties at Ambala where he was required to fly a short ten-minute dual check after his four months away from flying.

Joy would be at Simla for the final two months of summer (along with other British wives) in the cooler climate of the hill station at an elevation of around 7,800 ft. At that time Simla was the summer capital of British India with much of the government administration and the RAF Headquarters moving there for several months each year. Whilst at Simla, Joy celebrated her twenty-third birthday on 12th August; but without Hugh who was with the squadron at Ambala. However, she had a letter from him with a present of candlesticks; and in the evening Joy invited friends who were staying at a nearby hotel to join her for supper.

Hugh's return to flying was short-lived because at the end of August he contracted sandfly fever and was sent on sick leave to Simla to recuperate for two weeks. Joy went to meet him at Simla station on 4th September and commented in her diary: 'He does look awful and so fearfully thin, I want to cry when I look at him.'

On 13th September, Joy noted in her diary that she and Hugh had gone to Davicos restaurant in Simla; where they had met Sqn Ldr John Whittaker who confirmed that he had granted an extension to Hugh's sick leave. At about this time the CO of 28 Squadron, Sqn Ldr Mylne, had returned to Britain to begin training ahead of taking command of a Horsley torpedo squadron in Singapore. As his successor (Sqn Ldr Brooke) was not due in post until February it seems likely that Sqn Ldr John T Whittaker MC (who had been the CO in 1922) may have taken over command again temporarily to fill the gap.[18]

However, in a shocking note, two months later, Joy wrote in her diary that 'Bill had returned and told us that John Whittaker is dead – seems incredible'. There is no information about this, other than newspaper reports that he died in Bombay on 12th December.

After his recuperation Hugh had been back flying at Ambala from late September. With Joy still away at Simla, Hugh had also found time to go on a crocodile shooting expedition on the Sutleg river to the north of Ambala, which involved using a punt rowed on the river with the help of five locals. Once the weather on the plains began to moderate during early October, Hugh collected Joy from Simla by car and they drove back to Ambala on 9th October and moved into their new bungalow No. 74 in Paget Park.

By now it was only a few weeks until Joy was due to give birth and in preparation she arranged for a nurse to stay with them for a period afterwards. Then at 7 a.m. on the morning of Thursday 17th November Joy went into the British Military Hospital at Ambala and their son John was born at 1.30 p.m., weighing in at seven pounds. As was the custom in those days Joy stayed in hospital for the next ten days.

Although Hugh had been able to visit Joy and John each evening for the first few days, he was soon off again (24th – 27th November) to Kapurthala a hundred miles north-west of Ambala for the Golden Jubilee of the Maharajah who was a renowned figure of the British Empire in India at that time. His Highness Maharajah Jagatjit Singh had become the maharajah of the state of Kapurthala fifty years earlier in 1877 and ruled until his death in 1949 aged seventy-six. He had ascended the throne aged five and taken on full ruling powers in 1890 when he was eighteen. As a statesman and world traveller, he had built palaces and gardens in the city of Kapurthala, modelling his main palace on the Palace of Versailles. He was also a representative of India at the League of Nations in Geneva for three years during the late 1920s.

Ahead of the Golden Jubilee, Hugh flew to Kapurthala with Fg Off E A Healy and landed to inspect a proposed landing ground. However, the landing ground was evidently not suitable because a few days later on 24th November he flew with LAC Mathews as crew to a landing ground at Jullundur (now Jalandhar) a few miles east of Kapurthala and used this as his base. From there he provided an aerial escort for the train bringing the British Viceroy Lord Irwin to Kapurthala on

One of Hugh's oblique photographs of the palace at Kapurthala with white tented accommodation for guests during the Golden Jubilee.

25th November. Later that day he flew an aerobatic display over the garden party during the celebrations at the maharajah's palace. That evening Hugh attended a formal dinner at the palace, sitting at the end of one of the tables with the ADCs of senior visitors. On the following day Hugh carried out another aerobatic display and took oblique photographs over the city fair in Kapurthala. He landed back at Jullundur before returning to Ambala on 27th November.

Following the Kapurthala celebrations, Hugh's final long-distance flying in India began ten days later when his B Flight set off for a two-month detachment to an area some 900 miles to the south. With Hugh due to be away for so long Joy had been considering moving out of their bungalow which could make life simpler with a baby and less expensive without the need to retain staff. Indeed, ahead of John's arrival she had been looking at hotels and decided that Parry's Hotel would be most suitable. However, in the end she decided to stay put in their bungalow and a good friend who was the wife of one of the other pilots moved in with her for a time.

On 3rd December 1927, a few days before Hugh's flight was due to set off from Ambala, he had flown each of his four aircraft for a fifteen-minute engine and rigging air test to make sure everything was as it should be. Then on 7th December they took off and during the next three days (with Cpl Healy as his crew) Hugh led the four aircraft in seven stages from Ambala to Delhi, Agra, Jhansi (night stop), Sehore, Mhow (night stop), Deolali and Ahmadnagar. These flights varied in length from just over an hour to three hours. On 12th December, Hugh made a reconnaissance flight over the manoeuvre area for the forthcoming army exercise, before continuing on to Aundh near Poona.

A few days later AVM Sir Geoffrey Salmond, the AOC India since December 1926, arrived at Aundh. On 17th December he flew with Hugh to Ahmadnagar to inspect B Flight and to visit the army brigade with whom they were operating. On the return flight to Aundh later that day, Hugh and Salmond looked for suitable sites as potential landing grounds near Poona.

As no flying is recorded from 20th–31st December it is likely that B Flight spent the Christmas period at Aundh. On New Year's Day 1928 Hugh's B Flight detachment aircraft flew from Aundh to Sholapur to refuel before continuing on to Secunderabad. The following day they carried out a flypast over a Proclamation Day parade before landing back at Secunderabad. After a further overnight stop they returned via Sholapur to Ahmadnagar; before continuing to Aundh on 4th January.

No flying is recorded in Hugh's logbook during the period 5th–12th January, although his other crews and aircraft would have been busy flying. On 13th January Hugh flew the short distance from Ahmadnagar to land at Bhandi to inspect the landing ground, before returning to Ahmadnagar. Then on 17th January, Hugh made a two-hour flight from Secunderabad to Sholapur. After re-fuelling at Sholapur he continued to Aundh with another two-hour flight, which included inspecting the landing grounds at Patas and Yevat which were located close to the main road along the route from Sholapur to Poona. During this detachment he had also inspected a landing ground at Dhoud. The active part of the detachment was probably completed at Aundh in late January or early February and in due course B Flight returned to Ambala.

On completion of the exercises with the army, Hugh received a letter from the Army Headquarters of Southern Command at Poona thanking him and 28 Squadron for their help, instruction and the willing manner in which they had met the various tasks during this army co-operation flying. It was clear that the army in this southern location, remote from the RAF airfields in the northern half of India, had appreciated the opportunity to carry out live army co-operation training with the Bristol Fighters. The writer of the letter said that they looked forward to receiving Hugh's report and critique from the exercise which would be of value for when another RAF detachment might be in their area. There was also a letter from the Army Headquarters of the Deccan District commenting on the benefit of having the aircraft and crews to train with them and that their general had appreciated this.

Joy had dreaded Hugh going away for two months, so soon after the birth of their son John. On the day that B Flight left Ambala for this detachment Joy recorded in her diary: 'Watched them fly over the bungalow and pray God the time will go quickly until I see them come back again.' It must have seemed a long time for Joy on her own at Ambala (including over Christmas), especially as John was only three weeks old when Hugh had left. During this time Joy noted in her diary that she received a letter from Hugh almost every day; from Jhansi, Ahmadnagar, and other locations during the detachment, which is as much a tribute to him as to the Indian postal service and the railway network of the 1920s. Joy's final diary entry is for 29th December 1927, ending her only diary which survived.

Ambala 1928
Sqn Ldr A F Brooke assumed command of 28 Squadron on 23rd February. By now, Hugh only had a few more months to serve in India. Apart from flights he made from Ambala to Delhi and back in late February, in late March and early April, the rest of his flying around this time was routine army co-operation training, camera gun practice, an altitude test up to 13,500 ft, engine and rigging air tests and dual

instruction. There was also formation flying practice for a squadron flypast during a visit on 25th April by their AOC, AVM Sir Geoffrey Salmond.

Hugh's time with 28 Squadron drew to a close in May 1928 with his final flying of two short air tests on 7th May. During his four-and-a-half years in India he had flown 653 hours with the Bristol Fighters and used a total of sixty-seven airfields and landing grounds, namely: Peshawar, Risalpur, Dardoni, Dargai, Quetta, Dana, Jhelum, Lahore, Near Jhelum, Ambala, Shabkadr, Akora, Rawalpindi, Hassan Abdal, Hatti, Arawali, Kohat, Tank, Fort Sandeman, Chaman, Pishin, Sibi, Loralai, Hindubagh, Jacobabad, Pad Edan, Hyderabad (Sindh), Karachi, Sorab, Panjgur, Diz Perom, Nok Kundi, Koh-i-Taftan, Dalbandin, Nushki, Uttarlai, Jodhpur, Ahmedabad, Deolali, Aundh, Sholapur, Bellary, Bangalore, St Thomas Mount (Madras), The Island (Madras), Yaru, Ghulistan, Saranan, Zungi Nwar, Multan, Ferozepore, Delhi, Agra, Cawnpore, Kutwa, Delhi racecourse, Kapurthala, Jullundur, Jhansi, Sehore, Mhow, Ahmadnagar, Secunderabad, Bhandi, Yevat, and Dhoud.

Some of these airfields and landing grounds became international airports or major military airfields in later years. Others became disused when more modern aircraft required tarmac runways. But almost all of them are still traceable, near the villages which gave them their names. With a careful look, the tell-tale signs can be found such as the concrete ends visible of what was once a rough grit runway – similar to a square bracket at each end. If these are found, there is likely to be the circular or square shape of a fort alongside such an ancient flying strip. The signs are there if care is taken when looking at a satellite photograph.

In the months after Hugh returned to England, the number of RAF squadrons in India increased from six to eight during October 1928, when 11 (B) and 39 (B) Squadrons were established in India with the new Westland Wapiti. No. 28 Squadron continued to move to a different station in India every few years. In September 1931 their Bristol Fighters were replaced by Westland Wapitis and in June 1936 by the Hawker Audax. These army co-operation biplanes were replaced in September 1941 with the arrival of the short take-off and landing Lysander which the squadron flew in support of British forces in Burma fighting the Japanese advance until that country was overrun. No. 28 Squadron then re-grouped at Lahore in India and co-operated in a series of exercises until the end of 1941 when it re-equipped with Hurricane fighter-bombers. The 'Hurri-bombers' com-

Above right: Hugh on the left for King George V's levee at St James's Palace during May 1928.
Below right: Amelia Earhart at Northolt in 1928 – probably in late June while in England following her transatlantic flight as crew to become the first woman to fly the Atlantic 17th-18th June. Left to right: Hugh, Mr Don, Amelia, Mrs Don, Rita Sowrey, Joy, Captain White (no relation). D.H. 60 Cirrus Moth behind the group and another Cirrus Moth further back.

menced operations over Burma in January 1943 and continued through to the Japanese surrender on 2nd September 1945 – by which time 28 Squadron had started to re-equip with Spitfires. The squadron then returned to Burma as part of the permanent defence force, before moving to Hong Kong in May 1949 against the background of a challenging situation in China.

Although Hugh, Joy and their young son John (then seven months old) were heading home to England in May 1928, this was not the end of the family involvement with 28 Squadron. Some twenty-two years later in 1950, John (by then a newly graduated pilot officer from the RAF College Cranwell) joined 28 Squadron at RAF Kai Tak in Hong Kong, when it was one of the last of the RAF's Spitfire squadrons before re-equipping with the new Vampire Mk.5 jet fighter.

Hugh and Joy with their baby John travelled home to England on the P&O Troopship *Kaiser-i-Hind* (Hindi for Empress of India). When they arrived in England in late May 1928 Hugh had several weeks of disembarkation leave. This gave them time to catch up with family and friends in Kent and Sussex, who would also meet John for the first time. In addition Hugh attended King George V's first levee at St James's Palace.

These court levees were continued by the British monarchy until 1939. They took the form of a formal reception at St James's Palace at which officials, diplomats, and military officers of all three armed services, were presented individually to the sovereign. Full dress uniform or court dress was worn by the participants, who formed a queue in the Throne Room before stepping forward when their names and ranks were called. Each then bowed to the King who was seated on a dais with male members of his family, officials of the Royal Household and senior officers behind him.[19]

Hugh and Joy met Amelia Earhart at Northolt when they were visiting Hugh's sister Rita. At that time Rita and her husband Fred Sowrey were at RAF Northolt where Fred commanded 41 Squadron before becoming the station commander. There was also time in July for a holiday in the South of France, re-visiting Cap Martin, Menton and Monte Carlo where they had spent their honeymoon two years earlier. Finally, the family moved into a rented house on the outskirts of Letchworth in preparation for Hugh's two-year engineering course at Henlow which would begin in early August.

CHAPTER 11

THE 1930s
AND LIFE AS A TECHNICAL OFFICER

Changing direction for the future

When the RAF had been established as an independent air force in April 1918, almost all officers were active First World War pilots. With the arrival of peace a few months later Trenchard's plan was that in the years ahead most officers would continue to be pilots; with only a handful of non-flying specialists for the equipment branch (later for a period named the stores branch), medical, dental, chaplain and legal branches. With these exceptions, all other officers would be commissioned into the general duties branch which was responsible for all aspects of flying and engineering (including armament, wireless and photography) as well as all staff and administrative duties. While the small number of non-flying specialists would be limited in career terms for promotion to head of each branch, all general duties officers would be eligible for promotion to the highest ranks in the service.

This concept continued with very little change until the rapid military expansion of the 1930s, which required a considerable increase in officer numbers. These additional officers were required to manage functions as headquarters staff at each station to provide personnel and administrative support to the flying squadrons.

Trenchard's memorandum had placed emphasis on pilots gaining specialist technical training so that in addition to flying duties they would have broader capabilities. These additional skills and experience would also make them more suitable for higher command.

Short courses were provided for officers to gain a working knowledge of individual technical subjects, whilst long courses catered for those who would become expert in a particular field. Thus after officers had gained experience flying on squadrons and attended a specialist technical course, they would then alternate between flying and technical responsibilities.

This principle of alternating flying and technical appointments continued until 1940, by which time the growing complexity of modern aircraft and equipment was beginning to demand a greater degree of specialisation than could be provided by officers who were part-time technical staff. A separate RAF Technical Branch was then established with the sub-divisions of engineering, signals and armament.

Those officers suitably qualified, were transferred to this new technical branch, although for some years they might still move between flying and technical postings. In Hugh's case he would only have a few more years of flying duties after his time in India before his transfer to the technical branch at its formation on 1st April 1940 (following the creation of RAF Maintenance Command in 1938).

OFFICERS ENGINEERING COURSE AT HENLOW

As Hugh had completed a one-year engineering course at Cambridge, and then spent several years flying in Britain and India, it was now time for him to become more highly trained in his engineering specialisation. Therefore on his return from India he was selected for the two-year officers engineering course at the RAF Home Aircraft Depot (HAD) at Henlow.

The focus of the course was on basic engineering theory and the management of workshops. On completion of the course the outstanding students would be sent on to Cambridge to read for a degree. In years to come the officers engineering course would become the foundation of the RAF Technical College at Henlow established after the Second World War.

As can be seen in the photograph, most of the officers on Hugh's course have pilot wings on their uniforms in line with Trenchard's earlier policy for career pilots to gain a specialist qualification such as engineering.

In addition to Hugh's engineering studies at Henlow, he also kept his hand in flying a few times most months in a Bristol Fighter or Avro 504N (Lynx Avro)

Officers Engineering Course at Henlow 1928-30. Back row: Patterson, Boston, Battle, Hawkins, McEvoy (later ACM Sir Theodore), Greaves, Bardon, Shephard, Pankhurst, Melbourne, Fallick, and Elias. Centre row: Rodwell, Fidler, Vernon, Weedon, Mackay, Gadda, Prance, Ridgway, Perry Keene, Roland, and Beardsworth. Front Row: Foden, Lees, Williamson Jones, Levick, Norton, Williamson, H G White, Butler, Potter, Whitlock, and Strang Graham.

of the RAF Henlow practice flight, achieving seventy-five hours airborne during the two years. Apart from local flying with a variety of officers and airmen as passengers, many of the flights were to other RAF stations, often flying with Flt Lt Rodwell (who had been a pilot on his flight in India) or Flt Lt Wynne Tyson. These flying visits were made to a wide spread of RAF units, namely; Duxford, Northolt, Hendon, Digby, Upper Heyford, Halton, Tangmere, Manston, Catterick, Leuchars, Gosport, Andover, Martlesham Heath and Bircham Newton.

Henlow had started out as a Royal Flying Corps unit in 1917-1918 as a repair depot for Eastern Command. Following the First World War the RAF Officers Engineering School moved to Henlow from Farnborough in 1924 and in 1926 Henlow was renamed as the Home Aircraft Depot – which was the name when Hugh was there for the two-year course 1928-1930. For a short period (1925-1927) Henlow also had an operational role when 23 and 43 Squadrons were based there.

With the military expansion scheme in 1935, training courses were carried out at Henlow for aircraft fitters, riggers and mechanics. In 1936 Henlow also included the RAF School of Aeronautical Engineering. Then in 1938, with war approaching the Home Aircraft Depot at Henlow became No. 13 MU (Maintenance Unit) and some of the activities were dispersed for safety to St Athan in South Wales.

During the Second World War the main role for Henlow was unpacking Hurricanes which had been manufactured in Canada and shipped to England in crates. At Henlow the Hurricanes were assembled, tested and modified as necessary – and later damaged Hurricanes were repaired there. After the war, in 1947 the School of Aeronautical Engineering became the RAF Technical College. By 1953 the college was running courses for basic engineering, mechanical engineering, and electrical weapons systems, together with the Technical Officer Cadet Wing. After much discussion the RAF Technical College was amalgamated with the RAF College at Cranwell in 1965, and Henlow subsequently closed as a military establishment in 1983.

Hugh really enjoyed the engineering course at Henlow, while keeping his hand in flying. This was also a good stable period for Hugh and Joy with their small son John living on the outskirts of the attractive garden city of Letchworth a few miles from Henlow, after the many deployments which had taken Hugh away from his home base in India and Joy for long periods.

RAF COLLEGE CRANWELL

On completion of the Henlow engineering course, on 1st July 1930 Hugh was posted to the RAF College Cranwell on promotion to squadron leader to command the Workshops Squadron. As a substantive squadron leader aged thirty-two he was now back to what had been his acting rank as a front-line squadron commander aged twenty back in 1919. The commandant of the RAF College at that time was AVM Arthur Longmore. Hugh held Arthur Longmore in high regard and in time they became good friends.

Hugh's posting to Cranwell was an ideal combination for his engineering and flying qualifications. When his technicians had completed the repair and maintenance tasks in the workshops Hugh then flew the air tests. This was very practical and direct work to ensure that there were sufficient aircraft of the appropriate type available for the daily flying training of the flight cadets. As a part of his task it would have been crucial that the stores organisation at Cranwell always had available the correct tools and spares in stock for his team to use. This equipment and stores aspect would be an area in which he would be increasingly involved during subsequent appointments.

Hugh flew most days from the grass north airfield at Cranwell, usually on very short test flights of ten or fifteen minutes. His flying logbook lists the flying hours on the many different types of aircraft then at Cranwell (D.H.60 Gipsy Moth, D.H.9A, Bristol Fighter, Armstrong Whitworth Siskin III and IIIA, Armstrong Whitworth Atlas, Fairey Fox, Lynx Avro, Avro Tutor, Hawker Hart). He also had a short solo flight one morning in a Westland Wapiti during October 1931, which may have been an opportunistic flight when a Wapiti pilot was visiting – to add to his types flown. It is interesting to note that having stayed in flying practice continuously since he began flying in 1916 there was never a requirement for Hugh to have a dual check on arrival at Cranwell or before flying the many aircraft types there which he had not flown before. Indeed, once he had qualified as a pilot in 1916, about the only dual checks he flew during his RAF career look to have been on his arrival in India in 1924 when he flew for fifteen minutes in a Bristol Fighter for a 'passenger flight in accordance with regulations' and after spending four months at Lower Topa in India during 1927 when he recorded a ten-minute 'dual check after absence over four months'.

After the first few weeks at Cranwell Hugh's clerk maintained his flying logbook so there are none of the usual informative or cryptic personal comments about the characteristics of aircraft which he was flying for the first time, or of any particular occurrences. However, with the number of short air tests flown most days it is no surprise that he delegated log keeping to his clerk. For example, on 13th November 1931 he flew thirteen separate air tests on three different types of aircraft (six Atlas air tests, five Avro air tests and two Moth air tests) yet was only airborne for a total of three hours and fifteen minutes. During these air tests he usually took a technician as passenger, which he told me was useful for checking the rigging adjustment because when a technician was flying the aircraft he would not automatically correct for anomalies in flying characteristics as a pilot would.

During Hugh's time at Cranwell two new training aircraft types were introduced at the college, with the Avro Tutor replacing the Lynx Avro as the basic trainer and the Hawker Hart replacing the Armstrong Whitworth Atlas as the advanced trainer. Through March 1933 he air tested thirteen Tutors with consecutive airframe numbers (indicating that they were new aircraft from the production line) and in April he air tested five Harts with consecutive airframe numbers.

RAF College Cranwell Annual Inspection in 1932. Hugh in step with the commandant, Air Vice-Marshal Arthur Longmore, as he inspected Hugh's Workshops Squadron personnel.

The military site at Cranwell had begun as a Royal Naval Air Service unit during the First World War to train navy pilots to fly aircraft and airships, and to operate observation balloons. During 1915 the Admiralty requisitioned 2,500 acres of farmland, mainly from the Earl of Bristol's estate, to build a hutted camp with a grass airfield and hangars. This was named HMS Daedalus and comprised the RNAS Central Training Establishment and the Naval Boys' Training Wing (to train naval air mechanics and riggers). When the RFC and RNAS were amalgamated to create the RAF in 1918, HMS Daedalus was re-named RAF Cranwell.

The RAF College at Cranwell was opened on 5th February 1920, as the world's first military air academy and as part of Trenchard's vision to consolidate the RAF as a single, independent service. The flight cadets completed a two-year course for officer and flying training to create a core of potential future leaders of the RAF. In the years to follow Trenchard said that he had chosen Cranwell because 'marooned in the wilderness, cut off from pastimes they could not organise for themselves, the cadets would find life cheaper, healthier and more wholesome'. Indeed, his message to the first cadets left them in no doubt of his expectations:

'We have to learn by experience how to organise and administer a great Service, both in peace and war, and you, who are present at the College in its first year, will, in future, be at the helm. Therefore, you will have to work your hardest, both as cadets at the College and subsequently as officers, in order to be capable of guiding this great Service through its early days and maintaining its traditions and efficiency in the years to come.'

In 1922 work began to replace the wartime naval huts with permanent buildings. In time Sir Samuel Hoare, the Secretary of State for Air, took the architect James West to visit Wren's Royal Hospital in Chelsea, and the design for the new college building reflected this influence. The foundation stone was laid by Lady Hoare, wife of the Secretary of State for Air, on 29th April 1929 and the building work continued throughout Hugh and Joy's three years at Cranwell. Indeed, they would often walk across the grass airfield from their married quarter at weekends to see how the construction of the new college building was progressing. This impressive new brick building with Portland stone facing was finally completed in September 1933, a few months after they had left for the next posting. It was opened formally in October 1934 by the then Prince of Wales, later Edward VIII.

A few months after starting his tour at Cranwell, Hugh spent some days during October 1930 on board the battleship HMS *Barham* from Invergordon off the north-east of Scotland. It is not clear why this visit took place, which included operating at sea with other naval ships. HMS *Barham* had been built many years earlier and had taken part in the Battle of Jutland during the First World War. Some years after Hugh's visit HMS *Barham* would be in the Mediterranean Fleet during the Second World War. However, as reported by Pathé News HMS *Barham* had a tragic end in November 1941 when she was hit by torpedoes from a German submarine. As she capsized the main weapons magazine exploded killing 860 sailors – two-thirds of her crew.

When Hugh and Joy first moved to Cranwell with their small son John, they lived in a small terrace bungalow married quarter on what was known as 'Harmony Row', a small cul-de-sac at West Avenue not far from the college riding stables. These 'period' quarters were still there when I arrived at Cranwell as a flight cadet in 1959, but by the time I returned as a flying instructor a decade later they had been demolished and replaced by modern 1960s quarters. Although Hugh and Joy were very happy in Harmony Row, in due course they moved to a larger brick married quarter near the old airship concrete mooring blocks across the north airfield by Bristol Wood reached via the aptly named Lighter-than-Air Road.

Joy remembered their time at Cranwell as a settled and happy family period, with plenty of riding and hunting for them both, including riding in a RAF Point to Point. They enjoyed a good social life at Cranwell and during some long weekends with the Longmores and others (including Sir Geoffrey Salmond) on the Norfolk Broads when Hugh and Joy would sleep in the small caravan which Hugh had made in the workshops. On one occasion Joy flew as a passenger in Arthur Longmore's Blackburn Bluebird two-seater biplane during which he demonstrated the 'falling leaf' manoeuvre – as she recounted with relish in later years. In the years after Cranwell Hugh and Joy stayed in contact with Arthur and Marjorie Longmore as family friends. Indeed when Sir Arthur Longmore visited Cheltenham on business some twenty-five years later when I was at school there as a teenager, much to my surprise he took me out to lunch and quizzed me on my growing ambition to join the RAF.

The Belvoir Hunt moving off across the grass airfield from the meet at the officers' mess at RAF College Cranwell in 1931. Here they are passing Lynx Avro training aircraft.

Top: Belvoir Hunt 1932. From left to right: Hugh, AVM Longmore, and MacEwen.
Right: Joy at Belvoir Hunt in 1932.
Bottom: Hugh and Joy (in dark clothes) at Wroxham Broad with AVM Arthur Longmore and
AM Sir Geoffrey Salmond and their families..

Sir Geoffrey had been Hugh's AOC in India and on one occasion had flown as passenger in Hugh's aircraft. Salmond was now commander-in-chief of Air Defence of Great Britain Command – to where Hugh would be posted after Cranwell.

HEADQUARTERS AIR DEFENCE OF GREAT BRITAIN COMMAND

After three years at Cranwell, Hugh was posted in June 1933 to the headquarters of Air Defence of Great Britain (ADGB) Command at Uxbridge, where he and Joy (with John now aged five) lived in a spacious RAF married quarter. The headquarters was at Hillingdon House Uxbridge and used the nearby airfield at RAF Northolt for liaison flights to the various units within the command.

Having handed over the technical workshops at Cranwell to his successor, Hugh's posting for equipment staff duties at HQ ADGB would have continued to broaden his experience in his technical specialisation. He was now working within the Equipment Branch. His responsibilities would have been to ensure that the correct spares and equipment were at the appropriate depot or airfield within this rapidly expanding operational command at the right time to be fitted to aircraft, vehicles and other technical equipment.

ADGB Command had been formed in 1925 with operational responsibility for all home-based fighter and bomber squadrons. The command comprised Inner and Outer Artillery Zones and an Air Fighting Zone. The Air Fighting Zone was sub-divided into the Fighting Area and the Wessex Bombing Area. The Fighting Area comprised eleven fighter squadrons and two communications squadrons. The fighter squadrons were based mainly around the London area at Kenley, Biggin Hill, Northolt, Hawkinge and Duxford for the protection of the capital, and at Upavon and Henlow. During 1932 the Wessex Bombing Area in southern England was raised to command status with its sub-divisions of the Western Area with its headquarters at Andover and the Central Area with its headquarters at Abingdon. Each of these areas comprised ten bomber squadrons.

With the major expansion of the RAF which began during 1933 in response to the growing German threat, these two areas would become in 1936 Fighter Command and Bomber Command. Although the preparation for this change started while Hugh was at the HQ, the formal establishment of fighter and bomber commands did not occur until the year after he had moved on again.

When Hugh was at HQ ADGB the air officer commanding-in-chief was AM Sir Robert Brooke-Popham whom he had come to know during his time on 20 Squadron in France during 1916-1917. At that time Brooke-Popham had been a brigadier general as deputy adjutant and quartermaster-general at the headquarters of the RFC in France.

During Hugh's eighteen months at Uxbridge (June 1933 to January 1935) he was active visiting the stations within the command. He knew the importance of staff officers spending time out of the office to see the situation on the operational units and to have the opportunity to discuss issues with station personnel at first hand. For such visits Hugh generally flew solo or with a passenger in a D.H.60 Gipsy Moth of the communications squadron at nearby Northolt to visit a wide range of RAF units within the command. These flying visits included to Henlow, Andover, Upper Heyford, Norwich, Bircham Newton, Tangmere, Filton, Abingdon, Boscombe Down and on two occasions to Sutton Bridge near Holbeach.

Sutton Bridge was a seasonal tented camp within the ADGB Command which was activated for eight months each year to provide an annual armament practice camp (APC) for each operational squadron. The squadrons deployed in turn each year to live under canvas for two weeks of weapon training, firing guns and dropping bombs against targets moored just off the coast of the Wash. Holbeach range (and Wainfleet range) on the edge of the Wash are still in use today.

Annual APCs still took place for operational squadrons throughout my service in the RAF. While I was in the Middle East the two-week APCs were flown from Sharjah using Jebajib or Rashid range along the coast, with us junior pilots each spending a day each week as range safety officer and to oversee the safety and scoring. In later years three-week APCs were flown from the NATO airfield of Decimomannu in Sardinia using the range operated at Capo Frasca by the Italian air force.

It saved much travelling time and would have been enjoyable for Hugh to keep his hand in flying to the many outlying stations in ADGB Command. But even such routine flying is never risk free and Hugh and Joy's good friend Mike Moody had been killed two years earlier during such a visiting flight from Northolt in 1931. Mike Moody and his twin brother Charles had both been Royal Flying Corps pilots in the First World War, during which Charles was shot down and killed in 1917. Mike Moody stayed in the RAF after the war and in the 1920s was in India on 28 Squadron with his young wife, Bobbie, for much of the time that Hugh was there.

A few years after Moody had returned from India, he was posted to HQ ADGB. In April 1931 he was flying as pilot in a Northolt Communications Squadron Gipsy Moth for a visit to RAF Tangmere with the new AOC of the Fighting Area AVM Holt. Holt's ADC was flying with them in another Moth. As reported in *Flight* magazine on 1st May 1931, six minutes after leaving Tangmere on the return flight the two Moths were at 1,500 ft outbound when a pair of 43 Squadron Siskins returning to Tangmere saw the ADC's Moth and mistaking it for their commander dived in salute. The Siskin pilots had only seen one of the Moths and the wing of one of the Siskins clipped the wing of the aircraft they hadn't seen which was being flown by Mike Moody. Moody's aircraft went into a spin and although he recovered from this he had insufficient height to pull out of the dive. Meanwhile AVM Holt had baled out but his parachute had only partially opened when he hit the ground. Mike Moody and AVM Holt were both killed. The pilot of the Siskin was uninjured and was able to land at Tangmere.

Hugh and Joy's time at Uxbridge was a stable family period for them with John growing into a sturdy boy. There was also time for holidays which included a boating holiday during 1933 with another couple on the motor cruiser *Fantasy* owned and operated by a Mr Newgass. This trip took them along the Thames through London and out into the Thames estuary via Tilbury and Sheerness. From there they entered the Medway river towards Maidstone where Hugh had grown up. After Hugh and Joy completed the cruise it provided an opportunity for Joy to visit her family in Sussex, and her close friend Flora while they were in that area. Other boating holidays were to follow on the Solent and on the river at Littlehampton. While at Uxbridge Hugh also found time for skiing and tobogganing in Switzerland around Christmas 1933.

CHAPTER 12

BACK TO FLYING – RAF FILTON AND NO. 501 (CITY OF BRISTOL) SQUADRON

Final days of the biplane era

Despite the interest and challenge of his post at HQ ADGB Command, during which Hugh will have learned much about staff work in a busy operational head-quarters, it must have been a relief for him to leave the headquarters at Uxbridge and return to flying on his posting to RAF Filton in January 1935. He was to take command of 501 (Bomber) Squadron equipped with the Westland Wallace and he was also the station commander of RAF Filton. During this appointment Hugh and Joy lived in the station commander's quarter at Filton and John started at Clifton College Junior School.

No. 501 Squadron was a special reserve squadron of the Auxiliary Air Force with a mix of regular personnel for the key posts and volunteer part-time reservists drawn from the Bristol area. The Auxiliary Air Force had been created in 1924 through Trenchard's vision of civilians serving in flying squadrons in their spare time. This differed from the Royal Air Force Volunteer Reserve of former RAF servicemen who remained in the reserve and were obliged to return to service if required.

The Westland Wallace was the last of the RAF's two-seater general-purpose biplanes of the interwar years. During the 1920s the main general-purpose work-horses for army co-operation and air policing had been the D.H.9A (in service 1918-1931) and Bristol Fighter (1917-1931). These were generally succeeded by the Westland Wapiti (1928-1937) or Armstrong Whitworth Atlas (1927-1935). The design specification for the Wapiti was to use a high proportion of components from the vast RAF stock of spare D.H.9A wings, tails and other items already owned. In turn the Wapiti was replaced on some squadrons by its derivative the Wallace (1933-1943). In the case of 501 Squadron, which had only been formed in 1929, their D.H.9As were replaced by Wapitis in 1930, followed by the Wallace in January 1933.

During his sixteen months in command of 501 Squadron (January 1935 to May 1936) Hugh's main flying was on the Wallace, but the squadron also had two of the older Wapiti and two Lynx Avros used for instruction which he flew regularly.

The light and agile Lynx Avro was his preferred aircraft for aerobatic displays. He also flew a D.H.60 Gipsy Moth, probably of the Filton station flight, mainly for liaison visits to other RAF stations or outlying RAF units such as weapons ranges.

By 1935 when Hugh took command of 501 Squadron the strategic situation was changing rapidly in Europe. During October 1933 Winston Churchill (then an MP out of office) had made a speech in the House of Commons about Germany's expansionist plans towards becoming the most heavily armed nation in the world. Then in July 1934 the British government announced a major expansion of RAF squadrons, with the number of Home Defence squadrons due to increase from fifty-two to seventy-five, and the intention to increase the total first-line strength to 128 squadrons within five years. The following year, in May 1935, the government voted to treble the number of front-line military aircraft available to defend British soil – representing an increase of 1,500 aircraft of all types.

In parallel with this expansion, the reserve squadrons of the Auxiliary Air Force were also increasing in number. However, despite this very significant increase in tempo with RAF expansion in the face of German re-arming, this does not seem to have changed significantly the traditional army co-operation activities of 501 Squadron as a reserve unit, which also included involvement with other military units for ceremonial events during the mid 1930s.

As the squadron commander (and station commander) Hugh flew regularly to the RAF Central Area headquarters at RAF Abingdon in Oxfordshire for conferences or meetings with his air officer commanding, as well as taking candidate officers to be interviewed for a potential commission.

Flying for 501 Squadron involved the usual army co-operation activities such as W/T, photography, practice bombing and gunnery, high level flying at around 16,000 ft, giving dual instruction and liaison with other RAF units. It also included formation flying for formal flypasts which Hugh led and aerobatic displays (for which he used one of the two Lynx Avros). In addition there were air experience flights for the Clifton College Officer Training Corps cadets (although not for their son John who was at junior school and still too young).

The month of May 1935 was a particularly busy time with three major ceremonial occasions. On 9th May the squadron made an official visit to Cardiff with Hugh leading a formation flypast of nine aircraft before landing on the grass airfield where the mayor inspected the line-up of aircraft and talked with aircrew and ground crew.

Two days later, the squadron played a notable part in Bristol's Silver Jubilee celebrations for the twenty-fifth anniversary of the accession of King George V. This event was held on the plateau of Durdham Downs to the north-west of the city,

Hugh showing the mayor of Cardiff the rear observer/gunner's cockpit of a Wallace on 9th May 1935. (RAF photo).

comprising a military review with displays of pageantry involving 2,000 sailors, soldiers and airmen, the formation flypast by nine aircraft of 501 Squadron and a twenty-one-gun salute. Hugh led the formation flypast in Wallace K 3567 with his crew Flt Sgt Kemp for the rehearsal on 5th May and the flypasts on 9th May and 11th May 1935. These events were covered in detail in the *Bristol Evening Post* and *Flight* magazine, with their photographers flying as passenger during rehearsal flights.

Left: Rehearsal over the Cheddar Gorge ahead of the ceremonial flypasts during May 1935. (*Flight International*)

Overleaf:
A view from the rear cockpit. (*Bristol Evening Post*)

Close-up of a 501 Squadron Westland Wallace during the rehearsal. (*Bristol Evening Post*)

Hugh in Sidcot flying suit and harness by his Westland Wallace on the rehearsal day. (*Bristol Evening Post*)

Then on 25th May there was Empire Air Day. This was an Air League initiative which began in 1934 (and would continue until 1939) as an annual event for as many RAF stations as possible to be open for the public to see the everyday work of the RAF and promote a sense of 'air mindedness' in the public mind, with all proceeds going to the RAF Benevolent Fund. During the 1935 Empire Air Day at Filton Hugh again led the 501 Squadron formation of nine aircraft – but this time flying solo in one of their two Wapitis (K2236). He also flew an aerobatic display in a Lynx Avro (J2401).

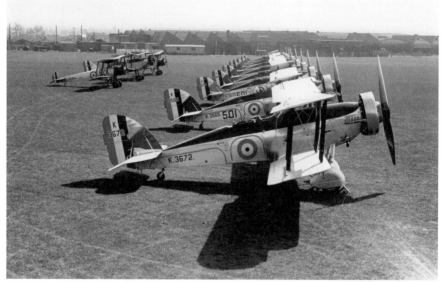

No. 501 Squadron Westland Wallace aircraft line-up at RAF Filton, with one of their two Wapitis and two Lynx Avros behind. Probably photographed for Empire Air Day on 25th May 1935. (*Flight International*)

Empire Air Day was a popular national occasion typical of this era. However, a downside of it taking place at so many RAF stations was that there were also flying accidents. This came to a head in 1937 when fifty-three RAF stations were open to the public and during the Air Day, or during the rehearsals, there were fatal accidents at several airfields which led to a debate in the House of Commons on the safety issues. These accidents caused eight deaths with two airmen killed at Odiham; one officer and one airman at Martlesham Heath; one officer and one airman at Farnborough; and one officer at Waddington and at Old Sarum.

There was a further ceremonial occasion on 6th July 1935 with a royal review of the RAF by King George V at Duxford and Mildenhall which included a flypast of

350 aircraft. Hugh was not involved in this massive flypast but was a part of the ceremony on the ground at Mildenhall. He had flown a Wallace to Mildenhall a few days ahead of the review and on the day stood by his aircraft in the extensive line-up of assembled squadron aircraft on the ground as the King was driven round during his inspection.

Following these four ceremonial events, during August 1935 the squadron deployed to RAF Manston near the north-east corner of Kent for an annual camp. These camps for reserve units provided an opportunity for them to spend time together and work as a cohesive team to hone skills and develop *esprit de corps* with the opportunity for some of the less experienced crews to fly in an unfamiliar area away from their home base of Filton. During the previous year's camp 500, 501 and 503 Squadrons had gathered at Manston for the annual air exercise to provide a sizeable auxiliary bomber force for 'Southland' against the 'Northland' fighter squadrons based at Biggin Hill and North Weald, but there are no indications of such a large-scale exercise during the summer camp of 1935.

After Hugh had taken off from Filton in a Wallace on 4th August for the camp at Manston, a sparking plug blew out and he had to turn back to Filton – before continuing to Manston. Two days later he flew a Wapiti from Manston to Eastchurch on the Isle of Sheppey (about twenty-five miles from Manston in the Thames estuary) where he landed to inspect the weapons ranges of the Air Armament School. Next day he was airborne in a Lynx Avro to carry out a dual check on an ab initio pilot before sending him solo. This mix of flying different aircraft types continued a few days later when he flew a D.H.60 Moth to land again at Eastchurch and the Leysdown range. The annual camp was completed after two weeks and the aircraft flown back to Filton on 20th August.

In early September it was time for 501 Squadron to head north to Catfoss in east Yorkshire for their annual three-week armament practice camp. Hugh flew via Halton to Catfoss in Wallace K3570 with LAC Green as his air gunner and continued to fly the same aircraft with Green throughout their time there. Flying from Catfoss the crews carried out practice bombing and front and rear cockpit gunnery against sand targets. The bombing involved the use of 20-lb practice bombs (including sometimes through gaps in low cloud) from 4,000 ft, 6,000 ft, 8,000 ft and 14,000 ft. They also carried out bombing with live 20-lb, 112-lb and 250-lb bombs from 4,000 ft and 6,000 ft. In addition they used an airborne towed target for air-to-air gunnery with Vickers and Lewis guns, including attacks from the rear quarter and beam attacks.

During the time at Catfoss Hugh flew to the headquarters at Abingdon on 18th September to attend an AOC's conference about the worsening political situation

HM King George V arriving at RAF Mildenhall for
the royal review on 6th July 1935. (RAF Museum)

with the Italian-Abyssinia dispute. The situation in that region continued to de-
teriorate and on 3rd October 1935 Ethiopia (then known in Europe as Abyssinia)
declared war on Italy, thus beginning the second Italo-Abyssinian War. With
differing views within Europe on this situation, one effect of this war was to en-
courage Fascist Italy to ally itself with Nazi Germany.

One of 501 Squadron's two Wapiti aircraft – 11th October 1935. (RAF)

The armament practice camp at Catfoss continued until late September when
the aircraft were flown back to Filton. Once back there the squadron continued
with routine army co-operation flying through the winter. In addition Hugh made
several flying visits to Hendon; gave flying instruction; flew air tests; inspected a
landing ground at Cirencester; inspected a civilian anti-gas range in the context
of future co-operation; flew Clifton College cadets and took a Clifton College

master in a Wallace to visit the RAF College Cranwell. He also flew a Hawker Audax (Hawker Hart derivative) solo on a delivery flight from the Bristol Works to RAF Sealand in north-east Wales, where he was met by a 501 Squadron Wallace to fly back to Filton.

Hugh's relatively short time in command of 501 Squadron drew to a close on 16th May 1936 on his promotion to wing commander and posting to the headquarters of RAF Far East in Singapore as the senior equipment staff officer and command engineering officer. It had been a busy sixteen months at Filton during which he had flown 157 hours (195 flights). Although he would continue to fly occasionally during later years, this was his final flying appointment before continuing his career fully as a technical officer.

Meanwhile 501 Squadron would continue to flourish in the years ahead. On 1st May 1936, not long before Hugh handed over to his successor, the squadron was re-named 501 (County of Gloucester) Squadron to embrace a wider area for recruitment than under its title of 'City of Bristol'. A few months later in 1936 the squadron would be flying Hawker Harts, and in 1938 Hawker Hinds. By early 1940, 501 Squadron had been transferred from Bomber Command to Fighter Command and re-equipped with Hurricanes. On 10th May 1940, with the German invasion of France, the squadron became part of the advanced air striking force and moved to a succession of airfields in northern France where it saw extensive action before France capitulated and the RAF squadrons involved in the action withdrew to England.

CHAPTER 13

SINGAPORE 1936-1939

The end of an era – colonial life in the Far East
while dark clouds gather over Europe

In the weeks after Hugh handed over 501 Squadron, he and Joy sailed from Liverpool to Singapore on the Blue Funnel Line troopship SS *Antenor* with a month-long voyage. Meanwhile, their son John, then aged eight, was left behind for nearly three years in England as a border at Clifton preparatory school and to spend school holidays with Joy's parents in Sussex where there would be cousins living nearby.

Antenor's standard route from Liverpool to the Far East was via Marseille, Port Said, Colombo, Penang, Singapore – from where it would continue to Hong Kong, Shanghai and Yokohama. It would then return to England with additional stops at Kobe (Japan) and Aden.

Hugh aged thirty-eight in 1936. Portrait photograph before leaving for Singapore. This uniform is now in the RAF Museum at Hendon.

THE RAF IN THE FAR EAST

During the second half of the 1930s the focus for the RAF was on increasing the number of squadrons in Britain as rapidly as possible and re-equipping them with more effective aircraft to face the growing German threat. These changes were far-reaching so that by the end of the 1930s there were many more squadrons available for the defence of Britain and the obsolescent biplanes were being phased out as faster and more capable monoplanes came into service.

Overseas, there was still a large RAF presence in the eastern Mediterranean, Iraq and India where the biplanes continued to be suitable for regional air control and air policing – and when necessary to carry out firepower demonstrations as a deterrent or to undertake operations to quell troublesome tribes. In contrast the

RAF only had a modest presence in the Far East where the situation had seemed more stable. However, the invasion by Japanese forces into Manchuria and China in 1932 had given a clear warning that there was a need to improve the security of Singapore and Malaya.

In Singapore an RAF airfield had been established during the 1920s at Seletar close to the north-eastern shore of Singapore island. On 1st January 1930 this became RAF Base Singapore and the headquarters of Far East Command. By then the RAF had Hawker Horsley torpedo bombers operating from the airfield and Short (Short Bros) Southampton II flying boats moored in the nearby Royal Navy harbour to fly from the waters of the straits between Singapore and Malaya.

In 1933 Seletar was re-named as Headquarters RAF Far East, with responsibility for the flying units in Singapore and Hong Kong. During the early years the officer commanding the headquarters also commanded RAF Base Seletar.

By 1936 the two land-based squadrons at RAF Seletar (36 and 100 Squadrons) had re-equipped with Vickers Vildebeest anti-shipping torpedo bombers. These single-engine biplanes (which had replaced the earlier Hawker Horsley torpedo bombers) had a crew of three.

The other two squadrons at Seletar (205 and 230 Squadrons) were equipped with Short Singapore III flying boats which were moored in the adjacent naval harbour. These large four-engine biplanes (which had replaced the Southampton II flying boats in 1935) had a crew of six and carried out regional survey work and reconnaissance patrols over Malaya. In turn these aircraft would be replaced during 1938 by the huge Short Sunderland flying boats with a crew of nine as the first monoplanes to operate in the region.

Despite the need to build up the RAF's capability in Singapore, it was not until 1937 that work began to clear rubber and coconut trees at the western end of the island to construct a second airfield, which in August 1938 would be RAF Tengah. Tengah became fully operational a year later in August 1939 with the arrival of two Blenheim bomber squadrons.

In Hong Kong, the airfield at Kai Tak had opened in 1927 with a slipway and seawall for the RAF's small flight of four Fairey IIIF fleet reconnaissance floatplanes, which operated with a crew of three. However, in 1930 the Fairey IIIF flight returned to Britain which left the colony of Hong Kong without a permanent RAF flying unit. The airfield became RAF Base Kai Tak in 1935, and during 1935-1937 there was just a small station flight located there with two former 36 Squadron Hawker Horsley torpedo bombers and two Tiger Moths for training flights.

During Hugh's time in the Far East the RAF also provided support to the Royal

Navy. This comprised two fleet spotter reconnaissance squadrons and two catapult flights, manned jointly by RAF and Royal Navy personnel.

To give an example of these joint RAF/RN units, 824 Squadron formed in 1933 at Gosport and embarked its Fairey IIIFs aboard HMS *Eagle* to sail for the China Station at Hong Kong. During the following years a replacement 824 Squadron was formed at Upavon, equipped with single-engine Fairey Seals. This unit sailed to the China Station, aboard HMS *Hermes* in 1934. Subsequently, in 1937, nine Fairey Swordfish and crews left Portsmouth aboard HMS *Eagle* and on arrival in Hong Kong took over the 824 Squadron number plate and were then engaged in the torpedo spotter reconnaissance role.

On 12th May 1937 four of these Swordfish from HMS *Eagle* flew a flypast over Hong Kong for the coronation of King George VI. This was led by a RAF squadron leader with a RN crew of two, so together with their mixed RAF and RN servicing crews this was a fully joint squadron. Similarly, 813 Squadron was also formed in January 1937 as a torpedo spotter reconnaissance unit at Gosport with Swordfish aircraft. In 1938 it embarked aboard HMS *Eagle* and sailed to join the China Station, to be shore-based at Seletar.

As well as operating from the aircraft carriers during this period (HMS *Hermes* during 1936 and HMS *Eagle* during 1937-39), these joint RAF/RN squadrons operated with the RN cruiser squadrons based at Singapore or Hong Kong. Their floatplanes were kept on board the cruisers from where they were winched over the side by a cable to take off and land on the water, before being winched back on board.

One of these units, 715 Squadron was built up during 1936/1937 with Hawker Osprey floatplanes which were allocated to ships of the RN 5th Cruiser Squadron on the China Station. The squadron operated the aircraft from the cruisers HMS *Berwick, Dorsetshire* and *Kent*; later replaced by HMS *Birmingham, Cornwall, Cumberland* and *Suffolk*. When not with the cruisers at sea, 715 Squadron was based at RAF Kai Tak. All of these combined RAF/RN squadrons were transferred to Admiralty control in May 1939.

HQ RAF Far East officers in 1936 (Hugh in front row fourth from right).

At HQ RAF Far East, Hugh was the senior equipment staff officer and command engineering officer. With the need to strengthen the RAF presence in the Far East the small headquarters staff, of which Hugh's technical team was a key part, would have been busy planning ahead to be ready to accept and operate additional aircraft numbers and new aircraft types in theatre.

The RAF presence in Singapore had grown substantially by the time Hugh arrived in Singapore in June 1936 and would continue to grow during his three years there. The number of RAF operational units in Singapore progressively increased and the headquarters structure was expanded to include additional branches and specialisations. The number of staff officers and warrant officers in the headquarters nearly doubled from twenty-four in 1936, when Hugh arrived, to forty in 1939 when he left. By 1938 the RAF Headquarters had moved from Seletar to the Union Building at Collyer Quay on the sea front of Singapore City. Meanwhile, the AOC was elevated from air commodore to air vice-marshal to reflect the increased importance and scope of the RAF's role in the region. Hugh's small team of five officers comprised an equipment section, an engineer section and a stores section.

With Hugh's responsibilities as the senior officer for equipment and engineering, and the very long supply line back to Britain, he would have been leading the forward planning for the necessary equipment and spares for new aircraft types, as well as continuing to support the existing aircraft. However, he also managed occasional flying with a total of forty-two flights during the three years. This was mostly local solo flying in a Moth from Singapore to keep his hand in and on one occasion in 1938 he flew in a Sunderland flying boat. During the latter part of each year he travelled from Singapore to Hong Kong by sea (a four-day journey each way) for an annual staff visit to the RAF station at Kai Tak. During his week or so there he flew a Tiger Moth or Avro Tutor a few times solo or with a passenger to inspect proposed landing grounds in the Hong Kong leased territory (also known as the New Territories).

Of interest, the pictured Tiger Moth, K2590, had been delivered from the de

Photo taken by Hugh of an unusual Sea Tiger Moth with floats over Singapore harbour.

Havilland factory at Stag Lane to the Home Aircraft Depot at Henlow in 1932. It went back to the company during June 1933 and was converted to a seaplane. It was subsequently sent to the packing depot at RAF Sealand in June 1934 and arrived at the air depot at RAF Seletar during January 1935 for allocation to the Air Headquarters, where at some point it was converted back to a landplane. In due course this aircraft was allocated to the Anti-Aircraft Co-operation Unit at Seletar and in 1941 was passed to the Malaysian Volunteer Air Force. It was finally lost in Singapore in January/February 1942.

For most of Hugh's time in Singapore his air officer commanding was AVM Arthur Tedder who would become the head of the RAF in 1946 as chief of the Air Staff. Some of the officers and their wives in Singapore were to become lifelong friends with Hugh and Joy; notably Edward (Teddy) and Blanche Addison, Henry and Peggy Scroggs, and the padre Rev John Jagoe (who christened Diana in Singapore and me a few years later in Cirencester).

During 1938 and 1939, Richard Longmore, whom Hugh and Joy had known as a teenager at Cranwell, was by then a flying officer as personal assistant to the AOC in Singapore. Richard was later an operational pilot during the Second

Sqn Ldr Ridley, Wg Cdr George, Padre John Jagoe and Hugh meeting Air Cdre Arthur Tedder when he took over from Air Cdre Sydney Smith (behind Tedder).

Admiral Yarnell (US Navy) meeting British officers, with Hugh and Teddy Addison on the right.

World War but tragically was killed in October 1943 together with the other seven members of his crew. They had taken off from Reykjavik in Iceland in their Liberator and were shot down over the Atlantic by the anti-aircraft guns of the surfaced German U-boat they were pursuing. By then he was a wing commander in command of 120 Squadron.[20]

A few years earlier, the *New York Times* had reported in 1932 that when Admiral Yarnell (pictured left with Hugh) had been in command of two American aircraft carriers that year, he pioneered tactics during an exercise to test the vulnerability of Hawaii to attack by naval air power. Instead of attacking as expected with battleships, Admiral Yarnell took his carriers to the north of Hawaii where they was less likely to be detected. With a storm as cover, his aircraft made simulated attacks on the harbour from the north-east. These tactics were successful – but his warnings of a potential Japanese threat from the air were ignored. Sadly, he was proved right when the Japanese attacked Pearl Harbor in a similar way nearly a decade later.

THE SOCIAL SCENE, TRAVEL AND FAMILY LIFE

Hugh and Joy lived well in Singapore. On arrival they stayed in a spacious airy flat at the Goodwood Park Hotel before moving into a house at 295 Thompson Road with local staff to help with the housework. They also lived for a time in Margate Road. The road bridge across the straits from Singapore to Johor in Malaya, which had been opened in 1924, enabled Hugh and Joy to spend weekend breaks and holidays in the invigorating cool air of the hill station at Fraser's Hill at a height of 2,600 ft (with peaks up to nearly 5,000 ft) some 150 miles north of Singapore, or to visit Kuala Lumpur sixty miles beyond. Photographs were posted by sea mail between England and Singapore to maintain contact with family back home and in particular for Hugh and Joy to see how their young son John was growing up.

In 1937, during their second year in Singapore, Hugh and Joy took the opportunity for an extensive seven-week holiday to visit Hong Kong and to see something of China and Japan. To achieve this, they joined SS *Antenor* as she passed through Singapore towards the end of the ship's routine passage to the Far East. At two stages along the journey Hugh and Joy would leave the ship for a few days and travel by land, before rejoining *Antenor* to continue the journey by sea.

This holiday began when they left Singapore on *Antenor* on 22nd March 1937 for the four-day passage to Hong Kong where the ship stayed for twenty-four hours, before continuing with the three-day passage to Shanghai where the ship docked for three days.

From Shanghai it was a further three days by sea to Tianjin, the nearest port to Peking (Beijing). At Tianjin Hugh and Joy left the ship for a week, going ashore by launch from the mooring on the Taku Bar buoy and travelling by train the hundred miles to Peking where they stayed for several days as paying guests with Dr Margaret Philips. While in Peking they visited many historic locations including the Great Wall of China, before returning by train to Tianjin.

Meanwhile *Antenor* had been to Darien (now Dalien) and back. Once back on board at Tianjin, *Antenor* made a twenty-four-hour passage to Tsingtau (now Qingdao) where they stayed for twenty-four hours. From this last Chinese port on the outbound passage they headed eastwards to Japan with a three-day passage to Yokohama where the ship stayed for about three days.

From Yokohama *Antenor* began the homeward journey along the south coast of Japan. At Nagoya Hugh and Joy left the ship for the second time. During two days they travelled by train to Kyoto (seventy-five miles) and then on to Kobe (sixty miles further west) to rejoin the *Antenor*. From Kobe the return journey to Singapore took twelve days with stops for a day or two at Shanghai and Hong Kong.

This was certainly a good opportunity for them to travel more widely in the Far East, although it may have been tiring at times for Joy during the early weeks of her second pregnancy. Judging by the number of items of Chinese and Japanese furniture and ornaments in the house when we grew up these journeys clearly had a considerable influence on them.

Joy continued horse-riding while in Singapore. Indeed, towards Christmas 1937 she was asked by an owner whether she would be willing to ride his horse in a race. Joy turned this opportunity down on the basis that she was soon to have a baby – as apparently he hadn't noticed! And so, midway through their three years in Singapore, Joy gave birth to their daughter Diana on 18th December 1937. Hugh and Joy were a family once again after such a long time without their son

John, so the arrival of Diana must have been a particular delight for them both. In the months to follow, a local amah (maid/nanny) was employed to help look after Diana, which enabled Joy to resume a full social and sporting life. Indeed, during August 1938 Hugh and Joy found themselves playing against each other in a mixed doubles tennis tournament.

THE JAPANESE THREAT TO SINGAPORE

The expansion and modernisation of the RAF in the Far East continued through 1938 and early 1939 while Hugh was working at the headquarters of RAF Far East, but by all accounts these developments were probably too little and too late for the defence of Singapore.

Hugh's three years in the Far East came to an end in April 1939 when he was posted back to England. Meanwhile, in the following years the situation in Asia would change dramatically for the worse as the threat grew from Japan which led to the Japanese invasion of Malaya and Singapore in December 1941. At RAF Tengah the two Blenheim squadrons were heavily involved in operations during the Japanese invasion. At Seletar the two flying-boat squadrons had by then replaced their Singapore III aircraft with Sunderland flying boats and been re-deployed out of the Far East theatre to Ceylon. Although 36 and 100 Squadrons had been due to have their ageing Vildebeest replaced in 1941 by modern Beaufort monoplane bombers, these aircraft had not arrived by the time the Japanese invaded. The heroic aircrew of these two squadrons attacked Japanese naval ships with their outdated Vildebeest aircraft and although they had some success most of the aircraft were shot down and the crews killed. The final two aircraft attempted to escape to Burma but were lost over Sumatra.

CHAPTER 14

BACK IN GREAT BRITAIN 1939 –
THE SECOND WORLD WAR

Wartime in Technical Training Command

By the time Hugh, Joy and eighteen-month old Diana had returned to England on HM Troopship *Lancashire* following the month-long journey through April 1939, the situation in Europe was menacing as the true nature of Hitler and his Nazi party had become ever more clear. But despite the threat of impending war, their return to England must have been a wonderful family time. Here they were, after three years away, being re-united with John (now aged eleven) and at last able to introduce John to his little sister Diana.

After two months of leave, when Hugh and Joy would have been able to catch up with family and friends, Hugh took up his appointment on 21st July 1939 at No. 13 Maintenance Unit (MU) at Henlow to command the general engineering squadron. This MU had only formed a few weeks earlier on 1st June with its main activity at that time being the maintenance of Hurricanes.

Although Hugh was only at Henlow for three months it must have been a tumultuous time with the outbreak of the Second World War occurring on 3rd September.

NO. 24 (TECHNICAL TRAINING) GROUP

Six weeks after the start of the Second World War, Hugh was promoted to group captain and posted to be the senior air staff officer (SASO) at Headquarters No. 24 (Technical Training) Group. This was one of four groups within Technical Training Command.

The headquarters of Technical Training Command was then located at Wantage Hall in Reading with a nearby airfield at RAF White Waltham. The other three groups in the command were 20 Group (located at Market Drayton, Shropshire); 26 Group (at West Drayton, Middlesex to manage its many outlying signals units); and 27 Group (at the Royal Agricultural College, Cirencester). When Hugh joined 24 Group his AOC was AVM P C Maltby. During Hugh's time there, AVM Maltby was succeeded in 1940 by AVM B E Sutton and towards the end of 1941 by Air Cdre G B Dacre.

When Hugh first arrived at the headquarters, it was located at RAF Quedgeley near Gloucester (also the home of No. 7 Maintenance Unit). But a year later on 3rd November 1940 the headquarters moved for a short period to the Bell Hotel in nearby Gloucester (demolished in 1968) and on 19th January 1941 to Hindlip Hall near Worcester.

The original Hindlip Hall had been built in the 1500s and after the Gunpowder Plot of 5th November 1605 some of those involved were found hiding there. Hindlip Hall was subsequently destroyed by a fire in 1820 and rebuilt. This large building made an excellent military headquarters in its rural location away from the likely target areas for German bombing. When the hall was requisitioned by the RAF in 1941, the owners moved into a separate part of the building. Following its use as a military headquarters during the Second World War Hindlip Hall was owned by Worcestershire County Council and since 1967 has been the headquarters of the West Mercia Police Force.[21]

Meanwhile, Headquarters No. 24 Group had continued to move its location after Hugh's time: from Hindlip Hall to Hereford in October 1944, then to Halton in February 1945.

Back Row:—F/O. B. Fellows. A/S/O. K. Brown. F/Lt. L. O. Glenister. W/O. J. Greeff. F/Lt. C. C. Aplin. S/Ldr. J. R. Morgan. F/Lt. W. Booth.
A/S/O. R. Fisher-Rowe. S/Ldr. H. Furner.
Centre Row:—F/Lt. P. R. M. Barker. S/O. M. S. Filgate. S/Ldr. F. T. Kitchin. S/Ldr. T, R. F. Brook. S/Ldr. J. A. Lennox. S/Ldr. R. H. Forster.
S/Ldr. K. W. Bransby. F/Lt. R. Eve. F/Off. G. P. Morgan.
Front Row:—Sq./Off. E. Balfour. W/Cdr. A. F. R. Bennett. G/Capt. H. G. White. A.V.M. B. E. Sutton, c.b., d.s.o., o.b.e., m.c. G/Capt. K. Biggs, m.c.
W/Cdr. E. A. Simson, a.f.c. W/Cdr. F. Susans.

Headquarters No. 24 (Technical Training) Group RAF at Hindlip Hall, October 1941.

No. 24 Group was responsible for a wide range of thirty units located at seventeen RAF stations spread across Britain, from south Wales to Scotland. Most of these units were specialist training schools and in addition the group was responsible for several RAF hospitals and other medical establishments. The main focus for the group was the RAF Schools of Technical Training at Halton, Henlow, Hereford, Innsworth, Melksham, Locking, St Athan and Hednesford. The other specialist training units comprised catering, physical fitness, administration, accounting and the RAF Polish depot at the Goodwood Hotel, Blackpool. As SASO Hugh had responsibility for overseeing all of these units, although his main focus is likely to have been with the eight technical training schools which would be his responsibility for the next few years.

Hugh remained in his appointment at 24 Group for three years (October 1939 to October 1942) during a time when it must have been strange for him after his combat flying as a young pilot in the First World War to find himself in a senior technical training role in the Second World War, and away from the operational scene. This is something I wish I had discussed with him in later years, but somehow it never occurred to me to delve into the vagaries of his RAF career as he had moved progressively from flying operations to technical. His record of service shows that he was transferred formally to the Technical Branch of the RAF on its formation in April 1940.

Whenever possible, Hugh visited the outlying units of 24 Group by air. He flew as a passenger in a two-seat Miles Magister training aircraft, and then as first pilot on this aircraft after a check-out during a flight from Ternhill to Halton. This was a new aircraft type for him and the first monoplane he flew as pilot. He also flew as a passenger in an Airspeed Envoy light twin-engine transport aircraft. After the 24 Group headquarters moved to Hindlip Hall, he generally flew on his own in a Tiger Moth from the elementary flying training school at the nearby small grass airfield at Perdiswell (now Perdiswell Park Golf Course) for visits to the Schools of Technical Training at Halton and Henlow.

On the family scene, Hugh and Joy's son John progressed in September 1940 from Clifton College Preparatory school to Cheltenham College (aged nearly thirteen). In 1941 they bought Ivy Cottage (a lovely stone house with small barns and a paddock) in the tiny village of Elkstone in the Cotswolds near Cirencester. By then Diana was three years old and I was born in Gloucester during July 1941.

RAF HALTON – NO. 1 SCHOOL OF TECHNICAL TRAINING (1942-1946)

After three years at 24 Group, Hugh was posted in October 1942 on promotion to air commodore to be the air officer commanding and commandant of No. 1 School of Technical Training at Halton where the RAF aircraft apprentices were trained. As technical training at Halton had been one of his prime responsibilities at 24 Group this was an ideal next posting on promotion. Hugh's return to Halton as the commandant, some twenty years after being there for a year as a young bachelor during 1920-1921 must have been quite a contrast for him.

During the intervening two decades there had been many changes at Halton while the apprentice scheme had progressed and flourished. During the 1920s permanent buildings had replaced the old hutted structures. This permanent layout had been designed so as not to appear purely utilitarian as had been the case with earlier Royal Flying Corps sites. The barracks, mess and NAAFI social and recreation buildings were in a composite arrangement around a parade square and the design of the new complex was highly significant because this concept was then used as a format for subsequent RAF units.

Hugh will have seen much of this evolving building work from the air because over the years he had made many flying visits to the grass airfield at Halton. For example, during 1929 when he was on the two-year engineering course at Henlow he flew to Halton in a Bristol Fighter on two occasions; then at various times during 1933 he had flown from Cranwell to Halton in an Atlas, in an Avro Tutor, and in a Hawker Hart. Then during 1935 he had refuelled at Halton when flying a Wallace from Filton to Catfoss in Yorkshire. He had also been a regular visitor during his three years at 24 Group, sometimes flying to Halton in a Moth from Perdiswell airfield near Worcester.

A large RAF hospital had been built on the Halton site which was opened on 31st October 1927 by HRH Princess Mary, after whom it was named. Later additions included the Institute of Pathology and Tropical Medicine, the Institute of Community Medicine and the Institute of Dental Health and Training. There was also a burns wing which did groundbreaking work during the Second World War. Great demands were made on the hospital during the war when it expanded to take 700 beds. By 1945 Halton Hospital had treated some 20,000 war casualties – and in the years to follow it continued to treat casualties from other operational theatres during the Cold War. After the creation of the NHS in 1948, local people were also treated in Halton Hospital.

Meanwhile, the aircraft apprentice scheme which Trenchard had launched in 1920 had achieved much as the RAF had evolved to become an increasingly powerful and flexible independent air force through the 1920s and 1930s. This was particularly significant with the RAF's major expansion during the second half of the 1930s, during which time Halton had grown and adapted in parallel.

When this expansion began in the mid-1930s, former apprentices numbered about half of the trained strength of the RAF. With recruiting buoyant, the size of Halton intakes ballooned, reaching over 1,000 boys per entry.

Although the main concept of the apprentice scheme had been to create future leaders of the technical staff who had an appreciation of the challenges faced by aircrew, a sizeable number of the boys who joined the service as apprentices saw it as a route through which they might achieve their real ambition to become pilots. From 1921, airmen had been able to volunteer for training as sergeant pilots and to serve as aircrew for six years before returning to their ground trades, retaining their rank achieved while aircrew. Several hundred former apprentices serving on these engagements at the start of the Second World War were subsequently retained in flying posts. Many were soon commissioned as officers and rose to executive positions on operational squadrons. Indeed, over a hundred former apprentices flew as pilots in the Battle of Britain.

With the rapidly growing numbers by then joining the service, many former apprentices found themselves racing through the ranks to senior non-commissioned officer and warrant officer rank to provide a vital source of experienced technical supervisors on front-line squadrons, maintenance units and as instructors for the growing number of technical training schools. Moreover, the introduction of the four-engine bombers in 1941 brought an urgent need for an additional crew member as flight engineer whose role was to assist the pilot(s) in managing the systems in these more advanced aircraft. Former Halton apprentices were ideally suited to this new challenge, and a large number of them transferred their engineering skills from the ground to the air in this role. In addition, the Royal Navy sent 400 directly recruited Fleet Air Arm apprentices to train with the apprentices at Halton.

When Hugh had been at 24 Group he had periodically flown up to Blackpool to visit the RAF Polish depot. Then in 1943 teenage Polish apprentices began to arrive at Halton. During that year hundreds of boys, mainly orphans and some as young as fourteen, were driven out of Poland by Hitler and after a tortuous journey through the Middle East ended up in Britain. Three hundred of these Polish boys were selected to train as RAF aircraft apprentices, with some 200 to train at Halton and 100 at Cranwell. They spent most of their first year in the RAF settling into their new country and learning English. At Halton, they joined the 49th and 50th Entries which graduated in 1947.

Sqn Ldr Henryk Wirszyllo was appointed as commander of the Polish squadron at Halton. On 13th September 1943, 264 boys aged fifteen arrived to begin their training. It was reported that they were given a warm welcome by Hugh and that the British showed great interest in them; providing considerable support and friendship throughout their stay. The Polish apprentice scheme continued until

1947, as recorded on a large plaque on a wall at the end of the 'Polish Avenue' between their accommodation block and workshop along which the Polish apprentices planted birch trees. The plaque states:

POLISH AVENUE
THESE BIRCH TREES WERE PLANTED BY THE POLISH AIRCRAFT APPRENTICES TO EXPRESS THEIR GRATITUDE TO THE BRITISH PEOPLE FOR THE HOSPITALITY CARE AND TRAINING THEY RECEIVED IN THE R.A.F. AT HALTON IN THE YEARS 1943 – 1947

Hugh built up a strong bond with the Polish Air Force apprentices who trained at Halton and when the Polish prime minister Mr Arciszewski visited Halton on 2nd February 1945 he presented Hugh with Polish Air Force pilot's wings in recognition of his strong personal support to the Poles for whom he had great respect.

VISITORS TO HALTON
The RAF had much to be proud of with the training of apprentices and other activities at Halton which inevitably attracted senior visitors from Britain and overseas, including senior visits during 1943/1944 from Poland, Turkey, Brazil, Bolivia and Persia.

Left: Hugh pointing out the control surfaces on a Cierva C.30 autogiro of 529 Squadron based at Halton. These slow-moving two-seat Cierva autogiros were used to calibrate the coastal early warning Chain Home radars. After the war this autogiro (AP510) was returned to the civil register as G-ACYE.

Right: Hugh listening to an address at Halton by Marshal of the RAF Sir John Salmond on 30th June 1945. Salmond had been the chief of the Air Staff 1930-1933 and again for a further short period later in 1933 after the death in post of his elder brother Sir Geoffrey. After final retirement in 1943 Sir John Salmond continued to have active involvement with the RAF.

JUBILEE CELEBRATIONS 25TH MAY 1945

Three weeks after the end of the war in Europe there was a major event at Halton with the Jubilee Celebrations on 25th May 1945 for the twenty-fifth anniversary of the aircraft apprentice training. The guest of honour and inspecting officer for the huge parade at Halton was Viscount Trenchard whose vision had created the aircraft apprentice scheme all those years earlier.

During the intervening years Trenchard had continued to take a keen and active interest in the progress and development of the apprentices and was proud of their achievements. It had always been his intention that the best of each Halton entry should be awarded a cadetship to Cranwell. Indeed, over twenty per cent of the apprentices were later commissioned as officers, with more than a hundred attaining air rank.

Above: On the dais, from left to right: AVM Izyicki (commander-in-chief of Polish Air Forces in Great Britain), Air Cdre H G White (wearing Polish Air Force wings above his RAF wings), Viscount Trenchard (then aged 72), MRAF Lord Portal (the chief of the Air Staff since October 1940), AM Sir Arthur Barratt (AOC-in-C Technical Training Command) and AVM Leask (AOC No. 24 Training Group) – at rear.

Right: Viscount Trenchard with Air Vice-Marshal Izyicki inspecting the Polish Air Force apprentices.

During the Jubilee Celebrations Viscount Trenchard paid tribute to Lord Portal for his leadership during the war years with these words: 'He has led the air force through its days of difficulty, sometimes almost of disaster. He has seen the result of the work you do here displayed by your predecessors.'

After the parade, Trenchard addressed the apprentices in the gymnasium during which he said: 'We celebrate not only a Jubilee but the part Halton has played in smashing Germany.' He went on to trace the progress and development of the apprentice scheme and emphasised his own phrases, 'All who wear blue are but one' and 'nothing but the best is enough for the Royal Air Force'. He concluded by reminding the apprentices that they should never forget that an efficient and happy spirit is the 'Halton Spirit'.

Viscount Trenchard was presented with a framed Roll of Honour which listed the names of former apprentices who had won decorations or commissions.

The chief of the Air Staff, MRAF Lord Portal, issued a message to Halton for the Jubilee celebration – which was also a tribute to Trenchard for his vision in creating the apprentice scheme:

> 'Although several Royal Air Force stations have shared the training of aircraft apprentices – Cranwell (where the first entry started twenty-five years ago), Flowerdown [near Winchester] and Cosford – it is with the name of Halton that the aircraft apprentice scheme is associated in our minds. It is fitting, therefore, that Halton should take the lead in celebrating this, the twenty-fifth anniversary of the foundation of this all-important part of the structure of the Royal Air Force. Since 1919 more than 18,300 aircraft apprentices have completed their training and have passed out to play that vital part in the service which was foreseen for them by Marshal of the Royal Air Force, Viscount Trenchard, and under whose leadership and inspiration this great school was planned and started.
>
> 'Now, after a quarter of a century, the last five years of which have seen the Royal Air Force serve our country and Empire in the greatest of all wars, we can review the record of apprenticeship training with satisfaction and pride. More than that, the consistent technical excellence of the service which has enabled the squadrons to meet and defeat the enemy in the air wherever they have met him, and to carry the war into the enemy's territory and at vast distances across the sea, has rested upon the skill and high devotion to duty of those who at Halton first learned their trades and first formed their sense of

service duty. Their success, in the air and on the ground, pays a finer tribute than any words of mine to the standard of Halton's achievement.

'I wish to congratulate all those who, whether as pupils or instructors, have helped to establish the outstanding reputation of Halton. Not the least part of that achievement has been the creation of the "Halton Spirit" which, though it cannot readily be described in words, has made itself felt wherever ex-aircraft apprentices are to be found. I am confident that this spirit will continue to make its influence felt during the war and be carried on by new generations of aircraft apprentices into the Royal Air Force of the future.

'I wish success and good luck to Halton and to all apprentices, past, present and future, wherever they are serving or may be destined to serve.'

The Jubilee celebration at Halton was certainly a day to remember.

HUGH'S FLYING AT HALTON
Whilst at Halton Hugh sometimes flew a Moth from the grass airfield for local flying or to provide air experience for Halton apprentices and local Air Training Corps cadets. He also used a Moth for occasional flying visits to the 24 Group headquarters at Worcester. He made several flights to other units as a passenger in a Proctor, in a DH.89 Dragon Rapide biplane (in its RAF guise as the Dominie) and an Oxford light transport and aircrew training aircraft. Hugh's logbook records his final flight as pilot was at Halton on 4th August 1944, flying a Moth.

Hugh's logbook also records a ten-minute local flight in a Sikorsky R-4 Hoverfly helicopter in April 1945 – which was probably visiting Halton from the RAF Helicopter Training School which had formed at Andover in January that year.

FLIGHT OVER GERMANY 9TH JUNE 1945
On 9th June 1945 Hugh was a passenger during a six-hour flight over Germany in a RAF Dakota, just four weeks after the end of the war in Europe. After nearly six years of war, it must have been a surreal experience to fly in a Dakota transport aircraft over war-torn Germany so soon after the end of hostilities; although it would still be a few more months before the war would end in the Far East. From being a young and precarious participant as a pilot in one war, here he was looking down over war-ravaged Germany after this later war. Hugh's logbook records the details for the flight from nearby RAF Westcott in Buckinghamshire.

Date: 9th June 1945
Aircraft type: Dakota
Pilot: ?
Passengers: Self, Sir Robert Brooke-Popham, Gp Capt Stevens, 2 others
Flight time: 6hr 30min
Route: Westcott – Aachen – Düren – Köln – Düsseldorf – Essen – Gelsenkirchen
– Münster – Dortmund – Ems Canal – Mouth of River Scheldt – Westcott

The purpose of the flight is unclear, but its route indicates a thorough look at a significant area of war-stricken Germany during which they would have seen at first hand the extent of the damage caused by allied bombing to the industrial Ruhr area. Whatever its purpose, Hugh was subsequently posted to Germany less than a year later on 1st March 1946 (his forty-eighth birthday).

It is not clear why ACM Sir Robert Brooke-Popham would have been on this flight. After his unusually long career in the RFC and RAF, during both wars, Brooke-Popham had retired from the RAF in 1942 (aged sixty-four) and became the inspector general of the Air Training Corps until 1945. Therefore he was no longer in a position of authority. His participation in this flight may have been through contact and friendship with Hugh dating back to the First World War (when Hugh first met him in France in July 1916 after making a forced landing in fog and sharing whiskies with the general before spending the night at the officers' mess of the General Headquarters for the RFC in France) and more recently during 1933-1935 when Brooke-Popham was the AOC-in-C of Air Defence of Great Britain Command where Hugh was a squadron leader on his staff. Maybe, this flight was simply to act as witness to the terrible effect of bombing in war. Having plotted the route on a flying map and checked it against the cruising range of the Dakota, it is evident that this extensive flight would have used most of the available fuel (less the necessary landing reserve).

FAMILY LIFE AT HALTON

During more than three years at Halton (October 1942 to January 1946) Joy carried out wartime social service activities. One such responsibility was staying in London overnight to escort evacuee children to the railway stations from where they were sent to safety in rural areas away from major cities. On one occasion Joy shared a bedroom in London with another Women's Voluntary Service helper who was apparently undecided whether to take out her teeth and remove her wig in case there was bombing in the night. Joy thought that she was teasing, but it proved to be a genuine dilemma!

At Halton, Joy organised the distribution of cod liver oil, orange juice and rosehip syrup for children. She co-ordinated working parties knitting sweaters, scarves, socks, over-socks, hospital socks, gloves, mittens and balaclava helmets – using hard-wearing RAF blue wool provided by the RAF Comforts Committee through the officer in charge of RAF Comforts at 20 Berkeley Square in London. Joy also worked in the library at the hospital and became skilled at repairing book bindings, as well as manoeuvring a trolley of library books around the wards!

During the Halton years Hugh and Joy's elder son John was a teenager boarding at Cheltenham College and spending his school holidays with the family at the commandant's spacious Beacon Hill House at Halton. It was during this time that he met his future wife, Patricia Hay, the younger daughter of Gp Capt 'Percy' and Mrs Elsie Hay at Halton.

Beacon Hill House was a lovely family home, albeit with the constant reminder of war by the many announcements from the tannoy loudspeaker on the wall in the hallway. I once overheard my mother saying on the telephone that a bomb had landed nearby. As a child aged four I had no idea of the reality of what she was saying and went outside to look behind a hedge where I thought the bomb might be. We were fortunate to spend the war years in such peaceful surroundings as Gloucestershire and then Halton, and to be there when the war in Europe came to an end on 8th May 1945 in what became known as VE Day for Victory in Europe. At Halton a Victory Day medal was struck and one given to each of the children on the RAF camp. My sister and I still have ours.

Occasionally a few apprentices would come to Beacon Hill House for tea. It was there that the term 'an Apprentice Slice' entered the family vocabulary to describe an extra large slice of cake!

As 1945 drew to a close, with the first peacetime Christmas since 1938, Hugh wrote a poignant Christmas message for the personnel at Halton which was published in the *Halton Magazine*:

'The period between the publication of this and the last issue of the *Halton Magazine* has been marked by a continual succession of events of national and local importance, amongst which V.E. Day, Halton's Silver Jubilee, V.J. Day, the participation of the apprentices in the Thanksgiving Parade at Hyde Park and the R.A.F. Pageant at the Albert Hall, were the most prominent.

'Thus, in this brief space of six months we have seen a world at war transformed into one that is striving to recover from its wounds and to construct an atomic-proof edifice of peace.

'Although Halton seems outwardly unchanged by these great events its internal organs are being severely racked by repeated and ever increasing doses of transition medicine.

Therefore we who expect to remain in the Service, to help mould the R.A.F. of the future into its peacetime form, we find ourselves more than occupied for many months to come before that long leave we have been looking forward to since Munich comes our way.

'So in taking this fleeting opportunity, before the last W.A.A.F. clerk leaves us and we disappear from sight beneath a sea of files, forms and syllabuses, I am sure that other regulars and permanent members of the station would wish to join us in thanking our war duration colleagues for their cheerful, willing and valuable assistance to us in particular, and their Service and country in general, during the dark war years now thankfully behind as, and to wish them all the very best of luck and good fortune on their return to civilian life.

'They have all done a grand job of work and I hope that life will reward them for their great efforts and sacrifices during the war years with the health, wisdom and ability to enjoy their civilian days to the full. Especially do I wish this for the gallant remainder who are still awaiting discharge from hospital and the regular service personnel, including civilian employees at this station, with whom lies the heavy task of ensuring the continued efficiency of Halton and the Royal Air Force.

'I wish all personnel a Happy Christmas and the very best of luck in 1946.'

HALTON – A POSTSCRIPT

The Aircraft Apprentice Scheme

By the end of the war, 18,499 apprentices had graduated from Halton since the start of the aircraft apprentice scheme in 1920. Meanwhile, former Halton apprentices had contributed to all of the major air campaigns of the Second World War, both in the air and on the ground.

While former Halton apprentices who became high achievers contributed much to its legacy, Trenchard's aim in founding the scheme had been to produce a cadre of well-motivated, highly trained airmen capable of becoming competent supervisors in the direction of work and control of men. Most former apprentices did exactly that. They were the true heroes, becoming senior NCOs and warrant officers whose training taught them never to accept second best in keeping the aircraft serviceable and safe. They gave of their best in the interwar years, during the Second World War, and would do so throughout the Cold War, and rightly earned the sobriquet 'The Backbone of the Royal Air Force'. It is therefore as an apprentice engineering school that Halton will best be remembered. Trenchard summed up the legacy of Halton in a speech he gave in the House of Lords in December 1944 on the air campaign during the war, as in this extract:

> 'Some of your Lordships will remember that after the last war we set up in the air force a very large training school at Halton. It was, I believe, the largest of its kind in the world. It was a great experiment and was bitterly criticised at the time. Nevertheless, I feel justified in saying that the experiment has richly justified itself. There is no doubt at all in my opinion, that Halton and the "Halton Spirit" have been a pillar of strength to the RAF all over the world. The Halton-trained men have provided the nucleus on which the great expansion of the air force was centred. They have set and maintained an extraordinarily high standard of efficiency. You have only to look at the promotions and honours gained. A large number of these men are senior air vice-marshals and air commodores running the highest technical offices in the air force. Surely the efficient maintenance of aircraft has also been one of the outstanding features of the war and that has been made possible by the Halton training of our men.'

Following Hugh's years at Halton, during which the Jubilee Celebrations had marked twenty-five years of apprentice training, the apprentice scheme continued to flourish for a further forty-seven years until the final apprentice course passing out parade in 1993 when HRH The Duke of Gloucester was the reviewing officer.

But this was not the end of RAF training at Halton, because Halton continues as the gateway to the Royal Air Force of the twenty-first century and upholds the Trenchard tradition of excellence. Halton no longer trains aircraft technicians, but today's curriculum includes the important support trades of administration, catering and logistics; together with leadership, management and career development. Following in the footsteps of their apprentice predecessors, young male and female recruits undergo nine weeks of basic training before embarking on their trade training.

The 'Halton Spirit', the seeds of which were sown in the Royal Flying Corps and nurtured to maturity by generations of apprentices, is still evident in all activities carried out at RAF Halton. However, nothing is forever and the renowned RAF Halton is planned for closure in 2022.

Halton Hospital

After the Second World War, Halton Hospital continued to treat casualties from many theatres of British operations for the half century of the Cold War. However, with changing national requirements and policies, most military hospitals were closed during the mid-1990s as part of a Conservative government Defence Review under Prime Minister Margaret Thatcher. All eight military hospitals in Britain were closed or transferred to the NHS by 1999, along with the closure of some British military hospitals overseas. These closures in the Defence Review, which followed the end of the Cold War in 1992, had been projected to save £500 million over ten years. Under this plan Halton Hospital was closed in 1996 and demolished in 2008 to make way for 400 new homes.

White Crescent

In common with the other commandants of Halton a feature on the site was named after Hugh White. Thus RAF Halton has a small curved road named 'White Crescent'.

Hugh's long tenure as AOC and commandant at Halton came to an end in January 1946. In March, Hugh, Joy and John (in his school RAF cadet uniform) went to Bucking ham Palace for an investiture ceremony in which Hugh received the CBE from King George VI for his achievements at Halton.

For the next four years the family home was to be the lovely rural cottage of North Lodge at Cayton Park near Henley, which had been bought as a long-term home – perhaps looking ahead to Hugh's retirement during the next decade. However, for much of those four years Hugh was only able to join the family at North Lodge for occasional leave and sometimes at weekends as, in a repeat of his time in Germany after the end of the First World War, he found himself posted back to an Occupied Germany some ten months after the end of the Second World War.

CHAPTER 15

POST-WAR GERMANY – THE BRITISH AIR FORCES OF OCCUPATION

Post-war occupation by the Allies

With the ending of the war in Europe the map of Germany had been re-drawn. The Allies (Britain, America and France) were now occupying and governing the western half of Germany, and the Soviet Union was occupying and governing the eastern half. The dividing line was drawn approximately north-south some fifty miles to the east of Lüneburg Heath; in the area which had been Montgomery's eastern flank between Wismar and Domitz. The Instrument of Surrender had been signed at Lüneburg Heath on 4th May 1945 by the German Admiral von Friedeburg and Field-Marshal Montgomery. This was followed on 7th May by a second signing at Eisenhower's Supreme Headquarters Allied Expeditionary Force in Reims. Finally the definitive text was signed at the Soviet High Command headquarters at Karlshorst in Berlin, just after midnight of 8th May (on what was now the 9th May and the date recognised in Russia as the end of the war). The eastern border of Germany now lay along the rivers Oder and Neisse, known as the Oder-Neisse Line. Meanwhile, on 5th May, the German forces in Bavaria and south-west Germany had signed an act of surrender to the Americans at Haar, outside Munich, which came into effect on 6th May.[22]

Some ten months after these momentous events, Hugh flew to Germany on 3rd March 1946 in a BOAC Dakota from Croydon to the RAF airfield at Bückeburg, to take up his appointment as the command engineer officer for the British Air Forces of Occupation at the headquarters in Bad Eilsen three miles from Bückeburg.

The airfield at Bückeburg had recently been built two miles north-east of the town at the small village of Achum, on a site already surveyed by the Germans as a future airfield. This new RAF airfield was constructed using manpower from the British-controlled German Civil Labour Organisation as an airhead for passengers, mail and some freight, to support the headquarters of four organisations:

> the British Air Forces of Occupation at Bad Eilsen
> the British Army of the Rhine at Bad Oeynhausen
> the British Zone of Occupation Control Commission at Lübbecke
> the British Element in the Allied Liaison Mission at Bad Salzuflen

There was a twice-weekly flight from Bückeburg to Northolt and the airfield was also the entry and exit point for all supplies to Berlin, some 200 miles further to the east. During the Berlin Airlift, which would follow, Bückeburg was one of the airfields used for supply flights to Berlin.

BRITISH AIR FORCES OF OCCUPATION

The headquarters of the British Air Forces of Occupation was three miles from Bückeburg, at Bad Eilsen. This small spa town, located in a pleasant hilly wooded area of Germany, was largely untouched by the destruction wreaked during the long war – despite the presence of the Focke-Wulf aircraft technical design team which had been moved to Bad Eilsen in 1941 from its vulnerable location at Bremen nearer the coast. This design team under Professor Kurt Tank (who designed the successful wartime FW 190 fighter) had comprised some 2,000 personnel from the technical department together with secretarial support, which had taken over the entire spa centre, nearby hotels and other buildings. Flight testing was carried out at Hanover's Langenhagen airfield some thirty miles to the north-east.[23]

With the ending of the war, the RAF headquarters was established at Bad Eilsen in the former Bade (Spa) Hotel and other buildings which had been used by Focke-Wulf. A small RAF camp area was established in an area now known as the Englischer Garten (English Garden). This comprised a mix of utility single-storey buildings and existing buildings requisitioned for the NAAFI and airmen's' mess; with the sick quarters (medical centre) located in a picturesque old building at the rear of the area. In time an air traffic control centre operations room was established in the Kurmittel Haus (the spa health and well-being 'cure' facility) for use during the Berlin Airlift. As with the Focke-Wulf team, some houses in the local area had also been requisitioned to provide accommodation for service personnel and a few British families. There was considerable relief in the local population that the occupying forces were British and not the Russians who imposed such a harsh regime on the population in the east of Germany.

In the nearby town of Bückeburg, with its newly constructed airfield, a NAAFI shop and other facilities had been installed in the large and elegant schloss (castle) which had also been requisitioned. The official residence for the air commander-in-chief in the grounds of the schloss was known as the Farm House.

To understand the background, it is necessary to look at how this RAF headquarters came to be established in a Germany occupied by the Allies.

THE ALLIED OCCUPATION OF GERMANY

As the war had progressed, the RAF created three discreet tactical air forces (previously known as expeditionary air forces) for specific tasks in the various theatres of war. Their purpose was to achieve air supremacy in their area and carry out ground-attack and reconnaissance sorties in support of land forces during an advance. Away from Europe, the Desert Air Force, which had been formed in 1941 to support land operations in North Africa, became the First Tactical Air Force; and the Third Tactical Air Force was formed in December 1943 to support operations in South East Asia.

Meanwhile in Europe, the Second Tactical Air Force was formed during June 1943 from units within RAF Fighter Command and RAF Bomber Command to support the allied invasion of mainland Europe planned for the following year. Its role would be to provide support and air cover as the invading allied ground forces under the supreme commander General Eisenhower moved eastwards across Europe following D-Day in June 1944. The British forces for the invasion were under the command of Field Marshal Montgomery with air support provided by the Second Tactical Air Force commanded by Air Marshal Coningham.

By the time the Allies achieved victory in Europe on 8th May 1945, the squadrons of the Second Tactical Air Force had been based at many airfields in the Netherlands, Belgium and the northern area of Germany. A peacetime headquarters for the Second Tactical Air Force in Occupied Germany was established at Bad Eilsen and re-named on 15th July 1945 as the British Air Forces of Occupation (BAFO) when AM Sir Arthur Coningham handed over command to ACM Sir Sholto Douglas.

At its formation in July 1945, BAFO had two distinct but vastly different functions. The first of these was to provide an effective RAF tactical air force to support the British Army of the Rhine (BAOR) and carry out air policing of the British Zone of Occupation. The second function was the destruction of the remaining Luftwaffe facilities. This latter task was carried out under the command of AM Wigglesworth.

During the war years from 1939, Wigglesworth had served in successive appointments in the Middle East and Mediterranean rising steadily from group captain to air vice-marshal. He had then become the senior air staff officer of the Allied Expeditionary Air Force when it was formed in 1943 in preparation for the D-Day invasion. Then in 1944, as an acting air marshal, Wigglesworth became the deputy chief of staff (Air) at the Supreme Headquarters Allied Expeditionary Force (SHAEF) commanded by General Eisenhower for the sweep across Europe. With the end of hostilities in Europe in May 1945 AM Wigglesworth was the deputy chief of the Air Division at the British Control Commission and the deputy air commander-in-chief of the RAF forces in Germany – which in July 1945 was re-named as BAFO.

On 1 February 1946, AM Wigglesworth (by now Sir Philip) took over from ACM Sir Sholto Douglas as the air commander-in-chief of BAFO at Bad Eilsen with responsibility for both of the functions of the headquarters. AM Wigglesworth was therefore Hugh's boss for most of his time with BAFO in Germany.

Meanwhile, on his promotion to Marshal of the Royal Air Force, Sir Sholto Douglas would take over from Field Marshal Montgomery on 1st May 1946 as the Military Governor for the British Zone of Occupation (with its twenty-two million inhabitants) and as the commander-in-chief of all British military forces in the British Zone. His headquarters was at the British Control Commission in Lübbecke and official residence at the Schloss Ostenwalde some ten miles to the west near Melle.

During this early post-war period, the war trials were taking place at Nuremberg in southern Germany of twenty-one of Hitler's men who had been charged as major war criminals. The indictments had been read out to them on 20th November 1945 and as the months went by official papers relating to the trials were flown daily by RAF Mosquito between Germany and London. After some nine months, the hearings were completed and the sentencing given during the two days of 30th September and 1st October 1946. Those who applied for clemency had their cases considered by the American, British, French, and Soviet military governors of the Occupation Forces Control Commission during two days of deliberations. Executions of those convicted of the worst war crimes were carried on 16th October 1946.

For BAFO's routine role as a peacetime tactical air force in the British Zone of Occupation, this overseas command was initially organised in four groups, made up of twenty wings with a total of sixty-eight squadrons across twenty operational airfields in northern Germany and the Low Countries. In parallel, the American Zone of Occupation was in the southern half of Germany, and the French Zone further back.

The BAFO airfields occupied by the RAF in the northern half of Germany stretched from Sylt in the north (on the island of Sylt near the Danish border) down to Gütersloh south of the Teutoburg ridge. In between there was Jever on the north coast; Lübeck, Oldenburg, Ahlhorn, Fassberg and Celle around the North German Plain; Wunstorf close to Hanover; Gatow in the British sector of Berlin, Wahn at Cologne further west. The squadrons based at these former Luftwaffe airfields were equipped variously with Tempests, Typhoons, Mosquitos and Spitfires, for the ground-attack and reconnaissance roles.

After the initial euphoria of victory, with many formation flypasts flown by individual squadrons to celebrate their success, the task of carrying out the

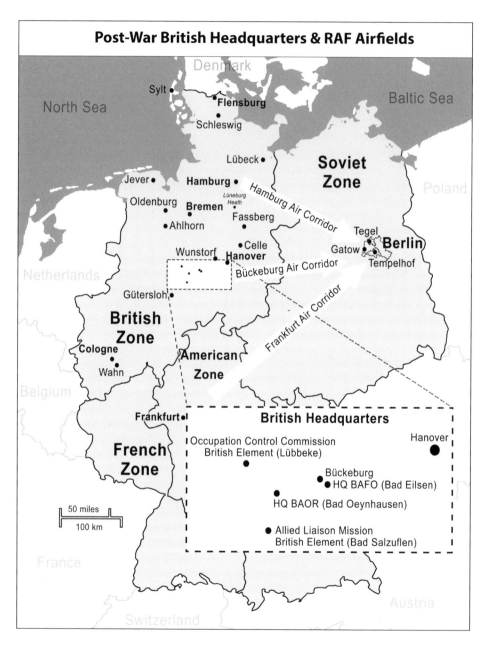

RAF Airfields, Berlin Air Corridors and British Headquarters.

flying commitments began. This was made difficult because of the widespread damage inflicted by the bombing during the war years, and the turbulence and disruption as squadrons and units began to disband, merge or were re-located or re-equipped. There was also the uncertainty of future roles for BAFO and even its place in the RAF. Moreover, the loss of expertise and dilution of skills over time posed a serious challenge for BAFO commanders. A further factor was that many of the RAF personnel were focused on returning home to seek new employment now that the war was over.

Each of the four groups within BAFO had an air disarmament wing tasked to search, identify and report war material; while the disposal of the most important material was directed by air technical intelligence. There was also the need for the German aircraft industry to be disarmed, and to dispose of the German signals and radar equipment and the associated establishments. By June 1946, 8,500 items of German equipment had been dispatched to the UK.

Another factor was that there were almost 5,000 potentially flyable German aircraft in the British zone. Some of these were taken to Britain for testing or to go to museums, but many others had to be destroyed. Then there was the danger-ous task of disposing of explosives, which included a considerable proportion of unstable munitions. This disarmament task involved over 8,000 people and was mostly completed by mid-1946.

On a lighter note, a little-known side-line of this early post-war period was that with the disbanding of the German military there was no longer an owner of the yachts in the Baltic which had been used for navigation and sea training by Ger-man naval and some Luftwaffe personnel during the 1930s. Most of the yachts were taken by the British as reparations; with a third going to Russia and a few to America. The majority were allocated to the British forces for offshore sailing. The British Kiel Sailing Club was formed and during 1946 the majority were sailed to England by servicemen, where they were known as windfall yachts. In later years most of them were transferred to private ownership; often in syndicates because of the work and expense of maintaining them. I occasionally saw them in later years when sailing with the Joint Services Adventurous Sail Training Centre at Gosport.

HUGH'S APPOINTMENT AT HEADQUARTERS BAFO

Hugh was the command engineer officer (later termed the senior technical staff officer) for the British Air Forces of Occupation. This was a complex appointment at a time of instability and change as events unfolded in Europe following the end of hostilities. It was certainly not a time for commanders to relax and enjoy the new peacetime in the challenging and continually evolving international situation.

Having arrived in Germany during March 1946, Hugh would have seen first-hand the complex post-war situation, but by then (some ten months after the end of the war) the number of former German airfields being used by the RAF was already beginning to decrease. However, there was much work to be done and with his responsibilities for all RAF technical aspects within BAFO he and his staff officers would have had their hands full. During this period Hugh would have worked closely with his colleagues Air Cdre George Scarrott who was the senior equipment staff officer; Air Cdre Hatcher the signals officer; Gp Capt Granville the armaments officer and the airfield works officer Air Cdre Doherty. During 1947 and 1948 the technical expertise of the headquarters staff increased with the addition of a second senior engineer officer and a radio specialist.

As one of the most senior officers in the headquarters, Hugh would have been involved in all forward planning in addition to his routine technical responsibilities. During his two-and-a-half years at Bad Eilsen he made 143 flights as passenger in a Dakota or Anson (and occasionally early on in a single-engine Proctor light communications aircraft) to visit RAF-occupied airfields and other destinations in Germany to see things for himself and talk with the individual unit commanders and technical officers and their specialists at the airfields. Topics of concern to discuss would have been wide-ranging including the current and future use of the airfields and aircraft, together with the technical issues such as the supply of spares and equipment for aircraft and vehicle maintenance, fuel, transport, manpower – and safety.

These flights were mostly to the British area in the north of Germany. In particular he made multiple visits to three airfields around the city of Hamburg (Hamburg/Fuhlsbüttel, Hamburg/Utersen, Hamburg/Starda) and to Lüneburg. But there were also visits to airfields around the North German Plain area at Celle, Fassberg, Ahlhorn, Lübeck, Wunstorf and Gütersloh. Other flights within Germany were to Cologne/Wahn, Nuremberg, Berlin/Gatow and Munich.

Outside Germany Hugh made flights to Ghent and Brussels in Belgium; to Eind-hoven in the Netherlands; and once to Épinoy near Cambrai in France. There were also some flights to the UK (with up to twenty fellow passengers) which may have included some personnel being posted in and out or going on leave; but the majority of travel for British military personnel to and from England was by rail and ferry.

In addition to these routine flights, Hugh also flew further afield to Occupied Austria during 1946 and 1948. The situation there had been far from straight-forward since Hitler had annexed Austria on 12th March 1938 and brought the country under his control with the Anschluss so that Austria became a federal state within Germany. This situation continued until the end of the war when the

Allies declared the Anschluss void and re-established Austria as an independent nation under allied occupation. In common with the four zones of occupation in Germany, the Allies also divided Austria into four zones; and Vienna was divided into four sectors in a similar way to Berlin. However, there were distinct differences in that Austria had been liberated by the Allies (not defeated) which meant that the nation was able to retain national unity and re-establish a democratic government early on.

During May 1946, two months after Hugh had arrived in Germany, he flew in an Anson with four staff officers of wing commander and squadron leader rank on an extensive six-day tour of the Austrian airfields in the British Zone of Occupation. They first flew from Bückeburg to Nuremberg, then onwards to Schwechat (Vienna), Klagenfurt, Zeltweg and Graz. From Graz they returned to Klagenfurt and Schwechat before flying back via Nuremberg to Bückeburg. This provided a comprehensive inspection of these Austrian airfields and their facilities, which would prove invaluable two years later when there was a potential threat of Soviet forces occupying Vienna and cutting off supply lines.

On 8th December 1947, Air Marshal Sir Philip Wigglesworth handed over command of BAFO (after two-and-a-half years as air commander) to Air Marshal Sir Arthur Sanders. By then Hugh had been at Bad Eilsen for nearly two years during which there had been much rationalisation of the RAF units in Germany. In Britain the economy was beginning to flag and the size of BAFO's forces had been much reduced. The individual group and wing headquarters were now gone and there were just ten RAF squadrons at three airfields (Wunstorf, Gütersloh and Wahn) under the control of the BAFO Air Headquarters at Bad Eilsen. Whilst these squadrons were sufficient for peacetime garrison duties, the division of Europe following the Potsdam conference held soon after the end of hostilities had required squadrons to patrol an Air Defence Identification Zone (ADIZ) extending thirty miles out from the East German border. By now Wunstorf only had a single squadron of ten Spitfire recce aircraft and two squadrons of Tempests with twenty-five aircraft total; further back from the border was Gütersloh with three squadrons of Tempests of fifty aircraft total; and back at the Rhine the airfield at Cologne/Wahn had four Mosquito squadrons with thirty aircraft total.

With these reductions, by the beginning of 1948 BAFO was down to 121 aircraft total; but with a shortage of manpower, spares and equipment, only half of the aircraft were serviceable. The manpower was depleted because of the extensive demobilisation of servicemen. Moreover, the hard-won lessons of mobility and ground attack learned during the fight across France and the Low Countries during 1944/45 were in danger of fading from the corporate memory; this knowledge and understanding was being lost with the change from offensive wartime operations to those of a peacetime force of occupation and as key experienced service personnel were posted out.

THE BERLIN AIRLIFT

But in 1948 there were other problems looming, because of the strained international relations in Berlin located perilously within the Soviet Zone of Occupation. This came to a head on 24th June 1948 when the Soviet authorities closed all road, rail and river/canal links to Berlin and the Western Allies began to re-supply Berlin by air with the Berlin Airlift.

The integrity of the Berlin air corridors had been enshrined in the Quadripartite Agreement signed in November 1945 by the four occupying powers (Britain, the US, France and the Soviet Union) which therefore enabled the Allies to supply Berlin with food and fuel by air. The Berlin Airlift began and during the next twelve months RAF Dakota, York, Sunderland, and later Hastings aircraft, together with US Air Force cargo aircraft and aircraft chartered from civil companies, supplied the city with food and fuel (including petrol and coal) by air.

As the situation had worsened during June 1948 a plan was prepared by the staff at Headquarters BAFO for the supply of British goods by air to Berlin. This plan was code-named 'Knicker', but more generally known as 'Carter Paterson' after the well-known British road transport company which had been a household name in Britain since the 1860s.

On 25th June 1948 (the day after the blockade of Berlin) RAF Dakotas were flown from Britain to Wunstorf; and three days later these aircraft began flying cargoes of food and fuel to Gatow in the British sector of Berlin. By then a British Army Air Transport Organisation and Rear Airfield Supply Organisation had been formed at Wunstorf.

At the beginning of July, RAF Avro York aircraft now based at Wunstorf began carrying freight to Berlin and RAF Sunderland flying boats were flying from the Elbe river alongside Finkenwerder airfield just west of the city of Hamburg to land on Lake Havel at the western edge of Berlin. Meanwhile, on 10th July the British Army Air Transport Organisation moved its headquarters from Wunstorf to Schloss Bückeburg and the overall British Airlift was re-named Operation Plainfare. By the end of July the first civil aircraft, a Lancastrian, flew cargo from Bückeburg to Berlin. (The Avro York and Lancastrian were derived from the Avro Lancaster bomber.)

As the airlift increased in intensity, the AOC of 46 Group in RAF Transport Command moved to Germany during September and set up his team in Schloss Bückeburg to take over controlling the British part of the airlift. Then during

October this team was combined with the American airlift team to form a joint American-British Combined Air Lift Task Force (CALTF) headquarters in the schloss under the command of US Major Gen Turner with the AOC 46 Group (Air Commodore Mercer) as his deputy. By now RAF Hastings transport aircraft had begun to fly freight to Berlin Gatow from Schleswigland (now Schleswig airport) south of Flensburg on the Schleswig Holstein peninsular. Meanwhile, BAFO fighter squadrons moved out of Wunstorf and Celle to make way for the USAF's four-engine C-54 Douglas Skymaster transport aircraft to fly supplies to Tempelhof in the American sector of Berlin. In parallel the French authorities flew freight into Tegel airport in the French sector of Berlin. However, it is understood that this was on a lesser scale because of the operations involving their transport aircraft in other theatres.[24] As time went by transport aircraft and crews also came from Australia, New Zealand and South Africa to provide additional airlift.

The Berlin Airlift was a remarkable success and this brief summary does not do justice to the extent of the extraordinary achievements made in preventing starvation of the population of Berlin and keeping the city going for nearly a year. Although the Soviet authorities ended the blockade on 12th May 1949, the airlift continued for many more months.

The statistics of the food and fuel carried are breath-taking. A total of 542,226 tons was flown to Berlin by RAF and British civil aircraft and 1,783,572 tons by US aircraft.

In addition, British aircraft flew 36,218 passengers to Berlin and 131,436 out from Berlin; while the Americans flew 24,216 passengers to Berlin and 36,584 out from Berlin.

To achieve this amazing airlift, British aircraft flew more than thirty million miles, spending more than 200,000 hours in the air and consuming thirty-five million gallons of aviation fuel. Sadly, thirty-nine British and Commonwealth men lost their lives in accidents in the air or on the ground; along with thirty-one American and thirteen German civilians

During the early months of the Berlin Airlift, before Hugh was posted back to England in October 1948, he made visits by Anson or Dakota to Fuhlsbüttel and Uetersen airfields at Hamburg, Lüneburg, Lübeck, Fassberg and Gatow (Berlin).

PLANNING FOR A VIENNA AIRLIFT

But such challenges were not confined to Berlin, because there had also been the possibility of Vienna being cut off by the Soviet authorities. During July 1945 agreement had been reached between the Allies to ensure that road access to Vienna would be available for the four occupying powers; because Vienna, like

Berlin, was located deep within the Russian zone. This agreement was followed up in June 1946 when the occupying powers established two air corridors to Vienna. One was in the American Zone from Hörsching (near Linz, some 100 miles west of Vienna); the other in the British Zone from Klagenfurt and Zeltweg (respectively some 145 miles and 100 miles by air south-west of Vienna). Both air corridors passed over Soviet-occupied territory when flying into Vienna.

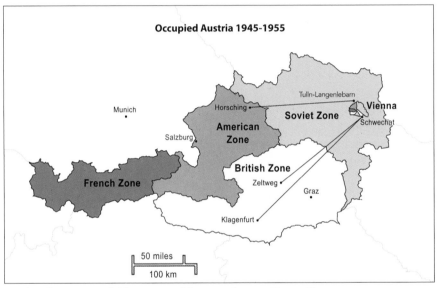

Occupied Austria 1945-1955

British and American airfields in occupied Austria and air corridors to Vienna.

Following a coup in Czechoslovakia during February 1948, the Soviets had begun to tighten their control over surface and air transport between the West and Vienna which followed a similar pattern to the build-up towards the blockade of Berlin. This situation raised concern that the Soviets might also blockade the city of Vienna; which would create a more difficult situation for the West because, unlike in Berlin, there were no airfields within the western sectors of Vienna. The reason for this was that when the borders between the zones of occupation were being drawn up during 1945 the Soviets had insisted on using the pre-1938 city boundaries. Had this not been the case there would have been four allied airfields available at Vienna. But with the pre-1938 boundaries there were only two airfields at Vienna available for American and British aircraft to land supplies; and these were several miles outside the city and could only be reached by road through Soviet-occupied territory. The airfield in the American Zone closest to Vienna was Tulln-Langenlebarn (some thirty-five miles by road north-west of the

Hugh (third from left with briefcase) visiting Zeltweg in Austria with Air Marshal Sir Arthur Sanders (in centre with back to camera) on 1st June 1948.

city centre); and in the British Zone there was Schwechat airfield (some ten miles by road south-east of Vienna's city centre).

During this uncertain time in Austria, at the end of May 1948 Hugh accompanied his new air commander-in-chief, Air Marshal Sanders, on a visit to the British airfields in Austria. On 31st May they flew in a Dakota from Bückeburg to Munich and next day to the airfields of Schwechat (Vienna), Klagenfurt and Zeltweg, which were all in the British Zone of Austria, before returning to Munich. Hugh remained in Munich, before returning to Bückeburg in an Anson on 5th June.

On 24th June 1948 (the day when the Soviets blockaded Berlin) the American army unit in Vienna warned that the Soviets might close all land routes into the city of Vienna and isolate the American and British garrisons there. By early July plans were being prepared for airlift support to the American and British garrison. Meanwhile, a survey had concluded that a parachute-drop of supplies to Vienna would not be practical because the city lacked the space for safe dropping.

During July a plan was devised to construct two 5,000 ft runways on farmland where an airfield had once stood at Kaiserebersdorf in the British sector on the south-east outskirts of Vienna (close to Schwechat). This would be constructed using perforated steel planking (PSP) to enable American C-54 cargo aircraft to land close to the city. This plan was later reduced to a single runway for use by the American aircraft (jointly funded by America and Britain) and a shorter runway for British cargo to be flown in by the smaller RAF Dakota aircraft from Klagenfurt and Zeltweg.

Although a large quantity of PSP planking was stockpiled (1.5 million square feet) to construct the proposed runways, this plan was not progressed further. As an additional safeguard, during April 1949 considerable stockpiles of provisions were brought in and stored in twenty-four warehouses in Vienna under the American operation 'Squirrel Cage'. Through much of 1948 and 1949 there had been a large amount of valuable planning and preparation, but in the event the Soviets did not blockade Vienna. In the years ahead the occupation of Austria continued by the four powers, until full Austrian independence was granted on 15th May 1955.

THE RAF IN GERMANY

Back in Germany, many of the airfields in the northern part remained in British hands through much of the 1950s with RAF squadrons operating variously from Sylt, Jever, Oldenburg, Ahlhorn, Celle, Wunstorf and Gütersloh. By then the wartime piston-engine aircraft had been progressively replaced by the jet-powered Vampire, and in turn by the more advanced jet Hunters, F-86 Sabres and Swifts. But apart from Gütersloh, these airfields together with Bückeburg were mostly returned to the Luftwaffe between 1955 and 1958. The airfield at Bückeburg re-opened in 1960 as a German army helicopter base.

In 1954 the RAF Air Headquarters at Bad Eilsen and the British Army Headquarters at Bad Oeynhausen were re-located to a purpose-built Joint Headquarters further west at Rheindahlen. The years which followed are another story, with the German air force re-established in 1955 as part of a NATO build-up to face the threat from the Soviet Union and its satellites of the Warsaw Pact nations which had been under Soviet rule since 1945.

Churchill had first used the term of the 'Iron Curtain' between east and west in his 'Sinews of Peace' speech at Missouri on 5th March 1946 – just two days after Hugh first arrived at Bückeburg. Subsequently, NATO was created in 1949 to provide collective security against the threat from the Soviet Union and over the years the international NATO structure continued to evolve in mainland Europe. This led to the creation of the international four-nation Second Allied Tactical Air Force (2ATAF). In time the re-born Belgian, Dutch and then German air force staffs were integrated into this new international command structure with Britain at Rheindahlen. The national RAF forces within 2ATAF in Germany were subsequently re-named in 1959 as RAF Germany.

Similarly, for the army, the British forces in BAOR were integrated into the four-nation Northern Army Group (NORTHAG) with the regional armies of Belgium, the Netherlands and Germany.

To the south of the 2ATAF and NORTHAG forces in the Central Region, the regional air forces of the United States, Canada and Germany were integrated into 4ATAF, and their armies made up the Central Army Group (CENTAG). Of note, the German air and land forces were split between the Northern and Central regions.

Throughout the decades of what had become the Cold War, the British presence in Germany was maintained with some 55,000 soldiers in BAOR together with the RAF Germany headquarters and squadrons of around 5,000 personnel – until the re-unification of Germany after the fall of the Berlin Wall in 1989 and the ending of the Cold War in 1992.

Finally, in 1993 the British forces of RAF Germany and a part of BAOR were re-patriated to the UK.

While he was in Germany, Hugh visited the memorial at Lüneburg Heath, where the German surrender had initially been signed on 4th May 1945. The plaque has this inscription:

HERE ON 4TH MAY 1945, A DELEGATION FROM THE GERMAN HIGH COMMAND SURRENDERED UNCONDITIONALLY TO FIELD-MARSHAL MONTGOMERY ALL LAND, SEA AND AIR FORCES IN NORTH-WEST GERMANY, DENMARK AND HOLLAND

In November 1945 the original wooden memorial plaque at Lüneburg Heath was replaced by this much larger memorial. However, after a visit to the memorial by Field Marshal Montgomery in 1958 it was moved from Germany to the Royal Military Academy at Sandhurst.

FAMILY LIFE IN OCCUPIED GERMANY

When Hugh began his time at Headquarters BAFO at Bad Eilsen in March 1946 the family remained at North Lodge until accommodation was available in Germany. At this stage their elder son John had just left school and was due to go to Cambridge University for a year as a RAF cadet, before joining the first post-war entry at the RAF College Cranwell. When accommodation became available in Germany during August 1946, Joy took my sister Diana (aged eight) and me (aged five) to Germany to join our father at Bückeburg. We travelled by train to Tilbury before crossing the North Sea on a trooping ship to the Hook of Holland. From there we continued across the Netherlands and Germany by train. At Bückeburg we moved into a large requisitioned house at 8 Georg Strasse in a residential area of the town near the schloss, two miles from the RAF airfield and three miles from the BAFO headquarters at Bad Eilsen.

This was an austere time with the German cities and economy in ruins and there was almost no contact between British military personnel or their families with the local German population. Indeed, with the Allied occupation after the war, Field Marshal Montgomery had imposed a rule for British military personnel of 'no fraternisation' with the local population. However, it was soon recognised that this policy was not realistic, because Germany was not some distant colonial outpost, and it was progressively eased in common with the Americans and not actively pursued by the time Montgomery handed over to MRAF Sir Sholto Douglas in May 1946.

The British Military Occupation authorities issued a temporary British Armed Forces occupation currency, known as 'BAFs' comprising shiny cardboard coins and paper notes valid in Sterling currency of pounds, shillings and pence. This currency could only be used in the services NAAFI shop, so there was no question of going into the local shops which had little enough stock for the local population who were desperately short of food. As in England our food was rationed, but with deliveries brought to our houses by a NAAFI vehicle (although with no fresh milk). The one thing in reasonable supply was sweets and our mother used to fill her pockets with sweets when we went for walks to give to any German children we met. The German cook in our house dried our used tea leaves to take home for her own use. The ration entitlement experienced by the German population was only a third of the entitlement in Britain, which was barely sufficient to sustain a working population. As the occupation organisation under the American, British and French military governors worked to restore Germany to a properly functioning nation again, the most pressing problem was the provision of sufficient food. Montgomery emphasised his concern about the lack of food in a memorandum to the Prime Minister Clement Attlee in February 1946, when he handed over as military governor to Sir Sholto Douglas (although Douglas did not know about this document until it appeared in Montgomery's memoirs a decade later).

Our time in Germany was a rather terrifying period of my life as a young boy as I had little comprehension of the destruction and turmoil around us. In particular I hated the Bailey Bridges (which we referred to as 'tin bridges'). These had been installed by the Royal Engineers as temporary replacements for the many bridges which had been destroyed. They rattled and shook as we drove over them which frightened me: if only I had understood the immense strength of these British structures!

The prolonged and severe winter of 1946/7 brought harsh weather to Germany and the British Isles alike. The River Weser froze solid so that the ice had to be dynamited by the Royal Engineers to keep the barges moving, leaving great blocks of ice on the river banks and floating on the water. RAF transport aircraft dropped supplies to the people on the Friesian Islands off the north coast of Germany. During these weeks there was no schooling for us children so we spent time tobogganing. This sometimes took place on a sloping track beyond the far side of the main road, which ran straight down into the road. There was little traffic then, although there was one boy whose toboggan continued onto the road when a car was coming.

During that winter we set out in our father's staff car (we had no private car in

Germany) for a short break in the Hartz mountains a little over a hundred miles east of Bückeburg. During the journey the snow on the only pre-war autobahn became increasingly deep so that we were eventually forced to turn back. Some vehicles had become stuck in the snow when crossing over the central strip to the return lane and I was frightened that we would also become stuck, but fortunately our German driver was successful. Our mother always disliked driving alone with him because she felt that he wanted to scare her by driving fast and would pretend not to understand when she asked him to slow down. Some weeks later, after the snow had thawed, we were able to travel to Bad Hartzburg for a few days to stay at the Red House which was being used as a leave centre for British families. By then the planned sleigh ride had to be a ride on a horse-drawn carriage and a visit to the quaint Cafe Winuwuk.

In contrast, during the summer of 1947 which followed, we had a day out with another family on a sailing cruiser on the huge inland lake of Steinhuder Meer near Wunstorf. It was a warm day with no breeze for sailing so we swam or waded from the boat in the warm shallow water.

In time, schooling for the British children had been organised in Schloss Bückeburg where the NAAFI was housed. The mothers took on the task of teaching but this didn't work well and eventually we had a German 'governess' who came to our house to give us lessons together with another boy who lived nearby.

Whilst in Germany our Springer Spaniel 'Vic' (so named because he was acquired on or near to Victory Day) died of poisoning. It was thought that this might have been done intentionally by locals who were antagonistic towards the British, but looking back I doubt this. It was certainly a strange and disturbing time, so it was no real surprise when another boy and I came across a stream in the undergrowth near the bottom of our garden with a thick layer of small-arms ammunition in clips along its bed. When I mentioned this find (not understanding what it was) it was speedily removed by a RAF team.

One notable feature of the house was its substantial Germanic tower, which we called the 'mystery tower'; but we children were not allowed to go up there. Our brother John managed to obtain a seat on a flight to Bückeburg to visit us when on leave from Cranwell during the summer of 1947 and of course he went up into the tower, but we had been told that it was unsafe to keep us from venturing there. Beneath the house was a huge cellar with a large and rather spooky collection of stuffed birds of all sizes mounted on stands.

Life in austere post-war Germany was difficult for our mother with her young family, in particular the makeshift schooling arrangements. Therefore, after a year at Bückeburg, we returned home to England in August 1947 to live at North Lodge until it was time for our father to complete his time in Germany. The journey home for us by train across Germany and the Netherlands was during a period of extensive flooding and for part of the journey the railway line seemed to be totally surrounded by water as far as the eye could see. After arriving at the Hook of Holland we went into a large crowded hall to wait before boarding the ship to Tilbury. While in the hall a tannoy loudspeaker message called for Mrs White to go to an office. As a small boy in those difficult times I thought that our mother was being taken away. It turned out that because she was the wife of a senior officer travelling alone the authorities wanted to make sure that she was being looked after properly. It was a relief to board the ship and travel safely back to England and North Lodge which had been let while we were away.

It would be over a year before Hugh handed over his duties to his successor (Air Cdre Frederick Vernon) on 13th October 1948 and flew by Anson from Bückeburg to Hendon after two-and-a-half years in Germany. In time, the Allies ceased to

Our requisitioned home at 8 Georg Strasse, Bückeburg – the top centre house with speckled roof and tow the far wall. Photographed during a routine training sortie in 1966, with one of the recce cameras on a Hu FR10 aircraft when I was a pilot with 4 Squadron at RAF Gütersloh.

be occupying forces in Germany, and as a part of this in September 1951 BAFO was re-named once again as the Second Tactical Air Force, before becoming RAF Germany in 1959. But this was all well in the future.

Hugh only returned to Germany on two occasions after this. In 1954 he flew for a short visit to RAF Oldenburg when HRH Princess Margaret presented a new standard to 20 Squadron with which Hugh had served during the First World War. Then, in 1973 he flew to RAF Wildenrath to spend a week with us at Rheindahlen when I was a staff officer there – but I regret that we failed then or later to discuss in any detail his time at HQ BAFO just after the war.

REFLECTIONS

As I write this some seventy years after our time in Germany during the late 1940s there are many unanswered questions from that period, in particular what happened to the family whose house was requisitioned for us and whether and when were they able to return to live there?

The Germany we saw in the late 1940s was a world away from the affluent and confident Germany I would come to know two decades later as a RAF pilot flying Hunters from Gütersloh through 1966 and a few years later when I was on the staff of the four-nation international headquarters of 2ATAF at Rheindahlen. At Headquarters 2ATAF we were a team of air force officers from Germany, the Netherlands, Belgium and Britain. In reconnaissance ops I shared an office with my boss, an Oberstleutnant (lieutenant colonel) in the German air force who had escaped from East Germany with his brother just as the wall was being built in 1961. Our international staff was headed by a German air force major-general who had been a fighter pilot during the war and had shot down many Russian aircraft while fighting on the eastern front. The attack ops team in our corridor was headed by a Belgian lieutenant colonel who had trained as a Spitfire pilot in Britain during the war. My Dutch air force colleague in attack ops had been a teenager in occupied Holland during the war, during which he was taken by the Germans and forced to become a truck driver.

One day at Headquarters 2ATAF I went to the transport office to arrange an official car for a visit to one of the air bases. The transport office was run by a German army warrant officer and when he saw the address of our rented bungalow in the village of Dalheim-Rodgen he said that we must be near neighbours as he lived in the adjoining village. As we talked I remarked on his excellent English. He smiled and said that he had learned to speak English when he was a prisoner of war under the British in Egypt. He said that this was one of the happiest periods of his life where he was well fed and safe from being sent to the Russian Front.

Being in a desert area there was no need for the camp to be fenced-in because there was nowhere for a prisoner to escape to and anyway no one wished to escape. In time we became good friends and my wife Diana and I used to visit him and his wife. He was an enthusiastic gardener but regretted that as a German he was not permitted to garden on Sundays.

Subsequently, for three years in the mid 1970s, I was back in modern Germany once again as a Harrier pilot at RAF Wildenrath and then RAF Gütersloh. During 1976 I took a detachment of four Harriers to the German air base at Fassberg towards the border with East Germany. There we took part in a five-day tri-partite flying exercise under the American, French and British 'Live Oak' organisation within NATO. (Live Oak had been created in 1959 under the auspices of NATO as a US, French and British contingency planning staff team to ensure that road, rail and air corridors remained open between West Germany and Berlin.) At Fassberg we flew in a joint exercise with American and French aircraft, to demonstrate our three-nation right to keep open the nearby air corridor to Berlin; a right established thirty years earlier in 1945. At the end of the detachment I led a mixed formation of our British Harriers and French Jaguars over the airfield as a symbol of our international unity. Although the American aircrew would have liked to fly their Phantoms in this formation, they were unable to obtain national authorisation and remained on the ground.

FAMILY LIFE BACK IN ENGLAND

Once we were back in England our family life at North Lodge was peaceful and secure. My sister and I went daily to school in Henley until we were old enough to go away to boarding school.

North Lodge had once been the gardener's cottage at Cayton Park, with its own large walled garden and orchard which needed restoring to productivity. Hugh and Joy (and John when he visited during leave) spent much time working in the garden and clearing the brambles and undergrowth around the orchard at the back of the house and in the surrounding woodland during the time before and after we were at Bückeburg. Hugh bought a red four-stroke Barford garden machine with various attachments to enable him to plough and tine the soil, cut long grass, etc. He loved this sturdy and flexible multi-purpose machine which stayed with us through the next decade. For a time he was thinking of making North Lodge into a market garden in his retirement years.

By now, John was a flight cadet at Cranwell (1946-9) and during the leave periods between terms he would arrive at North Lodge on his pre-war motorcycle; sometimes with close friends from his Cranwell entry Tim Tuke (also riding a

North Lodge, Cayton Park near Henley.

motorcycle) and Leonard Dixon (in his car with their luggage). These three were
lifelong friends during their RAF years and thereafter. As a small boy I would
hang around by the edge of the wood at the top of the narrow stony lane to our
house waiting for them to arrive.

While we were at North Lodge the corrugated iron roof of the huge barn was
painted with protective red-lead paint. One day, after John had graduated from
Cranwell and was converting to Spitfires, he flew high overhead in a Spitfire to
take an aerial photo. He said that the red roof on the barn stood out as a good

landmark. On another occasion we went to the nearby grass airfield at RAF White Waltham to meet John when he was due to land there. After he had taxyed in and come up to the control tower where we were waiting, he told us that this Spitfire was a 'clipped wing' variant which had a higher stalling speed than with the usual elliptical wing tip. As a young boy I had no understanding of whether this was a good or a bad feature. Only later, as a pilot myself, would I understand that this modification was to give it a slightly faster rate of roll, but at the expense of a slightly reduced turn rate.

John only stayed for a short time in the control tower before returning to his aircraft, so this flight was probably a land-away cross-country flight during his Spitfire conversion course at RAF Stradishall in Suffolk (April to October 1949).

Hugh could only occasionally travel home from Germany to visit the family during the year after we returned home, but we saw much more of him once he came back to England in October 1948 to be the air officer commanding of No. 43 (Maintenance) Group on promotion to air vice-marshal – taking over from AVM Harold Roach.

Family photo by Hugh's grape vine growing on the south inner face of the walled garden at North Lodge 1947-1948. Christopher, Diana, John, Joy, Hugh.

CHAPTER 16

THE EARLY 1950s – SENIOR APPOINTMENTS IN RAF MAINTENANCE COMMAND

Shaping the post-war RAF technical services

After Hugh's years in Technical Training Command through the war at 24 Group and then Halton, followed by the early post-war years in the operational theatre of BAFO in Germany, the rest of his RAF career was to be in very senior appointments within Maintenance Command.

At that time Maintenance Command comprised a headquarters and four groups with responsibility for controlling maintenance for all UK-based units. The command badge was a raven with the motto 'Service':

› No. 40 Group was responsible for all equipment except bombs and explosives.
› No. 41 Group was responsible for the supply and allocation of aircraft.
› No. 42 Group was responsible for ammunition and fuel depots.
› No. 43 Group was responsible for salvage of aircraft and equipment.

As the air officer commanding 43 Group and then 41 Group, Hugh was responsible for leading, directing and encouraging his headquarters staff and the many disparate maintenance and development units within his group. While his staff officers would work directly with these units as required, Hugh's role as AOC was to oversee the implementation of the overall policy.

It was therefore important for him to have a thorough knowledge of the work and activities of his units spread around the country, and to know their senior staff and understand the challenges they faced, whilst standing back to give them space to carry out their work under the guidance and direction of his staff.

The traditional RAF approach had long been for an AOC to carry out an annual inspection of each of his units, but otherwise only to visit when there is a particular need or a major event is taking place. The AOC's inspection is a formal occasion in the annual programme, always with a parade in those days, followed by a thorough look at the various activities of a station. It was also important for the AOC to meet and talk with as many of the officers, airmen and airwomen as possible. Another important aspect would be for him to gain a feel for the morale of a unit, including housing and family issues – so it was a matter of seeing, being seen, listening and talking. Hugh always took a close and personal interest in everything which was going on at his units.

NO. 43 (MAINTENANCE) GROUP (1ST NOVEMBER 1948 TO 30TH JUNE 1950)

No. 43 Group, which had been created in 1939, was responsible for the salvage of aircraft and equipment; with a number of specialist maintenance units under Hugh's command. In these years after the war there were many aircraft held by the group which were no longer required for front-line RAF service. These would be dismantled to remove any usable spare parts and for the recycling of the metals. The group headquarters was at RAF Hucknall, just north of Nottingham. The group crest comprised a strong arm wielding a hammer in front of the rising sun with the motto 'Servimus et Servamus' (I serve and I have served). This seems to symbolise very clearly the work ethic for the group of rising with the sun to get on with the task.

Hugh's logbook records his passenger flying in his Anson as he visited the widely spaced maintenance units within the group. These included Sealand and nearby Hooton Park (south of Liverpool), Rufforth (near York), Mount Batten (Plymouth), Aldergrove (Northern Ireland), St Athan (south Wales), Colerne (Wiltshire) and RN Arbroath (east Scotland). Hugh's personal pilot for most of these Anson flights was Flt Lt Ormston who was also his PA, as had been the tradition during pre-war years. On some occasions the Anson was used for Hugh to fly to White Waltham for weekends at North Lodge, which would have been a routine use of his aircraft in that era. These flights of an hour or less would have been a real boon for him. With a shortage of cars after the war and petrol rationing in force until May 1950 it might not have been practical to drive the 130 miles between Hucknall and North Lodge.

After Hugh had taken over as AOC of 43 Group on 1st November 1948, the final weeks of the year included flying visits to RAF Sealand and RAF Rufforth. The new year of 1949 began with a flight to RAF Mount Batten (Plymouth) for Hugh to carry out the annual inspection, where the combination of the Royal Marines band and the RAF contingent would have made an impressive parade against the backdrop of the traditional black wooden huts.

Then in early February 1949 he visited No. 23 Maintenance Unit at RAF Aldergrove in Northern Ireland, followed a week later by a flight to No. 32 Maintenance Unit at RAF St Athan in south Wales.

On 23rd February 1949 he flew in his Anson from Hucknall to Arbroath on the east coast of Scotland to visit the Royal Navy flying training unit of HMS Condor with its simulated aircraft carrier deck landing area. Following the visit, he flew back to Hucknall in a RN Beech C-45 Expeditor twin-engine eight-seat navigator trainer flown by a naval lieutenant commander. On 5th April 1949 Hugh carried out the annual inspection at RAF Sealand.

There were also sporting occasions such as the 43 Group athletic sports day. For 1949 this was held at RAF Hooton Park to the south of Liverpool on the Wirral Peninsular, a few miles from the airfield at RAF Sealand where the Anson landed – and not many miles from where Hugh had spent two years as a boy at the naval training school HMS *Conway* moored on the River Mersey.

The RAF Small Arms Association rifle shooting championships was a major annual RAF event held at the Bisley range in Surrey in June 1949. Here the chief of the Air Staff, Marshal of the RAF Lord Tedder, is being briefed by one of the organisers – Hugh (with pipe and shooting stick) is looking on.

Then in July 1949, within 43 Group, there was a competition between fire sections at the various stations, with the final being held at Hucknall at which Hugh presented the prize. The year of 1949 continued with a summer visit to No. 238 Marine Craft Maintenance Unit at RAF Mount Batten alongside the water of Plymouth Sound.

In the years to follow, RAF Mount Batten would become the RAF Marine Craft Training School; and from 1961 it was the main base of the RAF Marine Branch. Over the years the RAF Marine Branch, based at a number of locations around the coast, had an outstanding record for rescuing aircrew who had parachuted into the sea. The short but dynamic training course at Mount Batten for aircrew was second to none and saved many lives. However, with the improved capability of search and rescue helicopters and the superb Royal National Lifeboat Institution the RAF Marine Branch was disbanded in 1986.

The months went by with Hugh making a total of forty-five flying visits during his nineteen months as AOC of 43 Group. Some of these were day visits followed by staying overnight, whereas others were short – occasionally visiting two units during a single day. Sometimes his Anson would land at Andover on the way back to Hucknall to enable Hugh to catch up with his boss the AOC-in-C at the headquarters of Maintenance Command at nearby Amport House. It was certainly a busy appointment.

When 43 Group had originally been created in 1939 for the salvage of damaged aircraft and equipment through the war there had been much work to do, but by 1950 the significance of this task had reduced and the AOC's position was downgraded to air commodore. In line with this change Hugh relinquished command of 43 Group at the end of June 1950, handing over to Air Commodore H H Chapman. In the following years the salvage task for 43 Group continued to reduce and in 1956 it was absorbed into 41 Group.

When Hugh left the group headquarters at Hucknall he was presented with a large carved wooden crest with the 43 Group emblem. Below the crest is a metal plaque with the rather touching inscription:

Presented to Air Vice-Marshal H G White, CBE
by the Staff Officers of Headquarters No. 43 Group in appreciation of help and guidance received and as an expression of their sincere regret at his departure.
30th June 1950

During Hugh's time at 43 Group, their elder son John (by now aged twenty-two) had been posted as a newly trained Spitfire pilot to join 28 Squadron at RAF Kai

Tak in Hong Kong. Subsequently, during 1951 the squadron re-equipped with Vampire 5 jet fighters, which brought John into the jet era.

After leaving 43 Group in the summer of 1950, Hugh spent some time on leave at North Lodge and then attended a two-week Army/Navy/RAF Senior Special Study Period at the school of Land-Air Warfare at Old Sarum – so for a while he was back to his roots from the early 1920s when he had been at Old Sarum on the staff of the School of Army Co-operation. He then spent several weeks during the early autumn of 1950 working at the Air Ministry in London as the acting Air Member for Technical Services, standing-in for AM Sir Victor Goddard. Goddard held this appointment from August 1948 until 1951, after which this post was discontinued. During these weeks Hugh was able to use the 43 Group Anson with Flt Lt Ormston as pilot, to visit the RAF units at Martlesham Heath (Suffolk), Driffield and Leeming (Yorkshire), Kinloss and Turnhouse (Scotland), St Athan (south Wales) and Wroughton (Wiltshire).

After these few months of varied activities between postings, on 6th November 1950 Hugh took over from AVM Harold Roach as AOC of 41 Group – in a repeat of when he had taken over from AVM Roach at 43 Group two years earlier. Indeed, their careers had followed parallel paths for many years. Like Hugh, Harold Roach had been a pilot in the First World War (albeit in the Royal Navy) and had then spent time on the staff at Halton before training as an engineer at Henlow. Harold Roach had been in Singapore at the same time as Hugh when they were both wing commanders; with Roach as the senior engineering officer at RAF Seletar while Hugh was the senior engineering officer at the RAF Far East Headquarters. In Singapore they would have worked closely together in complementary roles. In common with Hugh, Roach had transferred to the Technical Branch on its formation in 1940. However, being two years older, Roach retired soon after handing over 41 Group. The most significant difference in their career paths was that while Hugh had spent most of the 1920s in flying appointments with the Bristol Fighter, and then the Westland Wallace in the mid 1930s, Roach had trained earlier as an engineer at Henlow and had remained in engineering appointments for the rest of his career.

NO. 41 (MAINTENANCE) GROUP (6TH NOVEMBER 1950 TO 5TH FEBRUARY 1953)

No. 41 Group had been formed in 1939, with responsibility for the supply and allocation of aircraft. The group headquarters was at Andover and as AOC Hugh was allocated Thruxton Manor as the family residence.

The emphasis for 41 Group was a notable contrast to that within 43 Group. Whereas the latter was focused on salvage of aircraft and equipment towards the end of the life cycle for many of the aircraft, 41 Group's role was to ensure that the front-line squadrons in Britain were kept supplied with the correct number of aircraft with up-to-date modifications to carry out the task. Thus, while the routine first-line daily servicing of aircraft and minor modifications was carried out at the flying stations, the deep servicing and major modifications for the aircraft were undertaken by the maintenance units.

This was a busy appointment with a very large number of widely spread maintenance units under the control of Hugh's headquarters. During a little over two years as AOC 41 Group, Hugh flew in his Anson (and its successor the Devon from early 1951) from the airfield at RAF Andover to visit his wide-ranging units within the group. He made a total of ninety-five visits (during 137 flights) to carry out annual inspections and to see for himself the work in hand. These maintenance units included: Wroughton, Colerne, Hullavington and Lyneham (all in Wiltshire); Kemble, Aston Down, Little Rissington and Brize Norton (Gloucestershire); Gosport and Farnborough (Hampshire); Henlow (Bedfordshire); Edgell (probably later RAF Wyton in Huntingdonshire); Martlesham Heath and Honington (Suffolk); Woodley (Berkshire); Defford (Worcestershire); Litchfield (Staffs); Silloth and Kirkbride (near Carlisle); Hawarden, Shawbury, High Ercall and Cosford (near the Welsh borders); Aldergrove (Northern Ireland); and Kinloss and West Freugh (Scotland). He also flew to visit the Armstrong Whitworth Aircraft Company at the two factory locations of Baginton (Coventry) and Bitteswell (Rugby).

For most of Hugh's time with 43 and 41 Groups of Maintenance Command, his AOC-in-C was AM Sir Thomas Warne-Browne. Hugh and Sir Tom got on really well and had an excellent working relationship; and socially Joy and Ruth Warne-Browne were good friends.

Sir Tom and Hugh were almost exactly the same age with Hugh a few months younger. Sir Tom had begun his military career as a pilot in the RNAS during the First World War before transferring to the RAF. He had then trained as a RAF engineering officer at Farnborough followed by some technical appointments. He returned to flying for a period in the mid 1930s as a Royal Navy squadron commander operating from an aircraft carrier (at a similar time to when Hugh was commanding 501 Squadron at RAF Filton). A few years later, having joined the new RAF Technical Branch at the same time as Hugh in 1940, Warne-Browne was a group captain at HQ RAF Technical Training Command in 1940 when Hugh was a group captain at HQ 24 Group in Technical Training Command; so they had been in similar areas within the RAF technical and technical training arena. Later, Sir Tom was AOC of 43 Group about three years before Hugh.

In common with Sir Thomas Warne-Browne, most of the air officers commanding-in-chief of RAF Maintenance Command had begun their RAF careers as pilots, with many undergoing engineer training in the RAF before transferring to the Technical Branch on its formation in 1940. One other such officer who had started as a pilot was AM Sir Grahame Donald who had been the AOC-in-C of RAF Maintenance Command from 1942 to 1947. It is said that in his younger years during 1917 Donald had a miraculous escape from death after falling out of his Sopwith Camel at 6,000 feet. On that summer afternoon he attempted a new manoeuvre in his Sopwith Camel and flew the machine up and over in a loop. As he reached the top of the loop, hanging upside down, his safety belt broke and he fell out. Aircrew did not have parachutes in those days; but, incredibly, as the Camel continued its loop Donald fell onto its top wing. He grabbed it with both hands, hooked one foot into the cockpit and wrestled himself back in, struggled to take control, and executed 'an unusually good landing'. In an interview fifty-five years later he explained: "The first 2,000 feet passed very quickly and terra firma looked damnably 'firma'. As I fell I began to hear my faithful little Camel somewhere nearby. Suddenly I fell back onto her."[25]

The Annual Inspection at the RAF Torpedo Development Unit at the Royal Navy airfield at Gosport (HMS Siskin) on 10th May 1951. This unit was jointly manned by RAF and RN personnel, together with scientists. A light moment ahead of the formal parade while Hugh is chatting with Captain Hawkins RN, the commanding officer of HMS Siskin.

The Annual Inspection of the RAF Marine Aircraft Experimental Establishment at RAF Felixstowe on 22nd June 1951. Hugh and the senior officers of the Marine Establishment leaving the parade. On the left of the picture is Flt Lt H J Sadd who had been Hugh's ADC since 1949. He retired as a wing commander in 1973 and remained in the RAF Reserve until 1981. Joy stayed in contact with Sadd and his wife into old age.

During Hugh's time as AOC 41 Group various options were considered for a crest and motto for the group. Of these, Hugh selected the emblem of a traditional work horse with the motto 'Provida Futuri' and he was very proud when this was authorised by Her Majesty the Queen in March 1953.

FAMILY LIFE IN HAMPSHIRE

With Hugh's posting to 41 Group in 1950, our delightful cottage of North Lodge had been sold (probably with some regret) and we moved as a family into Thruxton Manor in the small picturesque village of Thruxton near Andover. This was an idyllic place to live, in the elegant and spacious house, with a lovely main garden and thatched summer house, a separate walled vegetable garden, ancient coach house and orchard. By then, my sister Diana was at boarding school in Buckinghamshire (a few miles from Halton) and I had just started as a boarder at a prep school near Hindhead, so we children were only at Thruxton during the school holidays.

Thruxton Manor was provided with RAF staff of three and a local gardener. The staff did the cooking and cleaning. Although this was a wonderful service to have, it made meal times feel rather formal for us children. But life was busy for Hugh and Joy so it must have been a tremendous help for them. Hugh even came home for lunch some days, arriving in his black staff car with his driver and familiar number plate of 00 AB 50. While at Thruxton Joy was active helping with welfare aspects for local RAF families and providing a useful link with the service authorities to help resolve any housing or welfare problems.

The annual air show at RAF Andover each summer was a highlight for many – and certainly for me as an enthusiastic young aircraft watcher. I particularly remember one year when a Halifax bomber flew over the airfield with its four engines roaring; it then flew over on three engines, then on two – before a final flypast with only one engine powering. What a memorable sight! There were also flying displays by the early Vampire and Meteor jets.

A favourite part of the display for many was when an 'old lady' in a wheelchair would be pushed along in front of the seating stand. The person pushing the wheelchair would stop at the front of the seating area and, with back tuned, begin chatting with a technician in overalls who had been running-up the engine of a Tiger Moth parked nearby. After a while the old lady would notice the Tiger Moth and, looking cautiously to the left and then to the right, would ease herself out of the wheelchair – then with her ancient back bent, begin to hobble towards the Tiger Moth with its idling engine. The 'old lady' would then look furtively around, climb gingerly into the cockpit, open up the throttle and begin taxying erratically away. Of course at this point the technician would see what was happening and run after the slow-moving aircraft while waving his arms and shouting. By now the commentator on the loudspeaker would join in and be urgently calling out instructions to the old lady – but too late, the old lady had opened up the throttle further and with much yawing of the tail the aircraft became airborne and would be pitching and yawing as it flew uncertainly away. The pilot dressed as the old lady would then begin a series of apparently desperate attempts to land, with a great display of crazy flying while the commentator called out instructions – before eventually landing successfully and being taken away in her wheelchair. What a delight!

Each year there was an Auster to provide joy flights from the far side of the airfield and one year our father agreed to pay the ten shillings per head for Diana and me to have our first flight. It was late in the day and by then the joy flights had officially ended because the climax of the show was starting with the ground battle on the airfield and aircraft using flour bombs against the 'enemy' to the accompaniment of explosions being let off on the ground. Our flight was agreed and with this backdrop of the ground battle we took off on our first short flight.

Diana sat in the seat beside the pilot, but as the smallest and youngest I sat in a small side-facing seat behind them. Of course I had hoped to sit next to the pilot, but as I now know the centre of gravity restrictions in an Auster are critical and it would have been essential to have the minimum weight behind the front two seats. But what a delight it was to fly at last!

As a small boy during that time I remember Flt Lt Paddy Watson being my father's ADC. Some twenty-five years later in 1978, when I was a squadron leader, I spent a few months between flying appointments as a staff officer at the headquarters of RAF Strike Command at High Wycombe. One day I saw the name 'Sqn Ldr Paddy Watson' on an office door in one of the buildings. I went in to introduce myself – and Paddy talked about his time all those years earlier when he had been Hugh's ADC. By then Paddy had retired from the RAF and was working as a retired officer in

Hugh with his ADC Flt Lt E E 'Paddy' Watson, who had taken over from Flt Lt H J Sadd in June 1952.

the works services area. It was really good to meet him again and to have the opportunity for a good chat after all those years. By then Hugh was aged eighty and I telephoned to tell him, but I do not know whether contact was renewed.

While we were living at Thruxton, John and his fiancée Pat were married in Thruxton church on 8th November 1952, with their reception afterwards in Thruxton Manor. Following the wedding and their honeymoon, they did not have much time to settle into married life together at RAF Horsham St Faith because John had already volunteered for an exchange posting with the United States Air Force.

John's flying conversion to the F-86 Sabre began in January 1953 at Nellis Air Force Base in Nevada, before he joined the US Air Force 51st Fighter Interceptor Wing during the Korean War. He was based at Suwon airbase in South Korea from 3rd April 1953 until the peace treaty was signed on 27th July 1953. During his operational flying over Korea, John was often leading four-aircraft tactical formations with American pilots as his wingmen. In recognition of his achievements in Korea, including being credited with shooting down one MiG-15 fighter and a second 'probable', he was awarded the United States Distinguished Flying Cross and the US Air Medal. After John returned from Korea he was stationed again at RAF Horsham St Faith as a flight commander on 74 Squadron flying Meteors.

Meanwhile, by the beginning of 1953 Hugh had completed a little over two years as AOC 41 Group and on 5th February 1953 he handed over to AVM Gerard Combe. In common with Hugh and other senior technical officers of this period, AVM Combe was a former pilot who had transferred to the Technical Branch on its formation in 1940.

During Hugh's time as AOC 41 Group he was honoured by being appointed as a Companion of the Order of the Bath in the New Year Honours for 1952, giving him the letters CB after his name.

It had been thought that Hugh would move up to take over as air officer commanding-in-chief of Maintenance Command. However, that possibility was lost one foggy evening during 1952 when he was being driven across Salisbury Plain in his staff car on the way to or from a RAF boxing match.

In the fog his car collided head-on with an army tank transporter, which was coming the other way as it overtook a parked vehicle. As this was in the days before seat belts Hugh was thrown face first into the reinforced glass screen behind the front seats smashing almost every bone in his face. The other passenger in the rear seat was thrown forward breaking his collar bone on the edge of the open sliding window between the back of the car and the front seats. The driver was less seriously injured. They were taken to the army hospital at nearby Tidworth, where (apparently) it was decided not to operate on Hugh since he was not expected to live.

However, having survived flying during the First World War Hugh had other ideas about this and after a time he left his bed and was found walking in a ward. He must have terrified the other patients with his hideously swollen mouth and face and difficulty in speaking. Before too long Hugh's ADC Paddy Watson and Joy arrived at the hospital with his staff car and took him to the RAF Hospital at Halton. After an operation and the reconstruction of his nose without its bone, he returned home and was later able to go back to work. But the accident had taken a lot out of him, such that he found it difficult to concentrate for a full day without the need for a nap after lunch.

RAF MAINTENANCE COMMAND (5TH FEBRUARY 1953 TO 1ST FEBRUARY 1955)

Following his time as AOC 41 Group, Hugh was posted in February 1953 to the headquarters of RAF Maintenance Command at nearby Amport House as air officer administration (AOA). As a family we moved the few miles from Thruxton Manor to live in the AOA's official residence 'Winterdyne', a sizeable Victorian house with large gardens on the outskirts of Andover. In later years this house was demolished to make way for 'Winterdyne Mews'.

A few weeks before Hugh's posting, AM Sir Thomas Warne-Browne had retired from the RAF after handing over as AOC-in-C to AM Leslie Harvey (later Sir Leslie). In common with AM Warne-Browne, AVM Roach, AVM Combe, Hugh and others, AM Harvey had begun his career as RFC pilot before spending a year as an instructor at Halton and then undergoing engineering training at Henlow. After a number of engineering appointments, including in Technical Training Command, he too had transferred to the Technical Branch on its formation in 1940.

Although Hugh's appointment as AOA at Headquarters Maintenance Command would have been busy and demanding with the many personnel, organisation and administrative challenges, it would have been less strenuous and exhausting than his previous appointments as AOC of 43 and 41 Groups. For this reason it may have been the right posting for him after his very serious accident – from which he had been fortunate to survive. During just over two years as AOA Hugh made a handful of flights in the AOC-in-C's Devon aircraft to visit stations within the command, and for occasions such as being the reviewing officer at RAF graduation parades. In addition, Hugh and Joy attended the Queen's coronation in Westminster Abbey on 2nd June 1953 along with other senior military officers and their wives. They were seated on the row of dark blue velvet-covered stools which ran the length of the aisle. After this momentous occasion they were able to apply for a pair of these fine stools and my sister and I now have one of each.

After two years as air officer administration at Headquarters RAF Maintenance Command Hugh retired from the RAF on his fifty-seventh birthday, 1st March 1955.

In the years to follow, within Maintenance Command 42 and 43 Groups were to disband in 1956; followed by 40 and 41 Groups in 1961. Then on 31st August 1973 RAF Maintenance Command was re-named as RAF Support Command.

During Hugh's final year of service in the RAF he flew to RAF Oldenburg in Germany for the presentation of a new standard for 20 Squadron by HRH Princess Margaret. Thus, he was briefly back to his original Royal Flying Corps squadron with which he had flown for nearly a year during 1916 and 1917.

Opposite: Hugh with AVM Joe Hewitt, the Royal Australian Air Force Air Member for Supply and Equipment (1951-1956), during a visit to Headquarters Maintenance Command at Amport House. Amport House was later used as the RAF chaplaincy school before it became the Joint Services Army/RN/RAF chaplaincy school.

CHAPTER 17

A LONG RETIREMENT

A time to relax and reflect

When Hugh retired from the RAF the family moved to Budleigh Salterton in Devon. In time, Hugh had recovered completely from the effects of his injuries and lived a healthy life for nearly thirty more years, spending much of his time working with skill and dedication in his garden – including in the early years growing and processing four types of pipe tobacco which was possible with the mild Devon climate.

The White House, Budleigh Salterton.

By this time Hugh and Joy's elder son John was a squadron leader. During 1958-1959 he commanded 208 Squadron flying Hunters from RAF Nicosia in Cyprus, including a period detached to Amman in Jordan as part of the British Forces Jordan.

The new home at Budleigh Salterton was a few miles from Exmouth where Hugh's lifelong friend Quintus Studd lived after retiring from the RAF at the end of the Second World War. Quintus was five years older than Hugh and had been the senior cadet during their early years on the *Conway* training ship.

During the First World War Quintus had served as a bomber pilot. Then during the interwar years, he had spent much time in the Middle East as a transport pilot and then as the commanding officer of 70 Squadron. Later he became the station commander at RAF Habbaniya in Mesopotamia (now Iraq). Quintus was also stationed in Egypt as the chief flying instructor of No. 4 Flying Training School at Abu Sueir. As a group captain during the Second World War, Quintus was station commander of RAF Mount Batten. There the slipways from the two large hangars led down to the sheltered water's edge of Cattewater for use by his Catalina flying boats of Coastal Command – and from where he flew some wartime patrols.

The move to Devon also suited Joy whose good friend Hilda Corney lived nearby. Joy and Hilda had met in 1936 on the troopship *Antenor* travelling to Singapore. Later, when the Japanese invaders were approaching Singapore, Hilda fled to Australia with their daughter. However, her husband Len stayed on in Singapore and was subsequently interned by the Japanese. By the time we moved to Budleigh Salterton, Len was confined to a wheelchair, thought to be because of the effects of his harsh treatment in Changi prison.

After five enjoyable years at Budleigh Salterton, the White House was sold and in September 1959 we moved to the delightful Mill House on the estate of Plumpton Place, Sussex, where Hugh had accepted the position as manager for the gardens with its team of Italian gardeners. Although this might have seemed to be an idyllic retirement position for such a capable and enthusiastic gardener, perhaps the warning bells should have sounded when the post was advertised twice during the space of a year or so. Having regretted that he hadn't applied the first time, Hugh applied and was accepted when it was advertised for a second time. Alas, this did not work out as expected and after six months at Plumpton Hugh and Joy moved to East Dean, a few miles from Eastbourne.

The move to East Dean worked well. It was familiar territory for Hugh and Joy who had both been to school in Eastbourne and had relatives living in the area – in particular Hugh's sister Rita with whom he was very close.

By then I had left school and was a flight cadet at the RAF College Cranwell for three years of officer and pilot training. Hugh was a man of few words who rarely offered any comment or advice about my career in the RAF. However, when he did so, it was certainly worth taking careful note of what he said; because his advice was always constructive and very much to the point.

When I left home for Cranwell, his advice was simply *'never volunteer'* – this based on his experience from when he had arrived in France in 1916 and been 'nabbed' to march a group of soldiers to a rest camp several miles away.

A few years later, when I had completed flying training and operational conversion flying the Hunter, I told him that I was being posted to a squadron in Aden. His response was: 'In that case you had better write your will. Go and see my solicitor in Brighton and tell him to send me the bill.' This was certainly sound advice, because out of the four of us from my Hunter course who went to Aden in June 1963 for two years, only two of us returned.

His next advice came a few years later when I started working as an ADC: 'When you are travelling with your boss in his official car, never be tempted to start chatting because he will probably be using the journey as valuable thinking time.' This was important advice which I never forgot.

During Hugh and Joy's early years at East Dean in the 1960s their elder son John spent three years in the Far East as a wing commander. First, he was OC Operations Wing at RAF Tengah; followed by operations roles with Headquarters 224 Group at Seletar; then at Headquarters Far East Air Force at Changi; and finally in Bangkok with the South East Asia Treaty Organisation (SEATO). John's final overseas appointment during the 1970s was in the Regional Policy Section at the Supreme Headquarters Allied Powers Europe (SHAPE) in Belgium.

When John retired from the RAF in 1976, he moved with his family to Friston adjoining East Dean. Thus East Dean and Friston became very much a family home for the next two decades, with family weddings and christenings of grandchildren at Friston church.

Hugh and Joy lived in good health at East Dean for twenty-three years, during which Hugh spent much time gardening (and keeping abreast of world affairs), while Joy escaped from time to time to one of her favourite local racecourses such as Plumpton or Lingfield. Joy had an encyclopaedic knowledge of the horses, owners, trainers and riders, and loved her days out with her racing friends – especially in earlier years to her favourite course for the Gold Cup at Cheltenham.

Although Hugh maintained contact with Quintus Studd in Devon and a few friends from Royal Flying Corps days who lived locally and met up for occasional events in Eastbourne, in retirement he only visited the RAF for a few special occasions. During 1965 he flew to Cyprus for 29 Squadron's fiftieth anniversary celebrations held at RAF Akrotiri when they were equipped with Javelin all-weather fighters; and in 1980 he attended 29 Squadron's sixty-fifth anniversary at RAF Coningsby when they were equipped with Phantoms in the air defence role. By then I was commanding 41 Squadron at RAF Coltishall and during the afternoon of 29 Squadron's anniversary I flew one of our Jaguars from Coltishall to Coningsby and used a recce camera to photograph the visitors outside 29 Squadron's hangar as I flew over low. After landing at Coningsby I attended the anniversary dinner with my father, who was one of twelve former squadron commanders at this historic occasion. It was a pleasure to be able to provide the aerial photograph for the squadron's records.

By this time John's health had been declining and sadly he died in December 1982, just two weeks after his fifty-fifth birthday. John's cancer was attributed to his time in America in 1953 when he was converting to the F-86 Sabre and the American authorities were testing atomic weapons in the nearby Nevada desert. When I returned to our parents' home after visiting John shortly before he died, Hugh said that he wished it could be him instead of John.

Less than a year later, on 23rd September 1983, Joy took a mid-morning coffee to Hugh where he was working in the garden at East Dean and found him lying by an apple tree. This was a peaceful end at the age of eighty-five, to a long, eventful and very full life with all its hazards during the early years of flying through the First World War and in the years after. Hugh had known from an incident a few months earlier that his heart was weak and that he should take things more easily; but, typically, he had generally ignored his doctor's advice and continued to do as he pleased.

For some months Hugh and Joy had been preparing to move to Puddletown in Dorset to be near their daughter Diana and her family. The preparation was already well advanced and Joy duly moved to Dorset a few weeks later where she lived happily for the next fifteen years. Joy died at dawn on Easter Sunday 1999 aged ninety-four – the last of the eight brothers and sisters to go.

POSTSCRIPT

This book records the flying experiences of Hugh during the First World War and in the years to follow. But it is also a story about a young man growing up and facing considerable risk, danger and fear. Unlike so many young men who died after just a few weeks or sometimes only a few days of flying over the Western Front, he was lucky to survive and live a full life. It is also a story about a man and his family, with his sporting activities and other interests. Hugh's military service had begun on the Royal Navy training ship HMS *Conway*, and then after training at Sandhurst he began his flying career in the Royal Flying Corps. From there he served in the RAF from its formation on 1 April 1918 until he retired during the early jet age in 1955. He had therefore served in all three military services; navy, army, air force.

Many years later when Hugh was aged eighty-one, it was a very proud occasion for me when he came to RAF Coltishall to spend a few days with 41 Squadron during October 1979. Hugh had had little contact with the RAF since he retired twenty-five years earlier, but was really interested to find out what had changed and how we operated. I think what really struck him most was that despite the advances in technology with modern jet aircraft, the spirit and atmosphere of a front-line squadron was just as it had always been.

It was at about this time that I made the comment to him that none of us were getting any younger so perhaps he should write about his flying during the First World War. I am so glad that he did, otherwise his first-hand account in this book would never have been told.

At the time he simply grunted and I didn't expect anything further. It was therefore a total surprise when a year or so later he handed me a folder with a copy of his manuscript, complete with the photographs he had selected glued in place.

Hugh enjoying a drink at an informal party in the 41 Squadron pilots' crew-room, during a visit by a US Air National Guard squadron from Alabama. Seen here with Hugh and me, is our German exchange pilot Hauptmann Rolf Ahrberg and the US squadron commander Lt Col John Molini.

THE ROYAL AIR FORCE CENTENARY – 1ST APRIL 2018

On the morning of the RAF's centenary on 1st April 2018 I attended the opening ceremony of an exhibition at the Air Museum of Staverton Airport near Gloucester. One of the stands at this centenary exhibition was entitled 'An Early Royal Air Force Officer'.

The 41 Squadron dinner for Hugh and the US visitors during which I presented my father with a Bristol Fighter tie. Hugh is seated between my flight commanders Al Mathie on the left and Tim Thorn on the right. (I had just been presented with the Stetson hat by the US squadron commander!)

This stand was devoted entirely to Hugh because of his connection with Gloucestershire in 1917-1918 during his months as a Royal Flying Corps flying instructor at Rendcomb near Cirencester. The display included photographs of Hugh and some of the extracts from his flying logbook from that period and during his time flying on the Western Front. Hugh would have been surprised (but no doubt delighted) to have been remembered in this way so many years later.

Back in 1917, when the telegram about his brother Beresford's death was delivered to their parents at the Poplars, it did not name Beresford but simply stated, 'The King and Queen deeply regret the loss you and the army have sustained by the death of your son in the service of his Country. Their majesties truly sympathise with you in your sorrow.' (See page 220.)

With the very short life expectancy of a pilot in those days it was assumed initially that they must have lost Hugh. But this was not the case, as Hugh's long life still had many years to run.

Per Ardua Ad Astra

Letter of Recommendation – May 1918

Copy of original document in Hugh Granville White's personal archives

CONFIDENTIAL c.3/214.

To: Officer Commanding 11th. Wing R.A.F.
From: Officer Commanding No. 29 Squadron, R.A.F.

Sir,

      I have the honour to recommend the under-mentioned officer for immediate award:-

    2nd Lt. (T. Capt.) H. G. White   1 East Kent Regt.
    Hugh Granville   attd. R.A.F.

This officer served from July 1916 to June 1917 in No. 20 Squadron as a Pilot.

      On 5th April 1917 he drove down an Albatros Scout and forced it to land this side of the lines, near Neuve-Église. On 23rd May 1917 he crashed a hostile machine in the vicinity of Gheluvelt (unconfirmed).

      This officer has now served as a Flight Commander in this Squadron since 26th February 1918.

      On May 17th 1918 he drove down and completely destroyed a hostile machine (in flames) in the vicinity of Merville. On May 18th he drove down a hostile machine completely out of control and it was seen to crash in a field about 1½ miles west of Estaires. On 19th May he destroyed a hostile machine in the vicinity of Bailleul.

The following facts with regard to the destroyal of the last-mentioned machine:-

      Captain White was leading a patrol at 6,000 ft east of Bailleul and encountered nine hostile scouts. Three of his patrol were driven west almost immediately and Captain White was left alone. He dived on one of the E.A. and fired about a hundred rounds at very close range. The E.A. 'zoomed' to the left and its top plane caught the leading edge of Captain White's machine causing the E.A. to turn a cartwheel over his (Capt. White's) machine. The shock of the collision flung Captain White forward onto the gun mounting and stopped the machine. The E.A. went down into a dive and Captain White – expecting his machine to break up at any moment – dived after him, firing about a hundred rounds. The right wing of the E.A. fell off and it went down completely out of control.

Captain White then turned round, and turned West to endeavour to re-cross the lines. He was followed back by five E.A. scouts for some distance until they were driven off by friendly machines. Captain White managed to keep his machine fairly straight by putting on hard left bank, left rudder and leaning over the side of the cockpit. Near the ground the machine became uncontrollable and it crashed on landing near Ecke. The centre section wires of the machine were broken and the right-hand planes had anhedral instead of dihedral. The top right-hand plane was badly damaged but the main spars held. The fabric was completely torn off.

Captain White has led two attacks on hostile balloons, one on 18th May and one on 19th May. He drove down one balloon on 18th making the observer jump out.

> I have the honour to be, Sir,
> Your obedient Servant,
> (sgd) C.H. Dixon. Major.
> O.C. No. 29 Squadron, R.A.F.

In the Field. 20.5.18.

Royal Air Force War Communiqué 1918

Copy of original document in Hugh Granville White's personal archives

Extracts from Official Royal Air Force Communiqués concerning Capt. H. G. White.

Communiqué No.7. May 17th 1918

Capt. H. G. White, 29 Sqdn, managed to cut off an E.A. Scout from its formation and after manoeuvring for a short time got on to the tail of the E.A. and fired a burst into it, whereupon black smoke was seen issuing from the E.A. which went down out of control, followed by Capt. White still firing. The smoke from the A.A. gradually increased and when last seen the E.A. was still going down out of control and on fire.

No.7 cont. May 18th 1918.

Capt. H. G. White, 29 Sqdn, whilst leading an offensive patrol engaged one of a formation of E.A. Scouts and fired fifty rounds into it, following it down and firing further bursts into it at fifty yards range. The E.A. went down completely out of control. Capt. White followed it down to within five hundred feet of the ground and was forced to break off the combat owing to his gun jamming. Another pilot of the same patrol confirmed the E.A. as having crashed 1½ miles West of Estaires.

Lt. C. J. Venter, 29 Sqdn, dived on another E.A. firing seventy rounds into it. The E.A. went down emitting smoke which gradually increased and eventually burst into flames. This is confirmed by Capt. H. G. White as going down in flames.

Lt. R. H. Rusby, 29 Sqdn, got on to the tail of an E.A. Scout which was following down another of our machines. He fired a burst of a hundred and fifty rounds in to E.A. which went down completely out of control. This is confirmed by Major C. H. Dixon.

<u>No.7 cont. May 19th 1918</u>

Lt. F. J. Davis, 29 Sqdn, attacked an E.A. Scout at thirty yards range. After fifty rounds had been fired the E.A. turned on its back and was observed to crash near La Crèche.

Lt. C. J. Venter, 29 Sqdn, attacked an E.A. 2-seater over Nieppe Forest and fired four hundred rounds. The E.A. dived east with smoke issuing from it and was confirmed to have crashed by an anti-aircraft battery.

Capt. H. G. White, 29 Sqdn, dived on a Pfalz Scout. After firing fifty rounds he zoomed up and collided with the E.A. which rolled over and went down vertically, followed by Capt. White who, after firing another hundred rounds into it, saw the wings fall off in the air. Capt. White's engine stopped and he crashed on attempting to land as his machine was more or less out of control.

RAF operational message
dated 5th May 1918

Copy of original document in Hugh Granville White's personal archives

S E C R E T

To: O.C. No. 29 Squadron, R.A.F.
From: H.Q. 11th Wing, R.A.F.

      The following letter of instructions from the G.O.C. 2nd Brigade is forwarded for strict compliance and communication to all pilots.

In the Field   (Sd). H. A. VAN RYNEVELD, Lt Col
5.5.18   Commanding 11th Wing R.A.F.
GS/29

To: O.C. 11th Wing
From: H.Q. 2nd Brigade

      Several cases have occurred in the last few days of machines of this Brigade bombing and shooting our own troops.

      Until the weather completely clears up and visibility can be called good, no bombs of any sort will be dropped or MG fire opened at ground targets in the Corps Areas N of YPRES-COMINES canal. In this area our outpost line is some thousands of yards in advance of our main line, and most difficult to distinguish.

      On the rest of the Army front extreme caution must be observed by all pilots.

      The front-line trench system may not be bombed or shot at.

It must be made clear to all pilots that ill-directed bombing is likely to make low flying by our contact control machines impossible, owing to fire from our own infantry. If our machines cannot work in complete confidence over our own infantry, the results may be disastrous.

<u>Under no circumstances whatsoever may fire from the ground be taken as a reason for dropping bombs in that vicinity.</u>

All machines carrying bombs are to be given definite objectives such as dumps, villages, roads, etc. Bombing at the discretion of pilots is no longer permitted except during an attack by ourselves or the enemy. In cases of enemy attack all restrictions are removed from the threatened area for the time being, but the utmost attention must be paid to distinguishing friend from foe.

Squadron Commanders are to ensure that every pilot in their command understands this order, as a Court of Enquiry and disciplinary action is likely to follow the next bombing or shooting of our own troops.

In the Field.   (Sd). T. I. WEBB-BOWEN. Brig General,
5.5.18   Commanding 2nd Brigade, R.A.F.
G.14/227

RAF operational message dated 20th May 1918

Copy of original document in Hugh Granville White's personal archives

To: O.C. No. 29 Squadron R.A.F.

Can you please say if any of our machines have encountered anti-aircraft fire from shrapnel producing a pronouncedly pink burst? If so, can you give the areas over which this has occurred, as it would indicate the presence of Austrian A.A. Guns.

(H.Q., R.A.F. – F.I 33, d/d 19.5.18)

Please say.

	(Sd) HW Guy
	Capt & Adjt.
In the Field	for Lieut. Colonel,
20.5.18.	Comdg 11th Wing, R.A.F.

To: O.C. B Flight

Please let me have a report on the above no later than 12 o'clock noon tomorrow.

In the Field	(Sd.) C. H. Dixon, Major.
20.5.18	O.C. No. 29 Squadron, R.A.F.
G.14/1/227	

Royal Flying Corps (Military Wing): Rules for Flying (Aeroplanes and Airships)

ROYAL FLYING CORPS (Military Wing).

RULES FOR FLYING (AEROPLANES AND AIRSHIPS).

1.—Aircraft meeting each other.

Two aircraft meeting each other end on, and thereby running the risk of a collision, must always steer to the right. They must, in addition to this, pass at a distance of at least 100 yards.

2.—Aircraft overtaking each other.

Any aircraft overtaking another aircraft is responsible for keeping clear and must not approach within 100 yards on the right or 350 yards on the left of the overtaken aircraft, and must not pass directly underneath or over, save when the vertical distance is in excess of 800 feet. No aircraft shall remain persistently below or above another. In no case must the overtaking aircraft turn in across the bows of the other aircraft after passing it or move so as to foul it in any way.

3.—Aircraft approaching each other in a cross direction.

When any aircraft are approaching one another in cross directions, then the aircraft that sees another aircraft on its right hand forward quadrant—from 0 degrees (*i.e.*, straight ahead) to 90 degrees on the right hand constitutes the right hand forward quadrant—must give way, and the other aircraft must keep on its course at the same level till both are well clear.

4.—Distance to be maintained from Airships.

When one of the aircraft is an airship, the distance of 100 yards prescribed above shall be increased to 600 yards.

5.—Long glides and quick rises.

Except when pre-arranged for instructional purposes or in cases of emergency, long glides and quick rises will be practised only to and from the usual landing area.

6.—Position of other aircraft to be noted before starting.

Aeroplane pilots will when starting carefully note the position of other aircraft and will be responsible for keeping clear of them.

7.—Danger flag to be hoisted before aeroplane flying commences.

No aeroplane flying will take place without a red flag being hoisted at the appointed place as a warning to all concerned. In cases where the flag is likely to be mistaken for other danger flags, the flag of the Royal Flying Corps will be hoisted immediately below the red flag.

When the flag is flying, no unauthorised persons are to be allowed in the prohibited area.

8.—Officer responsible for regulation of aeroplane flying.

The senior officer belonging to an Aeroplane Squadron of the Royal Flying Corps (Military Wing) present on duty in the landing area will be responsible for and control the flying of all aeroplanes using an aerodrome or landing area reserved for War Department use (except aeroplanes flying at Farnborough under the control of the Superintendent of the Royal Aircraft Factory), and persons on duty in connection with such flying.

9.—" Stop " signal.

The " stop " flag (international code flag 'S,' *i.e.*, a square white flag with a blue square in the centre) will be the signal for all aeroplanes in the air to return to the landing area; it will be hoisted when necessary by the order of the Officer referred to in para. 8. This Officer may also suspend anyone from flying pending enquiry.

10.—Rolling practice.

Rolling practice will not take place on the landing area whilst aeroplanes are flying.

11.—Beginners practice area.

Beginners will be restricted to such area as may be prescribed by the Officer referred to in para. 8.

12.—Landing Marks.

Permanent marks will be made on the ground at the usual landing place to indicate the nearest points at which it is safe for aeroplanes to land in directions facing the sheds, etc. An aeroplane landing in such a direction must be on the ground before it reaches the point in question.

13.—Flying over towns.

Flying unnecessarily over towns and villages is to be avoided.

14.—Dogs.

No dog not on a leash is allowed in the starting and landing area while flying is in progress.

F. PARKER, PRINTER, FORTON, GOSPORT.

Copy of letter to a magazine about the R.E.7 Reconnaissance Experimental Aircraft

You may be interested to know that one of the 'remarkable' three-seat versions of the R.E.7, fitted with a Rolls-Royce Eagle engine, was in service with No. 20 Squadron in France from about August 1916 until it crashed on the date of its withdrawal on January 31st, 1917.

Its armament consisted of two free Lewis-guns and one fixed Vickers-gun firing through the propeller – including, on occasions, the blades. When in action the front gunner had to perch himself precariously on a Scarff ring fitted in the top centre-section, but all too frequently came adrift when rotating the gun mounting and invariably finished up in the pilot's cockpit.

The ingenious R.A.F. periscope bomb-sight was fitted for use by the pilot, but since not one of the many 500-lb bombs dropped from this aircraft was ever seen to explode, this excellent piece of apparatus proved to be entirely superfluous.

H G WHITE,
Air Vice-Marshal H.Q. Maintenance Command, Royal Air Force
(Written during 1953-1954)

Lieutenant Herbert Beresford White
23rd Brigade, Royal Field Artillery
3 October 1895 – 13 April 1917

Buried Chocques Military Cemetery (Grave Ref V.A.2)

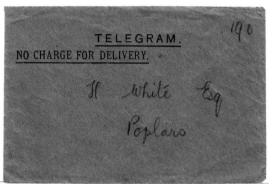

Beresford's death was reported in the local Maidstone newspaper, *South Eastern Gazette*, on Tuesday 24th April 1917. The newspaper reported that Beresford had been educated at Eastbourne College, where he had won the Duke of Devonshire prize for mathematics. It went on to say that after Eastbourne, Beresford had gone up to the Royal Military Academy at Woolwich from where he graduated in August 1914. The paper noted that Beresford had gone out to the Western Front in June 1915, but that during 1916 he had contracted trench fever and been sent home on sick leave for five months. It continued that Beresford had returned to France in November 1916. The newspaper also noted that during his time in France, Beresford had been involved in three great advances.

Beresford's lieutenant colonel wrote to his father Herbert White:

'It is with very great regret I have to inform you that your son, Beresford, was today accidentally killed. We were marching, and your son dismounted and was inspecting a gun team when the off-centre horse kicked out and caught him on the chest, just above the heart, and knocked him down. He got up, and then fell down dead. We all deeply deplore his loss; he was a very popular officer, very keen in his work, and took the greatest possible pride in his section. In action he always bore himself in a most gallant manner. We miss him very much, and we deeply sympathise with you and Mrs White in the great loss you have sustained. It is very sad to think that such a young life and such a promising career should be cut short in such a way. I can only hope that time will soften the blow which has fallen on you and yours.'

There was also a letter from Beresford's brigadier-general:

'I am writing to tell you how extremely sorry I am of the sad bereavement to you and your family in the loss of your son in the -----Battery, R.F.A. He was a most promising officer, and one of the best subalterns under me. He came under me soon after he came out here last year, and has done wonderful work ever since. He was very good and brave while with his Battery in the line, and managed his men so well. Under him they improved as soldiers, very much. He was proud of their work and they were fond of him. I sympathise with you and your family in your sad loss, and the country has lost a valuable officer.'

Colonel Frederick Minchin

During Hugh's leave at the Poplars with his sister Rita in late May and June 1918, they were visited by a Colonel Minchin who came to stay for a few days. Minchin had landed at Maidstone in an Avro 504K and during the stay he and Hugh flew to Langney airfield to the east side of Eastbourne and returned later the same day.

Coincidentally, Minchin and Hugh had both been educated at Eastbourne College, albeit not at the same time as Minchin was eight years older than Hugh. Minchin had subsequently graduated from Sandhurst in 1909 and later learned to fly at Langney airfield Eastbourne during 1912/1913 while on leave from the army. It is not clear how well Hugh and Rita knew Minchin but there are photos in Hugh's album of him in his Bristol Monoplane C4990 and having made a forced landing in a field with a Bristol Scout K1789 during July 1918.

Colonel Minchin had an impressive record as a pilot during the First World War having been awarded the MC and Bar and later the DSO. After the war he served in India and was appointed CBE before leaving the RAF and becoming an airline pilot with the Instone Airline at Croydon and Imperial Airways.

Flight magazine reported on 8th September 1927 that on 31st August Frederick Minchin had set off from Upavon in a Fokker F.VIIA tri-motor aircraft in an attempt to be the first aviator to cross the Atlantic from east to west. Flying with him were Captain Leslie Hamilton and Princess Anne of Löwenstein-Wertheim-Freudenberg who was also an experienced aviator. They were last seen by a ship some 800 miles west of Galway heading for Newfoundland, but they were not seen again and their fate is still unknown.

Hugh and Rita with Colonel Minchin at the Poplars in June 1918.

Colonel Minchin (flying as pilot from the rear seat) and Hugh (front seat) in the
Avro at Maidstone.

No. 20 Squadron casualties
(4th July 1916 – 3rd June 1917)

No. 20 Squadron casualties during the period Hugh was on the squadron 4th July 1916 – 3rd June 1917 (written in the back pages of his first flying logbook).

First page

Lt Fauvel (wounded owing to crash).

Sergt Mottershead V.C. D.C.M. (died of wounds received
during combat).

Lt Gower M.C. (wounded in aerial battle)

Capt Hartney ("   "   "   "

Lt Jordan ("   "   "   "

Lt Golding ("   "   "   ")

Lt Gibbon (killed   "   "   ")

Lt Dabbs (wounded by archie)

Capt Depuchar ("   "   owing to crash)

Lt Anderson M.C. (missing).

Lt Woolley (missing)

Lt Smith ("   )

Lt Irene ("   )

Capt Jones - . (killed in aerial battle)

Lt Moyes ("   "   "   ")

Lt Hampson ("   "   "   ")

Lt Lawson (wounded   "   ")

Cpl Reach (wounded by archie)

" Johnston (killed)

" Houghton (killed)

" Sergt Boyd ("   )

"   " Bird ("   )

Second page

Date and Hour	Wind Direction and Velocity	Machine Type and No.	Passenger	Time	Height
Cont^d.			Lt Robertson (wounded)		
Lt Bacon (missing)			Capt Knowles M.C (")		
Lt Martyn (")			Pte Blake (missing)		
Lt Burns (")			Pte Worthing (")		
Lt Story (wounded)			Pte May (")		
Lt Wilkinson (")			Lt Hazilline (wounded)		
Lt Conder (")			Lt Boucher (wounded)		
Sergt Attwater (missing)			Lt Cunnel (killed)		
Lt Davies (")			Lt Birkett (wounded)		
Lt Johnson (wounded)			Lt Stevens		
Lt Marsh (")					
Lt Neville (killed)					
Lt Scott (wounded)				75	
Capt Thayer M.C.² (missing)					
Lt Howarth (wounded)					
Lt Baring Gould (wounded)					
Lt Cogswell (wounded)					
Lt Perry (wounded)					
Pte Allum (")					
Capt Cubbon M.C.² (missing)					

Third page

Hugh Granville White Q&A

A resumé from Hugh's written answers to a researcher

With which squadron did you first serve and where were you stationed?

I was posted on 4th July 1916 to 20 Squadron – a general-purpose squadron equipped with F.E.2D pusher-type aircraft at Clairmarais airfield – between St Omer and Cassel. Duties included offensive patrols; bombing of enemy airfields, railway sidings and marshalling yards, ammunition dumps, etc.; general photographic reconnaissance; escorting and protecting aircraft of other squadrons engaged on distant bombing objectives, or on artillery co-operation duties. During the eleven months I was with this squadron, it operated on the same front from north of Ypres down to La Bassée in the south, although it moved to Boisdinghem in January 1917 and later to Sainte-Marie-Cappel.

In your opinion, what were the best combat types of the period?

Up to the end of 1915 air combats were few and far between as the only armament consisted of revolvers and shotguns. In the early part of 1916 the best combat aircraft on the Western Front in France – or elsewhere – was the German Fokker Eindekker E1 scout – to which the Dutch designer had fitted a workable interrupter gear to enable a forward-firing machine gun to be fixed along the line of flight and fire through the airscrew arc. The British reply to this was the D.H.2 scout and the F.E.2B and F.E.2D, which were all pusher-type aircraft so that fixed and moveable machine guns could be fitted to fire over a very wide field of fire in almost every direction except immediately behind and below the tail. The F.E.2D in my time had three machine guns: one fixed to fire forward and two moveable ones in convenient positions for use in other directions. Other tractor aircraft, like the Nieuport Scout and Sopwith Pup, had single Lewis guns mounted on the top plane to fire forward over the top of the propeller.

Thereafter first one side, then the other, produced new types of replacement aircraft with progressively improved performance; and all fitted with efficient forward-firing machine guns both through and above the propeller. Whilst in the case of two-seater aircraft a further machine gun, mounted on a moveable scarf ring was used by the observer/gunner to fire sideways, backwards, above and below. Pusher types faded out in the latter half of 1917 and thereafter until the end of the war the best British combat types of aircraft, but having different roles, were the S.E.5a, Bristol Fighter and Sopwith Camel.

How good were the aircraft in those days: were they fairly good or were they dangerous to fly?
Early types of aircraft were only dangerous to fly because until the latter part of 1917 pilots only received very elementary instruction before being sent off solo to 'juggle with death' as best they could. Thus, because they didn't know any better, they might lose flying speed at low altitude and dive into the ground, out of control; or again, through faulty flying, get into a spinning nose dive, from which no-one even knew, let alone told a pupil, how it was possible to regain control – for, by following the few control movements a pupil had been taught, the more certain he would never regain control before hitting the ground.

It was not until late 1917, when some of us got down to analysing the art of flying, and deliberately committed every possible fault to see what happened, and then discover the best way of getting out of the resulting difficulties, that a special School of Flying was set up, under Colonel Smith-Barry at Gosport, to train flying instructors who would be capable of teaching the whole art of flying from A to Z.

Another problem with earlier types of aircraft was a certain degree of engine unreliability, which often resulted in unexpected forced landings. Sparking plugs on rotary and radial engines were inclined to oil up, and petrol pressure systems were both complicated and unreliable. Also, with rotary engines, continual adjustment of throttle and air mixture levers was necessary to maintain full power and the engine would often cut out completely in the midst of a 'dogfight' when the mixture went haywire when alternately diving and climbing.

Was flying in those days as it is sometimes portrayed in films, or was it dangerous work with no frills?
Operational flying in 1916, 1917 and 1918, was always dangerous; and the aircrew suffered considerable hardship and discomfort, particularly during winter months. The issue of flying clothing hardly kept one warm on the ground at around zero temperatures, so that flying in the open air, with little protection at 12,000 ft to 14,000 ft with no oxygen or heating for up to three hours at a time was pure misery, and often resulted in severe frostbite. Added to this was that as all operational missions were carried out beyond the enemy lines, we were subjected to almost continuous anti-aircraft fire from the moment we crossed the lines until we re-crossed them on the way back. 'Archie', as we called it, only let up when we were being harried or attacked by a superior force of enemy aircraft

(EA), when we would either fly in a circle to maintain formation and to guard each other's tails and let them come and sample machine-gun fire from several directions; or else, if our objective had already been completed, and there was no need to maintain formation, we would make it a 'dogfight' and then head for home. There was definitely no frill or glamour in this kind of warfare, and the casualties and losses were severe.

How good were the German aircraft and pilots that you flew against?
There were a few very good German fighter squadrons, e.g. Richthofen's Circus and other star performers; but, through my time in France, German aircraft were seldom seen or able to penetrate over our side of the battle lines. We were always prepared to take on up to twice our number of Germans.

Much has been written about the chivalry in the air; is that the way it really was? Did many pilots have any personal animosity against the Germans, or were they just the enemy?
Yes, I think there was a certain degree of chivalry in the air. For instance, on one occasion I was attacked by two EAs when on my own directly over the trenches at about 10,000 ft. Having driven off one of them, I found, after firing a burst at the other, that he was in some kind of trouble and also his engine appeared to be failing. I therefore flew close alongside and conveyed, by pointing and shaking clenched fist, that if he glided down and landed on our side of the lines I would hold my fire; otherwise I would finish him off. He gave in and landed on our side, and I visited him next day in hospital and gave him a box of cigarettes. Was this chivalry I wonder?

Towards the end of the war, when some aircraft were equipped with parachutes I heard of a few instances when German aircrew had shot up aircrew members who had bailed out, so this chivalry may have started to wear a bit thin by that time. We treated the Germans as the enemy and nothing more.

In *No Parachute*, AVM Arthur Gould Lee wrote that 'there were few flyers with any degree of experience in air fighting who were not obsessed to some degree, though usually secretly, with the thought of being shot down in flames.' Was this something that you thought about very much?
Operational flying before parachutes were supplied was naturally full of all kinds of possible hazards, including being shot down in flames; but we never allowed our thoughts to dwell on such matters. I think most of us would agree that it was soon enough to worry about such things when, if ever, they actually happened.

In the same way as the average motorist doesn't dwell on the possibility of being trapped inside a burning car.

When you shot at an enemy aircraft did you think much about the man inside, or was it just a machine that had to be destroyed in order to survive?
We only thought about shooting an enemy aircraft or observation balloon down and not the man inside.

Do you remember any details of what you would consider to be your most dangerous or exciting mission?
The final now-or-never decision to descend through dense fog in a forlorn effort to land in unknown country could quite well come into this category. All too many of the squadron sadly failed to make it.

An equally unpleasant, but exciting experience, while it lasted, was colliding with a German aircraft in the midst of a 'dogfight'. Whereas his aircraft largely disintegrated, my S.E.5 with propeller smashed, some wing fabric torn away, rigging wires slack or missing – was just sufficiently controllable to enable me to get back across the front-line trenches before crashing. Although attacked twice on the way down, the first EA's gun luckily jammed after the first few rounds, and although another EA took his place close behind, I threw out an empty Lewis gun ammunition drum, and this damaged his propeller and caused him to turn away.

ENDNOTES

CHAPTER 3

1. Lt Frank Billinge was born in 1894 and commissioned into the Manchester Regiment in 1914. He was a founder member of 20 Squadron in September 1915 flying as an observer/gunner. He flew as Hugh's crew for a few weeks during July and August 1916 before returning to England for pilot training. He subsequently joined 32 Squadron flying the D.H.2 and was promoted to be a flight commander in 1917. In 1918 he joined 56 Squadron as a flight commander flying the S.E.5a. During the war he shot down a total of five enemy aircraft as air gunner and then pilot and was awarded a DFC in 1918. He died on 28th September 1928 aged thirty-three years. (Courtesy of The Aerodrome website)

CHAPTER 4

2. Wenman 'Kit' Wykeham-Musgrave (1899–1989) was a Royal Navy midshipman who survived being torpedoed when onboard or trying to board three separate ships during 22nd September 1914 (HMS *Aboukir*, HMS *Hogue* and HMS *Cressy*). He was eventually rescued by a Dutch trawler after hanging onto a piece of driftwood.

CHAPTER 5

3. Hugh flew his Nieuport Scout B3637 to Marquise on 19th April. From the next day his aircraft was a S.E.5a (D3942), which is depicted on the front cover.
4. My father told me that if there was a need to land on rough terrain the danger in landing straight ahead was the likelihood of the aircraft pitching forward heavily over the nose which would probably kill the pilot. By contrast the application of full rudder just before touching down would cause the aircraft to hit the ground sideways with a wing taking the initial impact. The aircraft would then cartwheel with the energy being absorbed by the wings as they collapsed. This might give some protection to the fuselage and improve the pilot's chance of survival.
5. This would have been caused by the differential in air pressure between the atmosphere and pilot's middle ear, which stretches the ear drum inwards during a descent. At this early stage of aviation it was not commonly realised that this pressure differential could be balanced out by squeezing the nose and blowing to 'clear' the ears (known as the Valsalva Manoeuvre).
6. While at No. 9 TDS Shawbury Hugh flew the R.E.8, D.H.6, B.E.2e, and Avro

504K.

CHAPTER 6

7. Hugh was billeted in a house at Lortzingplatz on the west side of Cologne near the Stadtwald park with tennis and other sporting facilities and a beer garden.

CHAPTER 7

8. The term 'shooting the pond' occurs many times in Hugh's logbooks, at various airfields. The prepared pond in a suitable location near the airfield would have a floating target so that the rounds could be spotted as they hit the water.

CHAPTER 9

9. Battle scenario on Brett Holman's website airminded.org 2011 from *Flight* magazine 5th July 1923.

CHAPTER 10

10. Derek O'Connor *Aviation History* magazine, July 2012.
11. Air of Authority – www.rafweb.org
12. Air of Authority – www.rafweb.org. Air Force list for 1924.
13. *The Royal Air Force: An Encyclopedia of the Inter-War Years. Volume 1: The Trenchard Years 1918-1929*, Wg Cdr I M Philpott, Pen & Sword Aviation, 2005.
14. Air of Authority – www.rafweb.org. Air Force list for 1924.
15. Air of Authority – www.rafweb.org
16. Derek O'Connor, *Aviation History* magazine, July 2012.
17. Air of Authority – www.rafweb.org
18. In support of this conjecture, there is uncorroborated reference on the internet that John T Whittaker took over as OC 28 Squadron for a second time on 16th September 1927.
19. *The Moon's a Balloon*, David Niven, Penguin, 2016, pp.125-126.

CHAPTER 13

20. www.rafcommands.com/archive/02280.php

CHAPTER 14

21. Bob Pooler, worcestershirepolicehistory.co.uk

CHAPTER 15

22. Military Histories – The Three Surrenders

www.militaryhistories.co.uk/surrender

23. Courtesy of Herr Manfred Tegge https://www.relikte.com/eilsen/

24. https://historum.com/threads/berlin-blockade-french-particiption-1948-1949.130286/

CHAPTER 16

25. *On a Wing and a Prayer*, Joshua Levine, Collins, 2008.

BIBLIOGRAPHY

Books and Journals

Cudmore, Michael, *The Windfall Yachts – A Legacy of Goodwill*, Topsy 11 Publishing, 2007

Douglas, Sholto, *Years of Command: A Personal Story of the Second World War*, Collins, 1966

Hargrave-Wright, Dr Joyce L., *The Bridge of Wings*, Abilitywise LLP, 2015

Larkin, Group Captain Min, 'The RAF Halton Aircraft Apprentice Scheme', *Royal Air Force Historical Society Journal*, No. 65 ISSN 1361 2431

Levine, Joshua, *On a Wing and a Prayer: The Untold Story of the Pioneering Aviation Heroes of WW1, in Their Own Words*, Collins, 2008

Miller, Roger G., *To Save a City: The Berlin Airlift 1948-1949*, Texas A&M University Press, 1998

Montgomery, Bernard Law, *The Memoirs of Field-Marshal the Viscount Montgomery of Alamein*, Collins, 1958

Philpott, Ian M., *The Royal Air Force: An Encyclopedia of the Inter-War Years. Volume 1: The Trenchard Years 1918-1929*, Pen & Sword Aviation, 2005

Philpott, Ian M., *The Royal Air Force: An Encyclopedia of the Inter-War Years. Volume 2: Re-Armament 1930 to 1939*, Pen & Sword, 2008

Royal Air Force Historical Society and Defence Studies, 'The Royal Air Force in Germany 1945-1993', Report of the seminar at the Joint Services Command and Staff College, Bracknell, 9th December 1998

Magazines and Newspapers

London Gazette, 1st November 1920

Air Ministry Weekly Order (AMWO) 624. 4th August 1921

Flight magazine

Bristol Evening Post

South Eastern Gazette

Aviation History July 2012, Derek O'Connor

Websites

Air of Authority (Malcolm Barrass) – https://www.rafweb.org/

Airminded – www.airminded.org

Britannica Encyclopaedia – Italo-Ethiopian War 1935–1936 https://www.britannica.com/event/Italo-Ethiopian-War-1935-1936

Hansard House of Commons debate 28th July 1937 vol 326 cc3095-100 https://api.parliament.uk/historic-hansard/commons/1937/jul/28/empire-air-day-displays-accidents

Hansard House of Lords debate 23rd October 1935 vol 98 cc1134-84 https://hansard.parliament.uk/Lords/1935-10-23/debates/967a24ea-1c58-436e-81e2-9f8962176f72/TheItalo-AbyssinianDispute

Historum.com Berlin Blockade French participation 1948 1949 – https://historum.com/threads/berlin-blockade-french-participation-1948-1949.130286/

Military.com – The First Attack: Pearl Harbor, February 7, 1932 –https://www.military.com/navy/pearl-harbor-first-attack.html

Military Histories – The Three Surrenders www.militaryhistories.co.uk/surrender

No. 529 Squadron (RAF): Second World War – http://www.historyofwar.org/air/units/RAF/529_wwII.html

Pearl Habor Visitors Bureau – February 1932: The Other "Attack on Pearl Harbor" https://visitpearlharbor.org/february-1932-attack-pearl-harbor/

RAF Commands Archive – Wg Cdr R M Longmore – www.rafcommands.com/archive/02280.php

Relikte.com Focke-Wulf-Flugzeugbau GmbH - Technical Directorate in Bad Eilsen 1941-1945. Herr Manfred Tegge (Bremen) – www.relikte.com

South-East History Boards – http://sussexhistoryforum.co.uk

The Aerodrome forum – http://www.theaerodrome.com/forum/

Wenman Wykeham-Musgave https://www.revolvy.com/page/Wenman-Wykeham%252DMusgrave

Worcestershire Police History – www.worcestershirepolicehistory.co.uk

Index

AIRFIELDS/ESTABLISH-
MENTS/MILITARY UNITS